DANIEL

A HISTORICAL NOVEL

DANIEL

THE MAN
WHO SAW TOMORROW

Thom Lemmons

QUESTAR PUBLISHERS, INC.

SISTERS, OREGON

This book is dedicated to Bo Whitaker,
who unknowingly helped me write it.

DANIEL: *The Man Who Saw Tomorrow*
published by Multnomah Books
a part of the Questar publishing family

© 1991 by Thom Lemmons

International Standard Book Number: 0-945564-83-X

Printed in the United States of America

For information:
QUESTAR PUBLISHERS, INC.
POST OFFICE BOX 1720
SISTERS, OREGON 97759

93 94 95 96 97 98 99 00 01 — 10 9 8 7 6 5 4 3 2

Acknowledgments

I MUST FIRST gratefully acknowledge the resources which were of so much assistance to me in the preparation of this manuscript:

"Daniel," *International Standard Bible Encyclopedia* (fully revised edition)

Keller, Werner; *The Bible as History*

Lamb, Harold; *Cyrus the Great*

Oates, Joan; *Babylon*

Pfieffer, Charles (editor), *Baker's Bible Atlas*

Saggs, H.W.F.; *Everyday Life in Babylonia and Assyria*

Shea, William; "Daniel as Governor," "Darius," "Dura," "Nabonidus," "Prince of Persis," and other related articles published in *Andrews University Seminary Studies*; 1982-1986

Wiseman, D.J.; *Nebuchadrezzar and Babylon*

Young, Robert; *Analytical Concordance to the Bible*

For their thorough scholarship and the insights afforded me, I owe a tremendous debt of gratitude to the authors of these excellent works.

As I do before any undertaking involving the Old Testament, I spent time at the feet of Dr. John Willis, professor of Old Testament at Abilene Christian University. I thank him for his kindness, his scholarship, and his serving spirit.

I must always thank and praise my wife, Cheryl, for her patience and support — despite the pacing, muttering, and hair-pulling which seem inextricably linked to my creative process. My dearest love on earth, how can I ever be sufficiently grateful?

THOM LEMMONS
Abilene, Texas
February 1, 1991

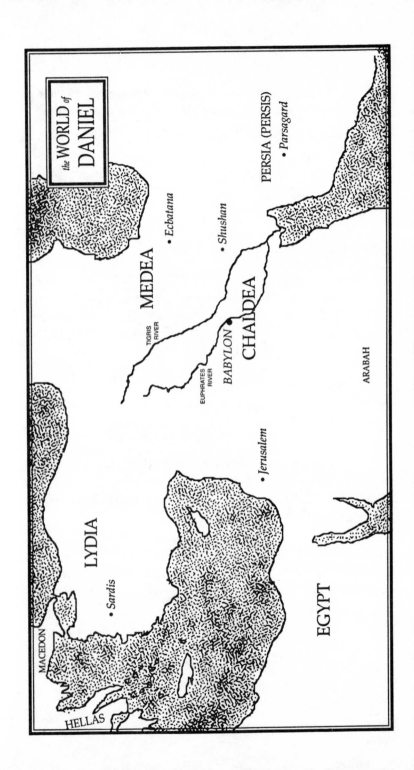

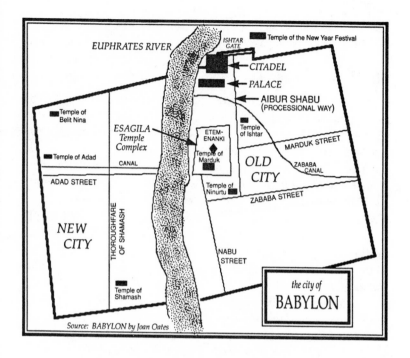

Source: BABYLON by Joan Oates

Notes from the Author

About Variant Name-forms

One of the most interesting aspects of the period of history portrayed by the events in this novel is the rich interplay between various cultures. I have attempted to preserve this flavor by sometimes using a few variant pronunciations of the names of people and places — in the naming of Persian rulers, for example, which have come down to us in their Hellenized forms. Thus, "Kurash" is known to us today as "Cyrus," "Uvakhshatra" as "Cyaxeres," and "Kanbujiya" as "Cambyses." The same thing happened when Chaldean names such as Abed-Nabu and Nabu-Naid were translated into Hebrew, becoming, respectively "Abednego" and (after Latinization) "Nabonidus."

I trust the use of different renderings of the same name will not be confusing to the reader, though parents in biblical times clearly did not choose names on the basis of ease for the western tongue. My intention is to capture for the reader a bit more of the flavor of the times — the better, hopefully, to launch the reader's imagination into the vistas of pagan grandeur which I have tried to portray.

About Darius the Mede

A number of the eminently qualified scholars whose works I consulted differ widely in their identity of the Darius named in Daniel 5:30 and later passages of the book. Two problems are primarily responsible for this lack of agreement.

First, Cyrus of Persia is the only conqueror of Babylon mentioned elsewhere in Scripture (as well as in extra-biblical sources discovered to date). The Darius mentioned in Ezra, Haggai, and Zechariah is a later Persian ruler who usurped the throne from Cyrus's son, Cambyses II. Cyrus, meanwhile, is mentioned in connection with Babylon in Ezra, 2 Chronicles, and quite impressively in the prophetic passages of Isaiah, which were written long before Cyrus was even born.

Second, the Darius mentioned in Daniel is presented as a Mede, while the conquest of Babylon was accomplished only after the subjugation of the Medean Empire by Cyrus, a Persian. True, the Medes and Persians were related peoples springing from a common ancestry. But it seems clear both from biblical evidence and extra-biblical sources unearthed in recent decades that the Persians and Medes regarded themselves as quite distinct ethnic groups. Certainly a chronicler of history who lived through the events described in this novel would have known the difference between Medes and Persians.

Scholars have attempted to resolve these difficulties in a number of ways. Some have tried to find Darius' identity in various characters known to have played a role in the events related here. Another view, which I believe to be reasonable and have followed in this text, is that Darius was a throne name assumed by Cyrus. This theory is given support by certain translations of Daniel 6:28, which equate the reigns of Darius and Cyrus: "Daniel prospered during the reign of Darius, even Cyrus the Persian."

Archeology may yet alleviate our present-day uncertainty in identifying Darius. For example, only fifty years ago Belshazzar (mentioned in Daniel 5) was thought by some to be a fanciful figure created by the writer of Daniel, since no extra-biblical reference could be found to such a character. However, more recent excavations and translation work on cuneiform cylinders found in the ruins of Babylon have uncovered several mentions of Belshazzar, the son and (presumably) prince-regent of Nabonidus, last Chaldean king of Babylon. The accuracy of the Scriptures is thus upheld in the matter of Belshazzar. It is entirely possible that such assistance in the matter of Darius the Mede may yet occur.

But I have chosen to write a novel rather than a scholarly treatise — fortunately so, for I am not qualified to attempt the latter. And for the sake of narrative clarity I have chosen to identify Darius the Mede with the conqueror of Babylon, Cyrus the Persian.

In light of the complexities mentioned above, I hope the reader will have no difficulty with my presentation of the fascinating events surrounding the conquest of Babylon. And I hope the overarching theme of God's absolute sovereignty will quickly clear away any momentary confusion which may exist.

CHARACTERS

♦Kings of Babylon♦

Nebuchadrezzar	Babylon's greatest emperor
Awil-Marduk	son and successor of Nebucha-drezzar; assassinated by Nergal-Sharezer
Nergal-Sharezer	son-in-law of Nebuchadrezzar; usurped the throne from Awil-Mar-duk
Labashi-Marduk	son of Nergal-Sharezer; deposed by Nabu-Naid
Nabu-Naid (Nabonidus)	originally prime minister under Nebuchadrezzar and his successors; later the last king of the Babylonian Empire

♦Hebrews in Babylon♦

Daniel (Belteshazzar)	wise man of the Babylonian and Persian courts
Mishael (Meshach)	friend of Daniel, singer of Babylo-nian court
Hananiah (Shadrach)	friend of Daniel, musician of Baby-lon
Azariah (Abed-Nabu)	friend of Daniel (called **Abednego** in the Bible) and aide to Nabu-Naid, Babylon's prime minister
Ephratah	wife of Azariah
Caleb	servant in the households of Daniel and Azariah
Ezekiel	Hebrew priest and prophet carried to Babylon by Nebuchadrezzar
Ezra	Hebrew priest who made the return journey from Babylon to Jerusalem
Jeconiah (Coniah)	deposed king of Judah imprisoned in Babylon
Jozadak	A Hebrew priest employed by the banker Egibi; later returned to Jerusalem

A HISTORICAL NOVEL

DANIEL

THE MAN
WHO SAW TOMORROW

A captive in the land,
a stranger and a youth,
he heard the king's command,
he saw that writing's truth.
The lamps around were bright,
the prophecy in view;
he read it on that night—
the morrow proved it true...

—from Vision of Belshazzar
GEORGE GORDON, LORD BYRON

PART I

Dreams

1

THE KING AWOKE wide-eyed and sweating, just as the last echo of his dream-shout dodged around the corner of his hearing. He sat bolt upright, panting with the terror of a night vision which evaporated even as he struggled to recall the alien images which had so frightened him.

The concubine, trained to deal with such matters, rolled over and gently stroked his chest, seeking to soothe the royal discomfort. Nebuchadrezzar impatiently pushed her hand away. "Leave me," he growled. He did not turn to look at her as she left the couch and quietly padded away, back to the harem.

Again the same dream, he mused. As his breathing slowed to normal, he pieced together the dim fragments of this strangely horrifying vision which taunted him night after night with its incomprehensible meaning.

He stood on a wide, open plain—much like the countryside round about Babylon—and the air was still. The sky was not blue with the fierce azure of the hot summer days, nor cloud-covered and heavy with threatened rain. Rather, it was oddly neutral—of no particular color or composition—as if the place in which he stood were not really the earth he knew, but a region somewhere between the kingdom of the gods and the nether world of the demons. It seemed a vast, silent hall with ceilings beyond the reach of his vision and walls so far away the horizon hid them from view. A waiting place. And that enormous sense of waiting filled him with a nameless dread.

He turned and saw a huge image. It stood like eternity upon the plain, and when his eyes fell upon it he felt joy and pride flooding into his breast. Its head, with fierce-staring eyes and noble chin, were cast in purest gold. He looked upon its face gazing bravely out over the plain, and knew the visage to be his own. A crown was set on the head of the statue; it was the crown of an emperor. Adamant dignity exalted the image, and he raised his fist in a fierce salute to this icon of his own majesty. Forgotten was the anxious suspense of moments ago, for now his eyes were filled not with the vast, humbling expanse, but with this noble monument to himself.

He admired the rest of the statue. Surely a master workman had fashioned such a brilliant creation! Its chest and arms were cast in shining silver and the right hand gripped a gleaming scepter of power. The torso and strong thighs were crafted of burnished bronze, the lower legs of iron. As he allowed his vision to drop to the feet and pedestal of the statue he was vexed to notice that the workman had apparently not planned adequately, for the bottom-most portions of the image were cast of iron mixed with clay. But again he raised his eyes to the heroic face, and soon forgot his momentary displeasure.

As Nebuchadrezzar recollected the rest of the dream, he felt his hands begin trembling. Sweat broke out anew upon his brow. He rose from his couch and paced nervously to the window of his chamber. Reluctant to rehearse the final, dreadful sequence, yet unable to resist its hypnotic power, his mind was pulled frantically forward.

As he stood smiling up at the statue, he heard behind him a rumbling sound, like thunder from a forgotten yesterday. Vaguely disturbed, he turned—and gasped.

A dazzling, shimmering rock the size of a fortress rolled toward him across the vast tableland. No cloud of dust accompanied its progress—in its purity it stirred not so much as a grain of sand as it wheeled with dire purpose toward where he stood. Nothing obscured his view of the juggernaut. And he felt it was coming…for him.

"No!" he heard himself scream. "Not me!" He began running away. "Not me! Take this," he shouted, pointing at the statue. "Take this as an offering, but only spare me, I beg you!" He tried to invoke Marduk, Nabu, any and all of the gods and demons, but the names stuck fast in his throat before the irresistible onslaught of the rolling harbinger of fate.

The glittering rock struck the statue with the force of a hundred thunderclaps. Before his horrified, cowering eyes, the mighty statue, the proud royal monument, collapsed and disintegrated. He felt a searing pain within his chest, as if his heart were being ripped forcibly from its cavity. Miniscule fragments of the once triumphant image rained down like dust. The wind of the rock's passing blew the fragments away like empty husks of grain.

He fell down, sobbing. From beneath his fingers he peeked abjectly at the rock. It grew—or did he shrink before it? It now appeared to him as huge as the snow-capped mountains of northern Lebanon, as vast as the searing dunes of the Arabah. The hugeness of its presence, the world-filling aura of its being, made him feel as insignificant as a speck of dust. He cowered before it. He screamed...

Nebuchadrezzar, Emperor of Babylon, Ruler of Lands, Master of the Two Rivers, huddled in a corner of his chamber, panting like a trapped bird. He hid his face in his hands, but the dream-terror exploded with relentless force inside his mind. He slept no more that night.

♦ ♦ ♦

ADAD-IBNI FELT A KNOT of apprehension gather in the pit of his stomach. Uruk, commander of the palace guard, stood in the outer chamber, bearing a message from the emperor. In other times this news would not have been particularly distressing, but in these days it was cause for some concern.

As chief seer, Adad-ibni enjoyed a high degree of access to the imperial presence. His was the responsibility for apprising the emperor of the disposition of the signs and portents of heaven, earth, and the netherworld. Heavy was the charge laid upon him, for Nebuchadrezzar's decisions affected the whole world, and Adad-ibni's counsel affected Nebuchadrezzar's decisions. Scarcely any event in Babylon—from reading the entrails of a sacrificed ox to the birth of a malformed child, from the tallies of the harvests to the formations of migrating birds— was overlooked by his agents or exempted from his calculations. Even the temple astrologers, perched at their posts atop the Etemenanki ziggurat and the lesser temple towers, dutifully reported their carefully logged observations and deferred to his interpretations. His post was the heart and soul of all planning and administration for the empire, and no one enjoyed higher prestige with the emperor than himself.

Or so it had been until the last few months. The emperor had grown increasingly difficult to deal with. Since the successful conclusion of his campaign to the Great Sea, he had seemed withdrawn, distracted. At times, when Adad-ibni had been closeted with him, Nebuchadrezzar had given the impression he was not listening at all—or, rather, listening to some other voice than Adad-ibni's. For the past several months his meetings with the emperor had been characterized by impatience and curtness from Nebuchadrezzar, and increasing frustration on the part of the chief seer. He very well knew what the emperor was capable of if his ire was aroused—but he felt helpless to eliminate, or even to understand, the source of Nebuchadrezzar's malaise. The emperor was not a man who allowed easy access to his inner thoughts—even to a seer.

He glanced a final time at the notes he had made from the information brought to him since his last meeting with the emperor. He had a bad feeling about this unexpected message from the imperial chambers. But failure to respond was a certain promise of doom, especially now. Sighing deeply, he straightened his shoulders, arranged his robes, and slowly paced into the outer chamber.

Uruk watched with a carefully neutral expression as the chief seer sauntered toward him. Inwardly he shuddered. He could never look on Adad-ibni's face without thinking of a sand lizard or a serpent. The chief seer's pate was clean-shaven, after the fashion of the mages and seers, and his face looked as if it had never sported a human emotion. His eyes were perpetually half-lidded, and his eyelashes so light they were invisible. Like a reptile, his expression never changed. If he was nervous or angry or elated, the smooth, cool exterior never allowed a hint.

Though he moved among the highest circles of power, the

chief seer was a relatively young man—disconcertingly so, as far as the commander was concerned. For one so young to have attained such influence, his abilities needed to be great indeed. Yet the soldier couldn't help wondering if the mage's advancement in court was due less to reading the stars than to divining the endlessly shifting winds of the emperor's favor. Uruk didn't trust Adad-ibni out of his sight. Unlike himself, a man of action and movement, the chief seer seemed to move entirely in a realm of thought and ideas, of muttered incantations and arcane knowledge. The bald one wielded words rather than swords.

"Good morning, Lord Uruk," intoned the chief seer smoothly. "I trust you rested well last night."

Thinking to himself that the mage might actually know the answer already, Uruk replied, "Yes, thank you. And good morning to you, Lord Adad-ibni. I hope I have found you well and happy."

Adad-ibni nodded serenely. A moment of silence ensued as the two powerful courtiers resumed the genteel feud—the ceaseless, polite war of attrition fought by the great and near-great in the imperial court of Babylon.

Uruk cleared his throat and said, "His majesty wishes to see you without delay."

Adad-ibni's stomach tightened another notch, but his face did not so much as twitch.

"He has not rested well of late—his dreams trouble him," finished Uruk.

Adad-ibni's mind began spinning. So—this was the trouble. This could explain the emperor's being out of sorts these last months. The apothecaries should be consulted. A potion, maybe...

"What is the nature of the emperor's dreams?" inquired the chief seer. "What has he seen—dragons flying, perhaps, or dragons reclining?"

Uruk held up his hands, shaking his head. "Lord Adad-ibni, I know nothing about such matters. The emperor has told me only as much as I have told you. What he has or hasn't seen you will have to ascertain for yourself."

Adad-ibni rubbed his chin and stared thoughtfully into the middle distance. This was important. He sensed that this dream of Nebuchadrezzar's would have far-reaching implications. Surely there was a way to turn this circumstance to his advantage.

Presently he looked up. "Very well, Lord Uruk. Take me to the emperor."

♦ ♦ ♦

AZARIAH CAREFULLY LAID the tablet on the cedar-planked table before his superior, bowing in deference.

The older man squinted at the cuneiform characters and asked, "Which dispatches are these, Abed-Nabu?" As always, he used Azariah's Babylonian name.

"These are from the western district, my lord Nabu-Naid," answered Azariah. "They concern the cities and territories of the Philistine plain, Syria, and..."—his voice hesitated ever so slightly—"Judah."

His master grunted, pursing his lips as he perused the summary tablet Azariah had prepared. It was Azariah's task, as his secretary, to digest the information contained in reports received from the emperor's agents scattered across the far-flung territories of the realm, from the edge of the plain of Elam to the shores of the Great Sea. From these reports, Nabu-Naid in his role as prime minister would formulate plans and strategies for the emperor's approval or disapproval.

Azariah's importance was compounded by Nabu-Naid's inclination to indulge himself in pursuit of his hobby. Descended from a long line of semi-royal priests and scholars, Nabu-Naid appeared to greatly prefer poring over musty potsherds to attending the affairs of state. When Azariah had a report to present, Nabu-Naid could most often be found where he was today—locked in his study, surrounded by souvenirs of antiquity dredged from the refuse heaps and dung hills of long-dead cities. Thus the prime minister allowed Azariah considerable latitude, not wanting his musings on the past to be too often interrupted by the annoyances of the present.

Still, no one made the mistake of thinking Lord Nabu-Naid was unaware of the realities of the court. Old was his family, and deep his connections. He was not, despite his outwardly quaint eccentricities, a man to be trifled with.

Now he aimed a crow-black eye at his aide. "The reports from Judah are not good, are they?"

Azariah allowed his face to show no emotion. "Apparently not, my lord."

Nabu-Naid allowed his intent gaze to settle on the stoic face of his assistant for several long breaths. "These are your people, are they not, Abed-Nabu? You don't feel concern for what may happen to them if this information proves true?"

Azariah's gaze flickered downward for an instant. He glanced at the noble, then returned to his impassive study of the air above Nabu-Naid's head. "I serve the emperor and my lord Nabu-Naid. My duty is to report the information given to me." Azariah paused a moment. "A prophet of our people has said we should seek the welfare of this land in which we live. This I have done, and this I will do."

A corner of the noble's mouth turned up, and his eyes flickered in the barest hint of a smile. "Well said, Abed-Nabu. Well said." He glanced back at the report, quickly noting the gist of its contents. "Everything seems to be in order here," the prime minister announced at last. "You may leave."

Azariah spun on his heel and left the chamber, closing the door behind him.

Nabu-Naid, locking the door behind his aide, quickly went to his table. Raking the potsherds impatiently to one side, he avidly scanned the summary report, his mind rapidly adding and subtracting columns of political fact and supposition. He squinted upward in calculation.

So the western territories were not so well in hand as the emperor had hoped. Could this be an opening? Probably not—they were too weak to create any appreciable rift in the pattern of probability. *But it is another piece to add to the puzzle*, thought the prime minister, idly sifting among the fragments of old pottery he had been studying so ostentatiously when Abed-Nabu entered. *Another piece to the puzzle.*

He was a man who possessed that most dangerous combination of attributes—patience and craftiness. He had a great deal of time at his disposal, this he knew. And one day, when the time was right...

◆ ◆ ◆

NEBUCHADREZZAR SAT PENSIVELY in his private chamber, scowling at a hanging on the far wall. It depicted the god Marduk, represented by a dragon slaying a winged bull. The hanging was intended to celebrate Nebuchadrezzar's victory over the Assyrians—the victory which had ushered in the Babylonian Empire. It had been achieved by means of an alliance forged with the Medes of King Cyaxeres—Uvakhshatra, as he was known in the outlandish tongue of his people. He remembered the lancers of the Medes, the way they rode laughing into battle on their majestic chargers, the Nisayan horses of the high eastern plains. He also remembered the cousin clans of the Medes—*Parsis*, they called themselves. These restless Persians seemed to chafe under the overlordship of Cyaxeres.

Staring at the wall tapestry, the emperor remembered the days of his triumphs, mentally tallying the cities and lands he had laid under tribute: Assyria and the wealth of Nineveh, the rich seaport city-states of Tyre and Sidon, Philistia and the coastal plain beside the Great Sea, Jerusalem...

And then the dream. What good was this empire, stretching from the Gulf of the South to the Great Sea, if he was held in thrall to the restless night wanderings of his own mind? Nebuchadrezzar recalled how he had huddled in his bedchamber, trembling like a slave before the tyranny of the horrific vision. Above all else, he hated weakness—in himself or in others. Yet this dream had brought him face to face with the stinking rot of fear within his own soul. And for that fear, that trembling frailty, he despised himself.

Try as he might, he could not dismiss the dream as a random occurrence. The vision was too fraught with awesome, inaccessible meaning. It inserted itself past his sleep into his waking, with the force of a knowing entity. It had about it the aura of something sent from the gods, yet his prayers—to Marduk and his son, Nabu; to Ishtar; even to Sin, the bringer of dreams—brought him no comfort. His armies, his wealth, his absolute authority—none could relieve his suffering. Even the Emperor of Babylon could not command a dream to cease.

He heard the sound of silk rustling, and looked up to see Adad-ibni prostrate himself before him. For a moment the emperor studied the prone form of his chief seer. This was the man who had predicted Nebuchadrezzar's rise to world dominion. He remembered the countless smooth words with which the seer had convinced him that his conquest, his dynasty, was assured. And Adad-ibni had benefitted handsomely from his foresight. But Nebuchadrezzar had begun to wonder: Did the chief seer's prescience have about it the scent of pandering?

Had the mages and astrologers ever averted a flood? Had their advice alerted him to the rebellious commanders whose uprising he had been forced to quell so violently some seasons past? What actual benefit had Adad-ibni ever been to him, other than as a flattering voice echoing the praises and aspirations of the masses?

It sometimes seemed to the emperor that mages invoked the heavens only to endorse the plans that kings and princes made. The astrologers and mages claimed to commune with the gods, yet often the visions they produced were no truer than praise odes sung by a paid minstrel. How often had a mage, acting upon his supposed knowledge of the gods, countermanded an undertaking of the king's? Nebuchadrezzar could not think of a time when Adad-ibni's reading of the signs didn't underwrite the plans he already intended to carry out. Was the authority and vision of the mages any greater than his own? A nagging doubt which had been gnawing at him for some time suddenly found words within his mind: Had the gods truly created men, or vice versa? Abruptly he closed his mind to further speculation of the sort—that way lay madness.

"Rise," he commanded, and the chief seer rose gracefully to his feet.

2

"HAS LORD URUK informed you of why you are here?" Nebuchadrezzar asked.

Adad-ibni nodded, a beatific smile gliding across his smooth features. Nebuchadrezzar felt a corner of his lip curling downward.

"My lord Nebuchadrezzar," the seer intoned in an unguent voice, "the interpretation of dreams is a study to which, as my lord knows, I have dedicated a considerable amount of time. Frequently dreams can tell us much about the disposition of the gods and of what may come to pass. And in the dreams of the Emperor..."—the mage made a slight bow—"messages may be read which will greatly alter the landscape of the future." Again came the honeyed smile, the deferential nod. "And now, if Your Majesty will be so kind as to describe the dream," the mage continued, "I will give such comfort as may be possible." Adad-ibni waited intently for the emperor to begin.

Nebuchadrezzar felt disgust clamoring at the back of his throat. This simpering, spice-anointed leech sought to pacify him with fancy phrases and erudite jargon! Had Adad-ibni stared, cowering, into the unknown? Had he felt his identity slipping away like desert sand through the fingers of a skeleton? Now the dandified bookworm wished to traipse about among the images of Nebuchadrezzar's terror, sorting through them like a collector, picking and choosing such elements as might fit the story he wished to concoct! The thought galled and angered the emperor. He would not willingly permit such offhand, avaricious gloating over the dread within his soul.

"Very well, mage," sneered Nebuchadrezzar, "since you are an expert, tell me this: What—exactly—was my dream? What were its images, and what did they mean? Tell me this, chief seer, so that I shall be comforted, and you shall be richly rewarded." Nebuchadrezzar crossed his arms on his chest and waited, his lips pulled back in a smile more akin to a snarl than a laugh.

Adad-ibni's comforting beam faded, evolving slowly into a wide-eyed look of panic. "My…my lord jests. Please…tell your servant the dream, and a true interpretation will be made." The mage's brow began to glow with sweat, though it was still early in the day and the summer heat had not yet penetrated the massive brick walls of the palace. Adad-ibni's blooming fear stank in the room.

"Perhaps the chief seer does not grasp my meaning," grated Nebuchadrezzar in barely concealed mockery. "I wish you to describe to me the dream—what it was, what transpired, what I saw—and then give me its interpretation. Thus I will truly know and appreciate the vast reservoirs of your skill and learning."

By now Adad-ibni was breathing rapidly, his fingertips trembling as he rubbed his hands together. Nebuchadrezzar saw his eyes twitch to and fro as thoughts scrambled furiously about beneath the bald pate of the the chief seer.

"My Lord Emperor," stammered Adad-ibni at last, "what

you ask your humble servant to do is without precedent. My studies indicate that such a feat has never before been performed—"

"Ah, but my lord mage," interrupted the emperor, beginning to take a perverse enjoyment from the wizard's discomfort, "you yourself have told me that my kingdom, my dynasty, was to be without precedent: 'Like no other king before you— so it is written in the stars.' Were those not your words?" Nebuchadrezzar paused significantly, allowing the pathetic seer to nod weakly. "Therefore, does it not follow," pressed Nebuchadrezzar, "that my chief seer's abilities should be also without precedent—like no seer before or since?"

Adad-ibni saw with terrifying clarity the trap Nebuchadrezzar had constructed for him with his own pronouncements. There had to be a way out of this box—yet his brain was addled by the absurd demand being placed upon him, and by the sudden, icy winds of the emperor's anger. To enter into the very mind of a man—no, of an *emperor!* Who could imagine such a thing?

"My...my Lord Emperor," he stuttered, "this...this will be very difficult. I shall require much more preparation for such an attempt than for a normal reading. Will your majesty permit his humble servant to retire for three days to prepare and fortify for this...this journey into the...the realms beyond?" Adad-ibni crossed his forearms on his chest and bowed his head, waiting in giddy panic for the words which would either seal his fate immediately or give him time to think of a way out of this tunnel into nowhere.

Nebuchadrezzar laughed within himself. Perhaps this blubbering hanger-on thought he, the king, actually believed the feat might be accomplished! He would allow time for this folly to ripen, and then Adad-ibni would taste the wrath of the emperor for such chicanery. "You have your three days, Lord Seer," the emperor growled. "Go and prepare..."

Adad-ibni bowed and scraped his way out of the chamber.

"...to die," finished Nebuchadrezzar under his breath, as the door closed.

◆　◆　◆

DANIEL LAID ASIDE the clay tablet and looked out the window, tiredly rubbing his stiff neck. He had risen early this morning to resume work on the accounts of the date harvest in the northern provinces—Lamech, his supervisor, wanted his report in two days—but the cuneiform columns had begun to look like tracks made by bird's feet. He massaged his eyes with his fingertips, then looked again out the window.

From his alcove in the citadel Daniel gazed out over the brown, sluggish Euphrates and the honeycombed streets of the New City sprawling beyond its western bank. He lived there, in one of the myriad tan, sun-baked brick houses that squatted in the harsh sunlight of the Chaldean plain. But this morning his eyes roamed past the streets and canals of Babylon, past the western wall of the New City, and far across the sparse landscape to the very horizon, and beyond.

Out there, he thought. *Out there calling silently with the urgency of a searching mother, with the constancy of a father whose son is lost, lies Judah.* Even now—after ten years in this bustling city, this throbbing center of empire—Judah still beckoned him with the voice of his own heart.

Daniel remembered a night in Syria, and a campfire. Again he heard the voice of a prophet retelling the legends of his people. Once more he felt within his breast the jarring sobs of a homesick, heartsick boy, heard the question: *How long, Jeremiah? How long will we be in the land of this foreign king?*

A servant shuffled into the room and waited, silently, for Daniel to acknowledge him. With difficulty, Daniel pulled his eyes away from the dim line of the horizon and turned in his seat. "Yes, what is it?"

"Honored Belteshazzar," the page began, "I was sent by Counselor Lamech. He wishes—"

"I have been working on the figures," interrupted Daniel, a

trace of irritation in his voice. "Please tell the honored counselor that I will bring him the report as agreed."

Nervously the page bowed his head and shuffled his feet. "It is not a report from you that Counselor Lamech desires. I am to bring you to him, as soon as possible."

Puzzled, Daniel stared at the top of the messenger's bowed head for several heartbeats. "Thank you," he said finally. "You may tell the honored counselor that I will come to him before the day's end."

Still the page did not take leave. "Honored Belteshazzar, forgive your humble servant," he began, more uneasy than ever, "but Counselor Lamech wishes you to return with me—immediately."

◆ ◆ ◆

DANIEL FELT HIS PULSE QUICKEN when he realized the messenger was taking him not to Lamech's offices—down in the lower reaches of the citadel, near the huge storage magazines—but rather to the chief counselor's private suite. Lamech, who had been in the emperor's highest circle of advisers since before Daniel came to Babylon, lived in lavish quarters in the upper level of the Citadel, overlooking the Ishtar Gate. It was a mark of his prestige that the emperor allowed him to reside within the very walls of the Citadel.

They reached the doorway. The messenger bowed himself aside, and Daniel walked forward into the silk-hung, myrrh-scented rooms of his overseer.

Lamech had his back to Daniel, staring out a window with his hands clasped behind him. Hearing the sound of Daniel's sandaled feet, he spun about. "Ah, there you are, Belteshazzar! Please, sit down!" Lamech beckoned hastily toward some cushions.

"Would you care for something to eat?" Lamech motioned toward an alabaster bowl full of various sweetmeats. Daniel shook his head. "Very well, then," said Lamech, peering intently at his younger assistant.

"Belteshazzar, a situation of gravest import has arisen. Unfortunately, it is also completely unfamiliar. In other words, we have no idea how to proceed. That is why I need your help."

Daniel felt strangely fearful, despite the high praise he had just received. His brow furrowed as Lamech continued.

"I believe you know the chief seer." He motioned toward a corner of the room, and Adad-ibni stood there, partially concealed behind a silk drape. Daniel involuntarily stiffened.

"Lord Adad-ibni had a frightening interview with the emperor. It seems that His Majesty has had a dream which has disturbed him profoundly."

Daniel felt something stirring deep, deep within him: a voice too faint to be heard. Then it was gone. Adad-ibni spoke. A sheen of sweat was evident on the chief seer's brow—an unaccustomed show of emotion on the part of the normally composed mage.

"Belteshazzar, the honored Counselor Lamech tells me you are one of the best and brightest of his young men. He says you have often succeeded where others have failed. You must exploit all your contacts in the palace and the city—anyone who might have the information we need."

"My Lord Seer," Daniel asked quietly, "what sort of information do you seek?"

◆　◆　◆

TWO HUNDRED LEAGUES to the east, in the land of the Parsis, Kurash, crown prince of Parsagard, laughed with glee as he vaulted to the back of the snorting charger. It was not yet midmorning in the valley of Anshan, but already the air had lost the coolness of the night. Long before noon, the heat would shimmer in translucent sheets against the rugged, mountainous backdrop of the Parsi homeland.

The child waved away the attendant who rushed forward with a saddle, gripping the bare-backed Nisayan steed with his knees as he leaned forward onto her neck and clicked his tongue. The high-bred mare vaulted forward at an immediate gallop, and Prince Kurash gave the horse her head as they raced pellmell down the long clearing toward a small creek near the stable.

Gobhruz, the prince's Medean bodyguard, stood with the stable lackey, staring after the vanishing horse and her rider. Gobhruz shook his head as he shaded his eyes against the bright sunlight. "That boy will not live to become king of Anshan," he said dourly. "He will cheat the lances of his enemies, but only by getting himself trampled to death."

"King Kanbujiya should take his son in hand," observed the stable attendant.

Gobhruz snorted. "That boy has not been 'in hand' since the day of his foaling." Grudgingly he smiled at the faint clouds of dust rising at the far end of the clearing—all that was now visible of Prince Kurash's progress. "Perhaps he is destined to take matters in hand, rather than be taken. Perhaps he spurns the halter the world would place about his neck."

The servant looked up at Gobhruz with a calculating squint. "If that is so," he observed to the bodyguard, "may the gods have pity on the world."

◆　◆　◆

DANIEL WALKED QUICKLY along the crowded Thoroughfare of Shamash. It was midday, and the Chaldean sun beat down in a merciless, brazen blaze. Every scrap of shade along the street was occupied, either by beggars, street vendors hawking their wares, or temple prostitutes conspicuously displaying the tattoo of their sponsoring deity. Even in the brutal heat of summer, commerce continued unceasing in Babylon. Though the wealthy merchants were in their houses, napping through the hottest part of the day, still there was business to be done, and the denizens of the streets of the imperial city lost no opportunity to get their share.

Daniel crossed the bridge over the Northern Canal and turned to his right, along the Street of Adad. Hurrying down the steps by his door, he heard a clear, high voice singing a familiar melody. The words to an ancient Hebrew hymn pealed bravely from the walls of the inner courtyard. *Good*, he thought. *Mishael has received his summons, and is already here.*

Passing through the vaulted doorway, he nodded at the doorkeeper and paced quickly into the sun-washed courtyard. Mishael broke off singing at Daniel's entrance. He turned and gripped the forearms of his friend in welcome.

"Whom were you serenading?" smiled Daniel, looking about quizzically. "I see no one else here."

Mishael chuckled. "I must sing at the court this evening. I was practicing."

"You will give them a song of David, then?"

"I sing for a king—so why not perform a song composed by a king?"

Daniel nodded approvingly. The four young men, friends since boyhood, lived together in this house. In their own minds, and when they were together at home, they clung stubbornly to their Judean names and culture. Always among themselves they were Daniel, Hananiah, Mishael, and Azariah —never Belteshazzar, Shadrach, Meshach, and Abed-Nabu. They might live in Babylon, but their hearts were tenaciously Hebrew.

"Are Hananiah and Azariah here yet?" Daniel asked.

"No. I received your message and came back from the court as soon as I could get away. I didn't see either of them on my way here."

An old man ambled from the kitchen with a bowlegged gait. "Will the young masters desire meat?" he asked in a tremulous voice.

"Yes, Father Caleb—please bring me some dates," said Daniel. "And stop calling me 'young master.' I have told you time and again, you are not a slave in this house!"

The old man stood a moment, nodding thoughtfully. "Very well, young master," he said as he turned back toward the doorway. "If you wish to wait, I will bring food when you ask." He shuffled back the way he had come.

"Caleb, I didn't say 'wait!' I said..."

The old man disappeared around the corner.

Daniel gave Mishael an exasperated look. Mishael only shook his head. "Deaf as a stone, and no mistake," he said.

Daniel's face creased in a wry grin. "Well, if Caleb is determined to deny us food, at least we have plenty of water." He went over to a large clay urn standing in the shade by the northern wall. Taking a bowl from a wooden peg, he dipped it in the water, first pouring it on his head and neck, then taking a long, deep draught. As he offered the empty bowl for Mishael's use, Azariah and Hananiah walked through the doorway.

"Why is there no food ready?" roared Azariah after he had greeted the others. "If I must leave the palace just before the midday meal, why may I not eat in my own house?"

Daniel and Mishael looked at each other and shrugged. Azariah snorted and strode into the kitchen. "Caleb!" he shouted. "You sly old cur! Have you eaten everything in the house?"

Minutes later, seated in the relative coolness of the main room around a low table and a huge bowl of dates and almonds, the three other friends listened as Daniel quickly related the story of the urgent meeting in Lamech's quarters.

"No one has any idea of the king's dream?" asked Hananiah.

Solemnly, Daniel shook his head.

"Even Adad-ibni is fearful?" asked Mishael.

"It appears so," Daniel nodded, "to the extent that anyone can read that one's thoughts from his words."

"I tell you this, my friends," mumbled Azariah around a mouthful of food, "these truly are uncertain days. In some of the dispatches we receive in our department, evil things are spoken of our homeland."

The others watched him as he swallowed, then continued. "Nebuchadrezzar's agents have perceived hints that Zedekiah is aligning himself again with Egypt."

"The fool!" hissed Daniel. "Will he never learn?"

"He will—one way or another," intoned Azariah ominously.

"The ones left behind in Judah—they haven't seen what we've seen here. They still don't fully understand the emperor's power, his determination…"

The four friends fell silent, pondering sadly the fate of their longed-for native land.

"What can we do about the immediate problem, Daniel?" asked Hananiah, returning their thoughts to the present.

"Keep your ears and eyes open," replied Daniel quickly. "Observe the courtiers, the guards, and especially the servants and…"—he continued, looking at Mishael—"the harem."

As a eunuch, Mishael was frequently called into the cloistered, tightly guarded women's quarters to sing for the wives and concubines. He nodded in understanding.

"Why should we assist Adad-ibni?" demanded Azariah. "What have we to gain or lose by the emperor's nightmares?"

Daniel remembered the faint tug within him as he had listened to the chief seer's predicament. His brow furrowed, and he sat silent for so long the others began looking at each other in misgiving.

"I…I'm not sure, Azariah," he answered finally. "But I cannot escape the sense that this summons from the highest circles of the court has some…meaning."

"And who knows?" Daniel finished brightly. "We may be witnesses of wondrous things. Who can say what the Eternal has in mind?"

The four friends fell silent, pondering the things they had heard. Azariah reached into the bowl for a last handful of dates.

3

THE HIGH WINDOWS of the imperial throne room framed hard, blue squares of Chaldean summer sky, and sunlight glistened on the glazed bricks of the facade behind the dais. Inlaid in the brick in vivid yellow were rampant lions which seemed to prance and lash their tails, and stylized palm trees that swayed in the rippling glare.

Uruk, the commander of the palace guards, stood on the lowest step of the dais awaiting the emperor's entrance. A tiny smile played about his lips in anticipation of what might transpire when Nebuchadrezzar convened the court.

The mages, beaten at their own game, were to sue for mercy. So his sources had informed him, and he had little reason to doubt the story's truth. For three days now the upper hierarchy of the mages and astrologers had been closeted in dire council. No one had seen more than a glimpse of any of the bald-heads since Adad-ibni's ill-fated interview with the emperor. As the hours passed and their fearful incantations and prayers proved ineffectual, their faces, said those few who had glimpsed them, grew longer and longer. Today, Uruk felt sure, they would crawl before the emperor and admit their inability to meet his demand.

Uruk was Sumerian. His ancestors had lived in the marshlands between the Two Rivers and along the Gulf of the South. His were the people who had built the ancient cities of the First Kingdom: Eridu, Ur, Lasar, and the ancient place which had given him his own name, Uruk. Almost instinctively, Uruk mistrusted the Chaldeans, a people who had settled to the north of the Sumerian territory and gradually usurped control over the whole region—even the cities built by his own people.

Despite his wariness of them, this was the age of the Chaldeans. Was not Nebuchadrezzar himself a Chaldean?

But the mages were not, to Uruk's mind, of half the measure of the emperor. The emperor spoke a word, and it was so. He said a thing, then performed it. Like Uruk, the emperor was a man of the open air, the light of day.

Not so with the mages. For Uruk, their influence represented the worst things of Chaldean society. Their power lay in the concealing darkness of a nether reality, in the occult practices of their midnight arts. Their stargazing and muttering over ancient, dusty texts, their incantations, their air of mystical conceit—Uruk found all of these profoundly suspect. And through the temples they maintained a stranglehold upon the economy of the empire. It was no coincidence that the houses of the gods, through their lending activities, controlled the lion's share of the slaves, land, and commerce of Babylon and her tributaries. Adad-ibni might whisper comforting oracles in the ears of the king, but Uruk was convinced that the good fortune which the chief seer was mainly concerned about was his own. Uruk was anxious to see the shaved-headed reptile get his comeuppance.

Glancing down a connecting passageway, he saw the bodyguard detail filing into formation before the door to the emperor's private chamber. Uruk knelt face down on the floor—the signal for all the courtiers milling about the throne room to make obeisance.

Flanked on all four sides by bodyguards, the emperor paced slowly down the hallway. Entering the huge room, he strode slowly to the dais and seated himself on the throne.

The ceremonial seat was of cedar wood overlaid with gold. Its sides were carved into the shapes of dragons, the emblem of the god Marduk. The beasts were fashioned so that the emperor's palms rested on their heads, and the jeweled facets of their eyes stared out from between his fingers. Beneath, their mouths gaped in a perennial snarl. Thus seated, Nebuchadrezzar was displayed as the Son of Marduk, earthly emissary of the god—his regent who reigned with his blessing and assistance.

Only when the emperor had taken his place did Uruk, as commander of the guard, announce to the prone assembly, "The Emperor Nebuchadrezzar, Ruler of Lands, Master of the Two Rivers and all the lands to the Great Sea; Beloved of Marduk, the King of the Gods.

"Let those who desire justice approach," continued Uruk. "Let the innocent trust in the wisdom of the emperor, and let the guilty tremble before his face."

When the commander had finished the formulaic invocation, Nebuchadrezzar announced in a ringing tone, "Come forth, chief seer!"

Adad-ibni and three other bald, perspiring men lifted themselves slowly from the floor and drew near to the throne, their faces downcast in submission. Uruk covered his grinning mouth with his hand—Adad-ibni's gowns clung to his sweat-sheathed body. The commander glanced quickly from the emperor to the four. Nebuchadrezzar's face was like a stone—impossible to read. Then the chief seer was speaking.

"O most gracious and merciful Nebuchadrezzar, a deputation of your humble servants comes before you, begging your clemency—"

"Will you now, before this august court, disclose and interpret the dream we propounded to you, in accordance with our command and your terms, as set forth these three days past?" Nebuchadrezzar's voice lashed across the wheedling voice of the chief seer like a white-hot scourge. Still his face showed no emotion.

Uruk shuddered, despite his dislike for Adad-ibni. The emperor fairly burned with authority—as if Marduk truly allowed his glory to shine from the face of Nebuchadrezzar. The gold crown on his head blazed like a sun against the dark blue tiles of the facade. Even those who were accustomed to the imperial presence were breathless with foreboding.

Adad-ibni's mouth moved, but no sound could be heard.

His three attendants had already dropped to their knees in fright, unable to control the trembling of their legs. At last, the chief seer managed to croak out a pathetic answer to the emperor's query.

"Your Majesty, the gods have...have not revealed to your humble servants the secret of the emperor's distress. The dream remains hidden from us."

A vast cloud of silence filled the hall. Uruk could fairly hear the beads of perspiration running down the necks of the miserable mages huddled before the throne. The only visible sign from the emperor was a tightening of the knuckles as he gripped the arms of the throne. The eyes of the dragons seemed to bulge in anger toward the four wretches as they waited for the voice of doom.

At last, Adad-ibni could endure it no longer. Falling headlong at Nebuchadrezzar's feet, he blurted, "My lord! Have pity on your humble servants! No man could do what my lord the emperor commands! None but the gods can discern the weavings of dreams, and they do not walk upon this earth! For the sake of the years of my loyalty, do not slay me!" The last phrase of Adad-ibni's plea dissolved into a blubbering flurry of kisses rained sloppily upon the feet of the emperor.

Nebuchadrezzar allowed the spectacle to continue for perhaps twenty heartbeats. Then he turned his face the slightest degree toward Uruk. Seeing the emperor's slightly raised finger, the commander of the guards strode forward, his lips curling in contempt. He gripped the chief seer's tunic and yanked him roughly backward, tossing him in a wretched bundle beside his three assistants.

"We are angered with you, lord seer," rumbled Nebuchadrezzar. "You have failed to perform the service we require, and yet you come before the court in an unseemly attempt to beg more time to accomplish your failure. We are not minded to be lenient."

Again Uruk shuddered inwardly. Nebuchadrezzar's face was as cold as the point of a spear.

"It is our wish," continued the emperor in an eerily flat tone, "that all the mages and seers in this city be slain, and their corpses ripped asunder by wild dogs. They are not useful to us, and we see no need for useless men to be maintained or tolerated."

The audience gasped silently in helpless empathy for the fate of the mages.

"Further, all their houses shall be torn down, and their wives and children sold as slaves. Lord Uruk," said the emperor, without shifting his gaze from the abject forms of the four condemned men, "your guards shall be responsible for carrying out the judgment rendered this day. So let it be done."

Uruk bowed in reluctant acceptance of the bloody burden. The emperor rose to exit the hall, and the bodyguards instantly formed around him. The courtiers flattened themselves against the floor in obeisance, as if each one wished to become one with the flagstones of the throne room—each perhaps with dread of being swept into the net of fate that just closed around the mages.

◆　◆　◆

AND THUS LED by the fravashi,
those benevolent spirit-servants,
good King Hakhamanish came here—
here to the land of the Parsi;
here to the shining mountains,
to valleys of fresh sweet water.

He lifted up his voice
to praise Ahura Mazda—
to laud the name of the Wise Lord
who led him on his journey;
who brought him past the dangers
and gave us this land forever.

The storysinger's last refrain—all about Hakhamanish, or Achaemenes, founder of the Persian royal dynasty—died away on the fading firelight in the Great Hall of King Kanbujiya.

Most of the old men were already snoring softly into their beards, their ale cups slipping from their somnolent fingers. But Prince Kurash, sitting raptly at the feet of the minstrel, stared into the darkness above the old man's head as if reading some vital message there, as if the flickering shadows whispered a message just beyond the threshold of his hearing.

"Arvanya," the young boy asked, "from where did the people of Hakhamanish journey to come to this place?"

"The songs do not say, my prince," said the grizzled old singer. He reflected a moment, then added, "Some of the old ones say our people came from the great grasslands of the far north. And certainly the Nisayan, the great treasure of our people, were bred for the endless vistas of the steppes, that their legs might reach out and devour the miles. But I cannot say for certain, young lord. It lies beyond my knowledge."

Kurash's eyes sparkled momentarily at the mention of the horses—always his first love. Then his young face grew thoughtful again. "Arvanya, did our cousins the Medes make the journey at the same time as our father Hakhamanish?"

The old minstrel chuckled deep in his throat. "So many questions, young lord! Doesn't that head of yours ever tire of thinking up puzzles for a tired old storysinger?"

The prince grinned, shaking his head.

"Ah, well," sighed Arvanya, "I suppose if you don't ask, you won't ever know." He scratched his head, looking up into the darkness, toward the center beam of the gabled hall. "Long ago, so long ago that the songs have almost forgotten, the Medes and the Parsi were one people—the Aryani. And I suppose it is likely that they journeyed into the land east of the Two Rivers at about the same time. But for scores of scores of years the Medes have kept to the plains of Elam, to the north of our mountain valleys. Though they still call themselves Aryani —just as we call ourselves—that is about all our peoples have in common. In the generations since, we have grown apart. Better answer than that I cannot give."

A shadow crossed the face of the prince. "And for how

long have our cousins lorded it over us, demanding their yearly tribute of Nisayan steeds and riders?"

"Enough, boy," called the king from his high seat at the head of the hall. "You have asked questions a-plenty for one night. Let Arvanya go to his well-deserved bed." Kanbujiya half-rose from his throne and beckoned toward his son, whose chagrined face was averted that his sire might not see the mouth he made. Reluctantly, Kurash rose from his seat, handing the old minstrel three silver pieces.

"Thank you, young lord," the singer nodded gratefully. "And may the *fravashi* guard your sleep."

The singer rose, bowed toward the king and then toward the prince, and hobbled off toward his house. Prince Kurash turned to face his father.

"Father," he piped impatiently, "why must we pay tribute to Asturagash? Why must we drive the best of our horses and men to the hot plains of Shushan? We are as good as they, are we not? Why should we play the bumpkin to them, and meekly surrender what belongs to us?"

Several of the graybeards were awakened from their doze by the insistent voice of the young prince. Wisely, they gave no sign. Instead, they waited cautiously for the king to answer his son's harsh query.

"My son," began Kanbujiya slowly, "I have told you before: You should leave such matters to me and my counselors. You are too young to trouble your head—"

"But my head is already troubled!" shouted Kurash impatiently. "I have been to Ecbatana with the yearly tribute! I have seen the way they look at us! Even the foot soldiers on the walls of the capital city gloat over us! 'There they are,' they say among themselves, 'those hayseed cousins of ours, who can neither read nor write! Let them bring us our mounts, and we will overlook their stupidity for another year.'" The young prince gritted his teeth, his nostrils flaring in indignation at the bitter memories. "All of them are not worth a single regiment

of Nisayan horsemen. They are not worthy to pick up the drop-
pings of our herds!"

"Kurash, I have told you," the king warned, raising his
voice. "Though a prince, you are not of an age to say such—"

"Was not Mandane, my mother, a daughter of Asturagash?
Did you think that because she died on the bed where I was
birthed, I would not know this of her?" the child shouted,
stamping his foot. "I am the son of a king, heir to the blood of
kings, by sire and dam! Why, then, must I be treated like a colt
too young to crop his own grass?"

"Kurash!" shouted the king, leaping to his feet, "I do not
wish to listen to any more diatribes from you this evening!
Now go to your bed!"

For ten breaths, the father and son glared at each other. At
last, with a disgusted snort, Kurash stomped from the hall.

"My king," ventured one of the old men quietly, after
Kurash had gone, "for one so young, strange thoughts run
about in the head of your son. I fear..." The courtier paused,
searching for words.

"Out with it," muttered Kanbujiya. "Most likely I have
thought it myself—give it utterance."

The graybeard looked at his king, then away. "My
lord...that boy is trouble." The old man waited, head down, for
the king's reply.

"Indeed," agreed the king, staring into the patch of darkness where his son had been. "But...for whom?"

4

STILL IN SHOCK from what he had witnessed in the court that morning, Daniel walked with Lamech his superior along Aibur Shabu—the Processional Way. At fifty-pace intervals, sputtering oil lamps burned atop ten-cubit poles. Months ago, the emperor had decreed that the broad way from the Ishtar Gate to Esagila, the temple of Marduk, should be kept illumined throughout the night—out of reverence for Marduk, Lord of the Sun. Frequent grumbling could be heard among the common folk about the expense of maintaining the scores of lamps with oil. Lately, oil seemed to rise in price daily—to the chagrin of all but the temples, who had vast holdings of olive groves and herds to supply the need. Of course, no one complained to the emperor.

"Lord Lamech, it is wrong for the emperor to order such a bloody deed!" Daniel was insisting. "The mages and seers are indeed a vain and supercilious lot, but they have done nothing to deserve this!"

Lamech, accustomed to allowing his young protégé to express himself frankly, shrugged as they walked beneath a smoking lamp flame. He stared at his feet, where the flickering light reflected from the deep blue glazed-tile walls on either side of the roadway. "He is the emperor, Belteshazzar," Lamech said, as they strolled slowly past one of the inlaid yellow lions, replicated every hundred paces or so along the walls. "It is so ordered. There is nothing we can do, no higher authority to which we may apply. And besides, this matter does not concern us."

"But don't you see?" pressed Daniel. "It *does* concern us! Suppose the barley shipments fall short unaccountably. Or what if the levies received from a province do not match the entries on the tablets prepared by the governor's agents? Will the emperor not do to us as he has done to the mages? Will we not feel the edge of the sword if we fail to perform satisfactorily?"

As they wandered along, Lamech raised his hand to rub his neck, uncomfortably contemplating Daniel's words. "Belteshazzar, it is the business of mages and seers to mind the hidden things," he rejoined finally. "What right have we to mingle in such affairs?"

Daniel snorted. "The mages and seers have always, I think, known far less than they allow it to seem."

Lamech glanced sharply at him. "Our astrologers are some of the most respected men in the world! Sages have come from Egypt and even the islands of the Greeks to study at their feet! How can you accuse them of fakery?"

Carefully Daniel looked into the eyes of his mentor, then away. They walked on a few paces, then the younger man said, "Lord Lamech, there is a God who grants visions, who causes men to dream dreams. He is the same God who raises up kings, and debases them. And it is He who gives true visions—not the stars, which He Himself created, nor the spirits, who are in submission to Him."

"More of that Hebrew strangeness," muttered Lamech.

Daniel smiled. "Yes, I suppose it does sound strange, my lord. But I have seen and heard things..." His voice died away as an old, blind beggar approached. Lamech turned and watched as the aged mendicant, his stick tap-tapping in front of him, moved in mincing steps toward them from the darkness beyond the lamplight. Five paces away, then four...three. He stopped.

The beggar looked directly at Daniel—or so it seemed to Daniel. He felt those sightless sockets upon his face as if he were being examined from the inside out. And he felt again a strangely familiar tug within his breast; again that faint voice... then silence. The old man nodded to himself, then picked his way carefully past them, without speaking, without asking for alms. Daniel had the strange sense that instead of begging, the old man had *given* him...what?

"Is something wrong?" asked Lamech, as Daniel stared, transfixed, at the departing, ragged back of the old man.

"I...it's...nothing," said Daniel slowly. Then he looked up at Lamech. "I must go to the emperor. I must cause him to reconsider this thing he has decreed."

"Daniel! You are out of your mind!" the chief counselor hissed. A passing foot soldier glanced at them strangely, then walked on. "If you place yourself between the emperor's wrath and its target, why do you think you will escape with your life? Don't do this mad thing! Stay out of it!"

Daniel looked away, and up—to the dark places between the stars, out and over the walls, to the west. Then he turned to face Lamech. "My lord—it is a thing I must do. I cannot explain." He turned and walked quickly back toward the citadel. Lamech stood staring after him.

"Belteshazzar," he muttered. "If ever that man needed his name to be true, it is now. *Bal-atsu-usur*," Lamech whispered in Chaldean. "Lord Bel, protect his life."

◆　◆　◆

HANANIAH ALLOWED the final tones of the harp to vibrate in the chamber before damping the trembling chords with his fingertips. He closed his eyes for a moment, then looked up at Mishael. A silent smile passed between them.

The music had been good. Song, singer, and player were welded into a single entity—borne aloft, to be lost in the diverse oneness of melody and phrase. The smile signified their communion, their appreciation of the selfless congruence of the music—they knew how rare are the times when the artist is privileged to feel himself a conduit for the creation of true beauty. For the brief time while they performed, beauty had lived, shimmering and evanescent, in the chamber of Nebuchadrezzar.

Even the emperor, accustomed to such nightly concerts,

was moved by the simple elegance of the ancient song. He stirred from his reverie to ask, "What was the tune you performed just now?"

Mishael bowed his head in respect. "My lord, it was an ancient song of our people. The melody is called 'The Death of the Son.'"

"Did you invent this melody?"

"Oh, no, my lord!" Mishael gave a small, downcast smile. "I could never compose a thing of such radiance. This air was conceived many, many generations ago by the first great king of our people—David, the Lord's Anointed."

Nebuchadrezzar peered closely at the musicians as he drummed his fingers on his thigh. "Ah, yes! You are of the Hebrews!"

Mishael and Hananiah bowed their heads in acknowledgment.

Nebuchadrezzar shifted on his cushion to glance at Nebuzaradan, the field commander of the armies of Babylon, seated behind his right shoulder. "Do you remember these fellows, Lord Zaradan? They must have come here at the same time you brought that young boy—what was his name? The son of that fool Jehoiakim?"

"Jeconiah, my lord," answered the commander.

"Yes, that's the one." The emperor looked from beneath his eyebrows at the two musicians, waiting to be commanded either to leave or to play another song. "You!" Nebuchadrezzar asked, looking at Hananiah. "What's your name?"

The harpist shifted uneasily. He was far less comfortable with words than Mishael. He preferred to speak with his fingers on the strings. Finally he mumbled shyly, "Shadrach, my lord."

"Tell me this, then, Shadrach: That frightened boy-king of your people who sits in my dungeon—was he anointed by this silent god of yours? What about Zedekiah, his ingrate uncle who now pretends to sit on the throne in your tiny homeland? Has this god of yours chosen him, as well?"

Hananiah turned red with consternation, his face firmly downcast as he searched within himself for an answer at once true and inoffensive. But the emperor didn't wait for his reply.

"And what good does it do them—this anointing? Will it save them from my anger? Does this god of yours do anything to preserve his precious 'anointed ones'?"

Nebuzaradan shifted uncomfortably on his cushion. The emperor was working himself into one of his bloody moods. It was frightening to be about when he was like this. Far safer, in fact, to be on the field of battle.

"Well, Shadrach?" demanded the emperor into the awkward silence. "What about this god of yours who places imbeciles and traitors on the throne of his little kingdom?"

Hananiah's heart pounded in fear, and Mishael's eyes were round and white with trepidation. Almost of their own volition, Hananiah's fingers went to his harp, plucking out the first few notes of a melody. Helplessly, his eyes pleaded with Mishael to join in. His was the music, the melody, but not the words. He desperately needed his friend to assist, to complete the message that was the only answer he knew to this moment of mortal fear.

Hesitantly, glancing back and forth from the emperor to his friend's face, Mishael began singing. It was another of the psalms of David:

> Listen to my prayer, O God,
> do not ignore my plea;
> hear me and answer me.
> My thoughts trouble me and I am distraught
> at the voice of the enemy,
> at the stares of the wicked;
> for they bring down suffering upon me
> and revile me in their anger.
>
> My heart is in anguish within me;
> the terrors of death assault me,

> *fear and trembling have beset me;*
> *horror has overwhelmed me—*

Abruptly they stopped after Nebuchadrezzar vaulted to his feet, his face white with fear. Covering his face with his hands, he turned away from the startled musicians and the confused general.

How could they have known? the emperor asked himself. *How could this harpist's fingers pluck from his instrument the very essence of my dream-terror? How could this alien eunuch speak the very words which are the quivering center of my nameless dread?*

This song, composed by a long-dead king of an insignificant people, had gripped his heart like a mailed fist. How was it possible?

◆　◆　◆

DANIEL CAREFULLY DESCENDED the stairs leading to the dungeon. At the bottom, seated on a straw mat in a shuddering circle of torchlight, was Uruk. The Sumerian commander glanced upward as he heard the footsteps coming toward him.

"Belteshazzar!" he greeted Daniel. "What errand brings you to this dismal place?"

"Lord Uruk," Daniel began, after swallowing several times, "I must speak with you about the emperor's decree."

"Which one?"

"The one concerning…" He took another deep breath. "Concerning the mages and seers. Your lieutenant told me I would find you here."

Uruk stared sidelong at Daniel, then glanced toward the massive doors behind which the chief mages and seers were being held. "And what have you to do with these charlatans?" asked the commander.

Daniel paused again before answering. "The emperor will sin greatly if he does this thing. I must tell him. Where is he?"

Uruk stared at Daniel as if he had just uttered gibberish. "You…you had best reconsider, Belteshazzar. You are not known for being a fool—don't begin acting that way. The emperor is the regent of Marduk. Their wills are one. Don't go in to Nebuchadrezzar with your Hebrew notions of right and wrong—he is not constrained by them."

Daniel shifted nervously on his feet before locking eyes with the commander of the guard. "My lord Uruk, I must go to him. If it is the will of the Lord that I live, I will live. If not, I will die."

"The lord will most certainly order your death, if you speak to him as you have spoken to me," retorted Uruk.

"You misunderstand, Lord Uruk. In Hebrew we have a word—*Adonai Elohim*—it means 'Lord of gods.' It is *this* Lord's will which preserves my life, or takes it. The emperor is but His servant, as are we all."

Uruk's hand strayed to his sword. He should summarily execute this young Hebrew for such treasonous talk of the emperor. But even as he gripped the haft of the weapon, his hand stilled. He studied the earnest, unswerving face of the counselor for ten, perhaps twenty heartbeats...then looked away.

"The emperor is in his private chamber," the commander husked. "Go to him, if you dare."

♦ ♦ ♦

IN THE SILENT CHAMBER, Nebuchadrezzar sat back heavily upon his cushion. Warily he looked again at Meshach and Shadrach, heads bowed in silence before him. "Who are you people?" he whispered. "What is it about you?"

His mind fled back ten years—to the time when his edict had summoned the best and brightest of the newly subject Hebrews to Babylon. Hardly had they arrived before they were creating consternation in the palace. Nebuchadrezzar remembered the nervous face of old Ashpenaz, his chief eunuch, now dead these three years. The man had come trembling before the king because he could not persuade his young Hebrew charges to eat the same ration as the other boys in training for the royal service. It was always something like that with this kind: They were bright, responsive, adept at almost any task given—and quietly adamant about the strange scruples of their nameless god. One might punish them for their obstinacy one instant, and in the next instant feel oddly unclean, chastised by their silent fidelity. They obeyed, but always in a way which reminded the emperor that, in their eyes at least, his was not the final word.

Mishael spoke softly. "My lord, it is not we who are of any account. It is our God, the Lord of heaven and earth, who kneads the hearts of men, who judges between the guilty and the innocent."

Nebuchadrezzar's nostrils flared, but he said nothing as Mishael went on.

"What Shadrach has attempted to say," the singer said, glancing at his friend and then back to the emperor, "is that our God humbles men who do not perform His will—even…" —Mishael took a deep breath—"even kings," he finished quietly.

At that moment Daniel entered the room, prostrating himself in the doorway.

Nebuchadrezzar glanced up. "Enter, Belteshazzar. For some reason, I am not surprised to see you."

Daniel stood, a slight smile quickly crossing his face as he recognized his friends kneeling in front of the emperor. Then his expression resumed the worried look of burdened purpose.

"My lord," began Daniel, "I have come to you to beg for the lives of the chief mages and seers."

Nebuchadrezzar stared at his counselor in disbelief.

5

DANIEL LAY TOSSING on his couch, restlessly watching the stars crawl slowly past the cracks in the ventilation grille just below the wood-planked ceiling of his bedroom. For the hundredth time since he lay down, he breathed a prayer: "Sovereign Lord, grant me the vision which will turn aside the emperor's wrath."

Nebuchadrezzar had heard him out, somewhat to Daniel's amazement. Again Daniel heard himself before the emperor requesting time to ask the Lord of heaven to reveal to him the dream that was causing the emperor's vexation.

Mishael and Hananiah had sat in slack-jawed shock as they heard their friend offer to ferret out the king's dream. They heard as well the dreadful certainty in Nebuchadrezzar's voice response.

"Belteshazzar," he had said, with a solemnity more fearful than open anger, "you have dared to reproach your sovereign. You have presumed to sue for the repeal of a decree which I have made and sealed with my own hand. You have come to me and spoken of the displeasure of this god of yours. Had you made such a disrespectful request in the public court, you would already be dead."

Again, lying on his bed, Daniel felt fear stinging his face as he remembered: The chamber had swirled about him while he awaited what he thought was certain and instant doom. Thoughtfully Nebuchadrezzar had studied the bowed heads of Mishael and Hananiah. Daniel felt sure the pounding of his heart had been audible in the chamber.

"But I know of your service to Lamech, and of your wisdom—a wisdom beyond your years," continued the emperor, more to himself than to them. He had looked at the three of them, studying each whitened face carefully, as if seeing them for the first time—or the thousandth.

His eyes returned to Daniel then, and he pronounced the next words in a ringing, ceremonial voice. "Know this then, Counselor Belteshazzar: I will grant you one night. If on the morrow you cannot bring me the solution to my problem, you …and you, and you," he said, pointing at Mishael and Hananiah, "shall suffer the same fate as the mages. Since you have taken up the cause of those I had determined to punish, you shall share their punishment if you fail. So let it be done."

The three had returned home with numb steps. When they told Azariah what had happened, the friends knelt, bound together in a fervent prayer for deliverance. Then, each dragging his own personal shackle of fateful resignation, they had gone to their beds.

Daniel rose now from his pallet. He paced toward his doorway, then back again. *Why?* he asked himself. *Why did I feel so strangely compelled to go to the emperor? What was this maddening voice within, calling so insistently, yet impossible to hear with clarity?*

He remembered the blind beggar on Aibur Shabu, and the chilling sensation that the old man's sightless eyes were actually seeing him in a way he could not see himself. An intuition of *choosing* had flowed from the seedy presence of the beggar; when the bedraggled old man nodded his head, Daniel felt he had passed some unknown, unfathomable muster. He would suit the purpose, the old man's nod seemed to say. But what purpose? Whose choosing? And after tomorrow morning, would it matter?

He flung himself back onto his bed, burying his face in his arms. "O God of my people," he half-sobbed, "I beg for deliverance, for knowledge—and for rest."

After what seemed ages, he drifted into a troubled doze.

He stood in a lofty place, though his feet rested on no surface he could see. Like a hovering bird he felt himself suspended above the ter-

rain—a familiar landscape, and yet as alien as the bottom of the Great Sea. The air was still, hushed. He was waiting for something unknown. Oddly he felt no fear, but rather a tingling in the pit of his stomach, a nervous anticipation, like that of a child waiting in the crowd at the edge of a wide street for the beginning of a royal procession.

Below him was a statue, and a man. The man was looking at the statue and smiling—admiring the image. Daniel looked closer, and felt his heart skip a beat. The emperor! He wanted to cry out, to warn his lord of whatever awaited. For he knew—how, he wasn't sure—that whatever came would come in awesome and irresistible change for the man and the statue below. Absolute destruction—or rebirth.

But he was mute. In the tableau played out below, he was intended to be a witness, not a participant. For a moment he struggled against the numbness in his throat before feeling a gentle, infinitely strong hand laid upon his lips. He ceased struggling, waiting in chest-pounding passivity for what would happen next.

When he heard the sound, he knew, with a knowledge beyond vision, what it was. Looking up with a grimace of fear, he saw the glittering stone rushing toward the figures below. He found himself nodding in recognition, even as he trembled to see the impossibly huge, white-hot gem bludgeoning its way toward the mark.

He heard screams from the tiny figure of the emperor, saw him flee in panic, cringing like a cur as the stone struck home.

"Daniel! Daniel!"

He snapped awake in a rush of half-choked cries. Azariah stood over him, gripping his shoulders and staring into his face with the intensity and concern of a worried brother. The rosy pigments of dawn collected on the grille above his bed, barely illuminating the shadowy outlines of his still-dark room.

"You were shouting, thrashing about," said Azariah in answer to Daniel's disoriented, questioning look. "You must have been fighting a demon in your sleep."

In a flash, it came clear. A bubble of excited joy lodged in his chest, and he smiled broadly at his friend. "Yes, Azariah!"

Daniel exclaimed, sitting bolt upright. "I fought a demon—and won!"

◆ ◆ ◆

TOYING PENSIVELY with the ivory hilt of his dagger, Nebuchadrezzar sat in his private chamber, awaiting the gathering of the court. The handle was carved from the tusk of one of the strange, huge beasts living beyond the cataracts of the Great River in Egypt. The design was of a rampant lion—an echo of the device in the throne room facade—and the beast's eyes were tiny emeralds. The butt of the weapon was of filigreed silver, the blade etched with mystical characters the smith had assured him would protect its royal wielder.

He pressed the tip of the blade into the heel of his left hand, drawing a tiny bead of blood. Indeed, he thought, the great Nebuchadrezzar bleeds like any other man. He smirked: *What would happen if this became public knowledge?* With the flat of the blade he smeared the blood across the pivot of his thumb, wiping the dagger on his sleeve and returning it to its sheath.

He bled—and dreamed—like all ordinary mortals. The three Hebrews, acting in unaccountable, unplanned consort, had reminded him of this. Had he been wrong to pronounce certain doom on them? They had not set out to offend him—he knew this deep in his heart. Almost, last night, he had been moved to clemency, and nearly to outright belief in Belteshazzar's mad promise. Even this morning he felt in his heart a tiny spark of fear: Perhaps the Hebrew could succeed. Nebuchadrezzar was not sure he really wanted the oracle of his dream proclaimed.

Belteshazzar and the two others had held up to his face the unwanted mirror of his own mortality and weakness. Without knowing it, each of the three had shoved him harshly against the cold reality of a huge, unrelenting Unknown. Though he did not taste in the Hebrews the conceited, self-serving air of the mages, still they, like those despised conjurers, had forced him to contemplate the unseen, uncontrollable tides of destiny and eternity. If they had no answers to offer, he thought, they deserved the same fate—however fair their words and music.

A discreet rap on the door told him the nobles and scribes were assembled in the throne room. He rose, gathering his purple linen robes about him, and paced to the door.

Tension crackled in the throne room of Babylon as the emperor seated himself. To one side, his left, crouched the chief mages and seers, rumpled and bedraggled from their sleepless night in the dungeon. To the rear of the hall were the nobles and attendants to the court, each waiting in stiff-faced uncertainty to see which way the wind would blow the blaze of the emperor's anger. Perhaps their apprehension was the reason for the wide, empty space before the dais.

On the other side of the hall, in a small group, were Belteshazzar and his friends. Their demeanor radiated an amazing air of calm, thought Nebuchadrezzar as he took his seat. It was odd—no more than a trick of perception, surely—but a beam of light from one of the windows appeared to fall upon the Hebrews as they prostrated themselves before him.

Commander Uruk uttered the customary invocation, and the throng raised itself slowly from the floor.

"Hear the word of the emperor," began Nebuchadrezzar. "The mages remain under the sentence of death." A muffled whimper could be heard from the wretched group on his left. "Nevertheless, for the sake of Belteshazzar, our counselor, we have agreed to stay the execution of the sentence until today. Belteshazzar, come forth!"

Lamech, standing rigidly in the back of the hall, felt his heart thud leadenly as Daniel strode forward to stand before the emperor. A knot of grief swelled in his throat: This good and honest young man did not deserve death. He murmured a fervent prayer to Adad, his patron deity.

"Belteshazzar has petitioned us for a hearing before this court. He has said that he will interpret for us the dream which these—" Nebuchadrezzar waved deprecatingly toward the mages—"could not."

The court buzzed with amazement at this unexpected development.

"Very well then, Belteshazzar," said the emperor, bringing his gaze to bear upon the fair, confident face of the young Hebrew. "Are you able to describe and elucidate our dream, according to your word?"

The court fell so silent that Lamech fancied he could hear a beetle scurrying along a window ledge high overhead.

Adad-ibni peeked from between his fingers, holding his breath. Who was this impetuous stripling, and why should he place his neck on the block alongside the mages? The chief seer found himself praying that this upstart might actually succeed —then, despite himself, hoping he would not.

The eyes of Azariah, Mishael, and Hananiah were glued to their friend. Daniel had always been the one they looked to, more than any other, for direction. Each found himself wondering, even as he beseeched the Eternal: Was Daniel about to blunder off a cliff, pulling them after him?

Nabu-Naid's black eyes flicked to and fro from the mages, to the emperor, and to Azariah, his aide. Could he rescue his own Abed-Nabu from the guilt of association with his foolish friend, this brazen interloper who now opened his mouth to speak? The prime minister rued the thought of losing so able an assistant.

"No man can read the signs of dreams, my lord," said Daniel in a clear, strong voice. Lamech felt his heart falling into his stomach. He saw Uruk's hand go to the hilt of his sword.

"No mage, astrologer, or diviner can explain to the emperor this mystery which confuses. But," continued Daniel, pausing as he drew a deep breath and squared his shoulders, "there is a God in heaven who can reveal mysteries."

Adad-ibni glanced about at his cronies. To what god did this boy refer? Which totem, which altar had been neglected in their feverish rush through the pantheon? A silent shrug passed among them as they turned to hear the Hebrew's next words.

"Your dream, O great Nebuchadrezzar, concerns the things that shall be: The Lord of Hosts has partly drawn aside the veil of the future, and has favored the king with a glimpse of years to come. As you lay upon your couch, my lord, this is what you saw…"

The visions tumbled from Daniel's tongue in a bright and terrifying cascade of splendor and awe. Every person in the court stood entranced as the young Hebrew described the flash of gold, the dull stolidity of iron, the telltale weakness of clay. As one man they sucked in their breath, fairly hearing the inexorable rumble of the rock as it bore down on the image like the fist of a god. Each felt his knees weaken as the stone shattered the image, each longed to cover his face and hide from the fearful grandeur of the stone which filled the whole earth.

When Daniel finished his depiction of the dream, the shadows had moved the length of a man's arm across the glazed brick floor of the throne room. Yet during the narration, not a muscle had moved, not an eye had stirred from the face of this young Hebrew. No one needed to observe the emperor's white-knuckled grip on the dragon throne or his amazed, unnerved stare to know the truth of Daniel's telling. Each one present felt its truth, its inevitability resounding within his soul.

"And now, O great king, I will give you the meaning of these things," said Daniel. The words were filling his mind, cramming themselves eagerly to his lips. He felt himself to be a funnel, a sluice-gate for a torrent from the very mind of the Eternal. He began to shake, to reel with the effort of expressing the vast sweep of time—of kingdoms, lands, and peoples—portrayed in the king's dream. It was like trying to capture the fury of the desert wind within a clay jar. And when he spoke of that final kingdom—that realm which would encompass the whole world, and even more than the world—he felt his heart would burst from the joyous and worshipful astonishment he felt toward the Eternal, the God of the Universe, *El-Shaddai*. Who else but He could bring such things to pass?

Daniel finished speaking, passing a hand wearily over his

eyes. He wavered on his feet from the exhaustion of the oracle, and Azariah rushed forward to steady him. When he regained his breath, he stared into the emperor's eyes, his face blazing with the potency of his message. "The great God has shown the king what will take place in the future," he said in a voice like a battle trumpet. "The dream is true and the interpretation is trustworthy."

With the gait of a crippled old man, Nebuchadrezzar rose from his throne. The court stood transfixed as the emperor of Babylon shuffled toward Daniel, his gaze locked onto Daniel's eyes like a lodestone. Slowly, almost in fear, Nebuchadrezzar approached this one who had just spoken aloud the stuff of his innermost soul. When he was an arm's length from Daniel, the emperor halted, looking at Daniel with an expression that defied description. And all Babylon would never forget what happened next.

The emperor did obeisance to his servant. Nebuchadrezzar, King of Lands, Emperor of the Two Rivers and the Shores of the Great Sea, bowed low before Daniel-Belteshazzar, and paid him reverence. One by one, every knee in the throne room bent in silent acknowledgment of the naked power of the words of this young Hebrew.

Adad-ibni raised his eyes from the floor just enough to see the feet of Daniel. Like a thieving dog who hears the steps of his master in the gateway, the chief seer was afraid—and resentful.

Nabu-Naid, for his part, surreptitiously studied the face of the Hebrew boy. The prime minister squinted, pursing his lips. *Another piece of the puzzle,* he thought.

6

THE TALE OF DANIEL'S FEAT ran from the palace throughout the city like a million scurrying ants. In the shops, in the bazaars, even in the temples of the lesser gods, the name of Belteshazzar of Judah was whispered in tones of awe. The young counselor's reputation took on the aura of a talisman, a wisdom-charm to be rubbed when one didn't know what else to do.

Within the Hebrew community Daniel's deed was a source of pride and a cautiously quiet boasting. His name even found mention in an oracle on the fate of Judah spoken by the wild-eyed prophet-priest Ezekiel. Overnight, Daniel's foreknowledge had become proverbial.

Daniel himself was placed in a peculiar position by his new-found notoriety. Lamech, his mentor, now looked at him askance, with a wary mix of malaise and respect. He felt this was not at all the same young man whom he had grown to like —even to value. A new and unsettling dimension of Belteshazzar's character had come to light in a way that left him unable to see his protégé with the same eyes. He found himself unsure whether to, as before, dispatch Belteshazzar on this or that errand, or to bow before him and receive orders from such a messenger of the gods.

Uruk the Sumerian was also confused. The commander of the guards had seen the Hebrew youth act the part of a mage and perform duties in the fashion of a mage—yet Daniel did not claim to be such. Uruk felt he ought to place this young prodigy in the same category of mistrust in which he held the abashed Adad-ibni and his ilk, but something about Belteshazzar's openness, his lack of pretense, made this impossible. The commander even heard that the boy refused to be consulted by those who now eagerly pressed him for advice on other matters. Hardly a day went by when Belteshazzar was not accosted by some young functionary who wished the Hebrew's input on whether he should take this or that post, or by some aging, anxious merchant who wanted the meaning of a troubling dream or imagined omen. Belteshazzar steadfastly refused to be dragged into such matters, on the grounds that his eerily accurate vision of the king's nightmare was a special dispensation by his god, not a freshly tapped reservoir of augury, to be turned on and off like the spigot of a beer cask. Nothing was so sure a passage to the topmost levels of Chaldean society, if not of the royal court itself, as being recognized as a new seer —but Daniel did not deign to play such a game.

Such refusal of proffered advantage lay beyond Uruk's experience. In the imperial court of Babylon, one did not ignore such opportunities. One grasped the mantle of influence whenever it was available—ripping it off another's shoulders if necessary.

Even among his friends, Daniel felt himself adrift on a raft of strangeness in a sea of sidelong glances. Whatever Hananiah, Mishael, and Azariah thought of recent events, they did not feel at liberty to discuss it with him. He heard the quiet conversations which ceased suddenly upon his entering the room; he felt the back of his neck itching from the thoughtful stares when he walked away. He longed to talk to them as before, without the unseen barrier of intimidation which rose up involuntarily when he approached. He began to resent the heavy gift the Eternal had placed upon his shoulders.

One day he sat alone in the main room, halfheartedly picking at a meal of salted lamb and dried figs. The other three friends' duties kept them away. His old servant Caleb shuffled in, carrying a bucket of dates for sorting. He had been working in the courtyard, but the midday heat had driven him to a cooler place.

Thoughtfully Daniel observed the slow, patient toil, the

wrinkled old hands of Caleb. He had not seen Daniel, who was seated in a far corner of the room, leaning against an inside wall to savor the lingering night-coolness within the two-cubit-thick walls. Quietly the old man worked, inspecting each piece of fruit, tossing the spoiled dates aside, saving the good to be stored for later use. Daniel, starved for human conversation, began talking softly at the deaf old man.

"Once, when I was a boy, my father told me the story of Joseph," Daniel mused. "Have you heard that story, Caleb? No, of course not. You haven't heard anything in such a long time I doubt you'd even remember. In any case, I remember that my father—this was in our homeland, Caleb. In Judah. Do you even remember Judah? My father often told me how Jacob's youngest son had dreams. And those dreams drove a wedge between Joseph and his brothers..."

The old longing, the aching sorrow for Zion, fell about his shoulders with its well-worn, familiar creases of poignant loss. He thought of his father—he of the strong hands and easy laugh—whom he hadn't seen since the last, lingering glance over his shoulder as the hostage-train departed Jerusalem. He remembered his mother, too—her soft hands, her ready lap. And he remembered her raw wails as he walked away from her under Chaldean guard. Her face that day was an open wound, as if her life bled away through her weeping eyes.

Daniel watched Caleb's patient hands as they sorted and sifted—tossing this brown, wrinkled lump aside, placing this one in the storage jar. "Do you ever feel that way, Father Caleb? Do you sometimes sense the chasm of silence dividing you from the world through which you move so slowly and quietly? Do you ever wish for better hearing, Caleb? Do you wish to be able to respond to something other than shouts and gestures?" A moment more Daniel watched Caleb contentedly dividing the good from the bad. "Or do you enjoy your solitude, your apartness?"

Daniel sighed, turning his head away from the servant and his task. "I never wanted apartness, Father Caleb. I wanted only to do the will of the Eternal. Yet it seems that apartness is the fruit of such labor." Daniel closed his eyes, listening to the soft plop-plopping of the good and bad dates.

Then the sounds of Caleb's toil ceased. Daniel opened his eyes and looked back toward the old man. Caleb was returning his stare. Apparently Caleb had just noticed he was not alone in the room.

"Young master!" he crackled in his liver-spotted voice, "I didn't know you were here!"

Daniel smiled at the wispy old man. "I came in here to take some food," he half-shouted. "I was eating when you came in out of the heat," he said, gesturing toward the courtyard.

A slow, considering look crossed Caleb's face, and Daniel grimaced inwardly. He knew the signs: He was about to get one of Caleb's nonsensical replies to the question he thought he'd heard. Caleb began nodding sagely.

"Yes, young master," the old man opined carefully. "Perhaps you should speak to the Teacher. Ezekiel is a wise man, besides being a prophet of the Most High. Yes," Caleb finished matter-of-factly, as if the matter were settled, "I think it would be a good thing for you to speak with Ezekiel."

Daniel began to chuckle, then caught himself up short. Hadn't he been longing for counsel, for guidance through the bog of confusion in which he found himself? Who would know better how to advise him than one who had felt, at least as keenly, the burden of the Lord? With new eyes, Daniel studied Caleb. The servant sat as before, studiously sifting through the pile of fruit. The good here, the bad there. Who really knew what went on beneath the thinning white hairs of that old skull?

Shaking his head and smiling sardonically, Daniel rose to take his dish to the kitchen. Caleb glanced up as he passed, giving Daniel a quick smile before returning to his work.

"And stop calling me 'young master,'" muttered Daniel as he stepped into the glare of the courtyard.

♦ ♦ ♦

AT THE ENTRANCE of the counting-house stood Jacob bar-Uriah, or Egibi as he was known in the Aramaic dialect of the empire. As was his habit, he was watching the faces of Babylon passing in the street. He and his sons ran a moderately prosperous lending and buying trade, and the counting-house was located on a street just off Aibur Shabu, in the financial district which centered around the Esagila temple complex.

Egibi, unlike the latecomers making the trek from Judah with Daniel and his peers, had lived in Babylon for two score of years. His people traced their roots to Shechem in Israel, not far from Samaria, capital of the mostly forgotten northern kingdom of Israel. Since the conquest of Sargon the Assyrian almost three generations past, Egibi's clan had been Babylonians—first as subjects of the kings of Nineveh, then as citizens of the kingdom of Nabopolassar and his son, the great Nebuchadrezzar. In his youth Egibi was a traveling merchant, plying the trade routes from the spice kingdoms of the Arabah to the bustling seaports of Phoenicia. He had finally grown too old for such wandering, settling here in this thriving metropolis on the banks of the Euphrates. Like his father before him, he decided Babylon was where he belonged. He took to wife a Chaldean girl; then, as his fortunes expanded, he took two more. Truth to tell, he rarely thought of himself anymore as Jacob bar-Uriah, son of Israel. For many years now he knew himself mostly as Egibi, merchant and lender of Babylon.

The temples had the bulk of the moneychanging trade, but Egibi and Sons managed to make a more-than-adequate living from their particular niche of the business—lending to those who were either unwilling or unable to approach the temples' agents. Perhaps the borrower had already defaulted on a debt to one of the god-houses. Or perhaps, like the pious among the Hebrews, they were loath to obligate themselves to an agreement with one of the deities of the imperial city. Though gods from a myriad lands had found a home in Babylon, still some folk felt disloyal to their upbringing or customs if they literally or figuratively indebted themselves to the gods of Babylon. To Egibi it was all the same—business was business.

Egibi had a shrewd eye for human nature. By observation he could usually tell if a prospective borrower presented a potential collection problem. Where another banker might be misled by fine clothing, the flash of jewelry, and a confident facade, Egibi could study such an applicant and decide he would not allow his silver to leave the counting-house without a significant security pledge—a slave, perhaps, or a yoke of oxen, depending on the size of the loan desired. Egibi had rarely been left with a bad debt he couldn't turn to profit by selling repossessed property.

As Egibi continued watching the street, one of his scribes touched him lightly on the shoulder and held out a clay cylinder. The merchant turned to take the ochre, sun-baked article. It fit easily in his palm, being of about equal length to the span from his fingertips to the heel of his hand. He turned it over, studying the cipher scrawled about the outside of the cylinder. "Whose loan is this?" he asked, squinting at the cuneiform crow-tracks scribbled all around the document. "Either your handwriting is getting worse, Shatak, or my eyes are."

The Chaldean scribe smiled. "It is the loan of Sin-malik, the weaver. He is two cycles of the moon past due."

Egibi grimaced. He sincerely liked the weaver. This loan was one of the very few he had allowed himself to make in violation of his instincts. The tradesman had borrowed up to his limit with several temples, and had even had property remanded to the house of Sin, his namesake deity. But then he had approached Egibi with a proposition: He had secured an agreement to provide a Tyrian linen merchant with a large quantity of finely woven cloth. The partner would then dye the cloth with the coveted Phoenician purple, and ship it back for resale. The profit, it was assumed, would be enough to repay Sin-malik for the cost of materials and provide a generous return for himself and the partner in Tyre.

Alas, the Tyrian merchant proved less than trustworthy. He

had originally agreed to pay a substantial deposit for the cloth, enabling Sin-malik to build larger looms to accommodate the increased volume of production he must undertake. Then things started to go awry. Sin-malik had already commissioned and begun the construction of the looms when word arrived from Tyre that the partner would not be able to make the initial earnest payment. Then he wheedled Sin-malik into accepting smaller and smaller shipments. It seemed the market for purple linen was much stronger in the cities of the north, and the partner assured him they would both benefit more handsomely.

The final upshot was that Sin-malik had come in desperation to Egibi for ten *mana* of silver to pay the craftsmen who had built the looms. The fellows were getting dangerously impatient for their money. Because of his personal regard for the hardworking, if too trusting, Sin-malik, Egibi had agreed to the loan.

"Break it open," Egibi now said to the scribe, handing over the clay cylinder.

In Babylon, business contracts and almost everything else were written on tablets of dampened clay, the arrow-shaped characters inscribed with pointed sticks. Both parties to the agreement affixed a name or totem to the pancake-shaped tablet, which was then carefully rolled into a cylinder while still moist. This was then sun-baked, then wrapped inside another clay tablet on which was inscribed identifying and descriptive information. This second, outer layer was then baked into place around the actual contract. This method prevented tampering with the original document.

Egibi watched as the scribe carefully cracked the clay envelope surrounding the loan agreement. Glancing at it to ascertain that it was undamaged, the scribe offered it without comment to his employer.

Egibi scanned the cylinder, then looked away, clucking his tongue and scratching his beard in consternation. It was as he had remembered. He had given Sin-malik the silver with no security other than the weaver's solemn oath to repay. Such cases could get unpleasant, usually involving litigation of the matter before a mutually recognized authority. In this instance, the situation was further complicated by Egibi's reluctance to take Sin-malik to law. He asked himself which he wanted more: the continued friendship of Sin-malik, or the return of the ten *mana* with an additional two *mana* in interest which the weaver owed him. It would be difficult to have both.

Egibi was roused from his quandary by the clopping approach of a squad of horsemen. He looked up and saw six Medes approaching, the reins dangling loosely from the necks of their statuesque mounts. The horses moved with loose-jointed grace, their ears flickering eagerly this way and that. From the orange-hued dust on their gear and the crusts of dried sweat on the horses' flanks and withers, Egibi surmised the riders must have traveled hard, perhaps day and night, from the Medean capital of Ecbatana more than a hundred leagues to the north and east.

Possibly it was their fatigue which allowed the riders to ignore the uneasy glances of the passersby. Asturagash, heir of Cyaxeres and now king of the Medes, was in name at least an ally of Nebuchadrezzar like his father. But the Medean hegemony arched far along the eastern border of the Chaldean lands, and away to the north. Like a fat serpent it lay along the frontiers of Akkad and the old territories of Assyria, reaching to the edge of the Lydian domain of King Croesus. It was said that Ecbatana controlled unimaginably vast tracts to the east—stretching over endless ranges of rugged, desolate mountains. The emperor's announced purpose for the recently completed fortifications along the Tigris River between Opis and Sippar was defense against the steppe-dwelling nomads who periodically made incursions into the rich cities of the alluvial plain, but few were under any delusions about the real threat. Nebuchadrezzar doubtless felt the ominous weight of his supposed ally leaning against his eastern flank.

The leader dismounted, grimacing at the kinks in his joints, and approached the merchant. "Peace to you, Egibi," he said in eastern-accented Aramaic, bowing slightly in greeting.

Egibi returned the salutation. "And peace to you, worthy Indravash. I trust the road was kind to you?"

"Not so kind that a cup of beer would be unwelcome," responded the Mede.

"Of course!" Egibi motioned to a slave who had materialized just inside the doorway. The boy wheeled and dashed off to perform his errand. "Please come in," continued Egibi solicitously, motioning toward the interior of the counting-house. "It is far cooler inside, and one of my servants will attend your mounts."

"No," said the Mede firmly. He turned to one of the members of his party. "Kurash," he called, "you will stay with the horses. See that they are watered and fed."

A rider, startlingly young to Egibi's eye, swung down nimbly from the back of his steed. Egibi thought he detected the merest flash of resentment in the youth's bearing as he gathered the reins tossed at him by the other dismounting riders, and it struck the merchant as odd. One seldom if ever saw such in the strictly disciplined corps of the Medes... Then Indravash was talking, and Egibi's attention shifted away from the young boy with the smoldering eyes.

"I come on an errand for my lord Asturagash," the captain remarked as they strode through the entrance court of the banker's establishment. Indravash paused, seeking Egibi's eye. "I can, as always, depend on your discretion?"

Egibi shrugged nonchalantly. "Of course." The servant he had dispatched earlier was beside Indravash, pressing into his hand a clay cup of beer fetched from the cool storage vaults below ground. The Mede took three deep, long draughts, swallowing noisily. "Ahh..." he sighed gratefully. "Much better. Lead on, Egibi." Wiping his mouth with the back of his hand, he followed the banker into a private alcove.

Egibi turned to the servant. "See that we are not disturbed." The boy nodded, stationing himself firmly outside the door.

The Mede was speaking again. "How much can you give the king for these?" The rustle of parchment was heard. Then the door closed, cutting off the sounds from inside.

7

DANIEL PECKED NERVOUSLY at the door, half-hoping no one was home. He looked about: The sluggish water of the Zababa Canal oozed past, fetid with the heat and stagnation of midsummer. Ezekiel's house was a rundown, patched-together affair situated in a less-than-desirable corner of the Old City. Not many of the Judean importees had become prosperous, and the relative squalor of Ezekiel's circumstances attested to this. As priest of a nonfavored people, he could hardly command the respect and tithes he might have received in a better place and time.

Following the forced march from Judah, Ezekiel had originally been settled in Nippur, many leagues south of Babylon in the flat plain between the rivers. Following the death of his wife, however, the prophet had relocated to the capital city, where a few of his kinsmen lived.

The door creaked, and Daniel turned, startled. Standing in the open portal was Ezekiel.

The priest-prophet's face was drawn, his eyes dark sockets of almost unbearable anguish. His beard, though still dark, showed at its edges the early hoarfrost of impending autumn. He wore a soiled, threadbare cloak of rough-woven wool—much mended, though none too skillfully. He radiated such an air of fatigue, of utter exhaustion, that only the unyielding urgency of his inner vision seemed to be holding him upright. From Ezekiel's haggard, resolute bearing, Daniel had the impression of a man who had been worn away, like a plowshare dulled and abraded by too many seasons of struggle against rocky soil.

Only his eyes showed life, and these burned with an exigency made the more disturbing by juxtaposition against the weariness in his other features—as if something inside him burned too hot to be quenched, undiminished even by the shell of spent flesh which housed it.

The voice of the prophet glowed just as hot as his eyes. "You are Daniel—the one they call Belteshazzar."

It was not a question. Daniel shuddered. "Yes, rabbi. I have come—"

"I know why you are here," interjected Ezekiel abruptly. His words issued forth in a tone full of bright light and sharp edges; they were impossible to ignore, like the cry of a hunting bird.

Ezekiel turned about and went back inside, leaving the door ajar. Daniel was uncertain whether he had been dismissed or allowed—certainly not invited—inside. After an uncomfortable moment or two, he hesitantly entered the house of the prophet.

The interior was dark and not much cooler than the afternoon street. Lacking the niceties of heat-conscious design, Ezekiel's house provided shelter—nothing more. There was no entry hall to shade the inside from the invasive heat of the sun. The door opened onto the west, which made for greater and greater discomfort as the afternoon's rays became more and more direct. The dwelling was constructed of mud-brick, the most plentiful and inexpensive material in the riverine low-lands, but Daniel noticed light—and heat—seeping through gaps in the roof wattle.

If Ezekiel was aware of the slovenliness of his estate, he showed no sign. In fact, the prophet's ramshackle hovel was matched by his appearance and manner. Daniel sensed that the affairs of daily life held but a tired disinterest for Ezekiel—as if he would rather be in another world, where one had no need of houses. Perhaps the darkness and nothingness of Sheol was more suited to the care-worn rabbi's tastes.

Daniel remembered what he had heard of Ezekiel's reputation: of his exotic, mystical visions of flaming wheels and frightening creatures of the air, and of how he had endured the death of his wife with no more weeping than if she had been a stranger to him. On that occasion he had indeed proclaimed an oracle upon his bizarre behavior: In the same fashion, he declared, the Lord would take away from Israel the delight of her eyes and the joy of her heart. Daniel thought of this, and of Azariah's news from Judah, and shuddered.

Daniel also found himself remembering another prophet, another message. Jeremiah, too, had seemed forever weary; the sadness of his burden had dragged at the corners of his eyes, thickened his steps with a mourner's heaviness. Yet there was also a tenderness about him, Daniel recalled: Jeremiah had been able to summon the strength to tell stories to a group of frightened boys.

Ezekiel appeared beyond the ability to give such solace. He sat now, staring a challenge at Daniel. Or perhaps his eyes were those of a man who, having seen too much, craved only rest, resenting those who intruded upon his solitude. Then he broke his own silence with a pronouncement.

"You have seen, Daniel son of Kemuel."

Daniel sucked in his breath—he had not heard his father's name spoken aloud in the decade he had been in Babylon.

"You have seen," continued Ezekiel in his cawing voice,

"and now you cannot go back, cannot live as if you knew nothing."

For twenty breaths, Ezekiel peered into Daniel's soul, nodding slightly at what he saw. "You have seen," he mused, in a softer voice, "yet yours is not the burden of a prophet."

Daniel looked quizzically at the older man. With the same type of surety with which Ezekiel gazed truly into his soul, he knew he had seen. Adonai had shown him, if only for a moment, the disturbing, immense shapes hidden beneath the tidal surges of days to come. What had he done in the court that day, if it was not prophecy? "What is the difference, Rabbi Ezekiel?" he asked.

A mirthless chuckle grudgingly escaped Ezekiel's lips. He looked away. "The difference? What is the difference?" His eyes bored in on Daniel, giving him the uncomfortable impression he had offended in some unintentional way.

"To be forged upon the anvil of God's purpose, to be at once His hammer, His tongs, and His molten iron; to hear words that rend the heart, see visions that pierce the chest; to be emptied like an urn, again and again and again until one desires only rest, only an end to the refilling—and to know one cannot live without the refilling. To be given words that one dare not speak, and to feel those words churning and boiling in the belly until one must speak them aloud, or die. To be despised, soon or late, by everyone except Adonai—and to desire it so, while hating it. This is to be a prophet." Ezekiel's eyes misted over. He withdrew from Daniel, from the present. For several moments the past claimed him—or the future.

Then his fever-bright gaze snapped back to the young man who sat in his house. "When you were granted your vision—did you receive a call, a sending?"

Daniel's face tilted again in uncertainty. "A call...?"

"No, I thought not," snapped Ezekiel decisively. "When the Eternal summons a prophet, always the prophet is commissioned—summoned to a task and a people. And the people, it seems, are foredoomed to be heedless."

Again the faraway look stole over the prophet's face. Daniel felt deep pity stirring within him for the inexpressible sadness which cloaked Ezekiel. He searched for words to bring comfort, to signify sympathy.

"Rabbi, I...I cannot believe that the Hebrews in this place have been entirely ungrateful for your—"

"You think not?" barked Ezekiel. "You think they hear, really discern what the Lord says?" He stared at Daniel a moment more, then snorted in disgust. "Your easy words don't comfort me, boy. I have seen too much, drunk too deeply of the Eternal's anger toward those faithless impostors. No," he continued, shaking his head in tired resignation, "they *merely* attend. They gather in their little groups on the day of *shabbat* and listen politely to the reading of the Law only because they are nostalgic for the trappings of the simpler times. Their hearts are not there. As long as the Temple still stands in Zion, they will not listen with the ears of their souls. As long as they can delude themselves into thinking the covenant remains unbroken..."

The prophet stared vacantly past Daniel into a corner even darker than the rest of the disheveled room. He was quiet for so long Daniel began to quietly gather himself to depart and leave Ezekiel alone with the broken, jagged edges of his pain. Then the prophet spoke again, in a voice tempered into mellowness by the ancient bludgeoning of grief.

"A healing time will come, son of Kemuel. It will be too late for me, but it will come. This, too, I have seen. The dead bones will again be covered with flesh; the city will be rebuilt." He looked carefully at Daniel. "And I think it may be your destiny to be an agent of renewal for Israel. Perhaps it is for this that the Eternal has placed you here—for this moment in history."

Daniel slowly turned these words over in his mind. "But rabbi, if I am not to be a prophet—?"

"Not only to prophets are visions vouchsafed," Ezekiel said, "and not only kings achieve conquests. Adonai is Lord of all, and His providence may not be denied. His victory is sure."

Daniel felt his chest throbbing with the implications of Ezekiel's words. He was not certain he wanted to hear more, but the prophet was not finished.

"He is molding you into His tool, Daniel-Belteshazzar. He is fashioning you for His work. But beware! Stumbling blocks lie before you, and many trials will seek to entangle your feet."

The dark, smoldering eyes of the prophet lanced toward him; he felt the force of their impact pinning him to the place where he sat. It was too much. He scrambled to his feet, afraid of staying here another moment. Here in Ezekiel's hut he felt as if the cords which bound him to the earth were stretched thin, frayed to the breaking point. He had the dizzying sensation that he might snap loose at any moment, careening away into another reality, one for which he knew he was not prepared—yet.

As Daniel backed toward the door, Ezekiel held up a hand. "Wait! There is something you will need!"

Despite himself, Daniel froze, his hand on the latch. The prophet scrambled to a corner of the hovel, scratching through piles of dirty parchment and writing utensils until he found what he sought. He stalked toward Daniel, who waited, heart hammering, by the doorway. "Here. Take these."

Daniel looked down. In Ezekiel's hands he saw two scrolls covered by lambskin sheaths. Slowly, tentatively, he reached out and accepted them. "Rabbi—what are they?"

"The book of the prophet Isaiah," replied Ezekiel, his eyes lovingly caressing the scrolls he had just given away, "and the letters of the prophet Jeremiah." His glittering eyes sought Daniel's. "Read them. Carefully. In them lie the keys to your destiny."

Despite his desire to yank the door open and run away from the otherworldly eyes of the prophet, Daniel tarried a moment more. Staring at the scrolls, his mind formed a timorous query. "R-Rabbi Ezekiel," Daniel stuttered. The prophet, who had half-turned away, halted, his head cocked in a listening attitude. His tongue sticking to the roof of his mouth, Daniel continued, "Rabbi...if you please... Where is the scroll of *your* words? May I be favored with your teachings as well?"

Ezekiel appeared lost in thought, swaying on his feet. Once Daniel thought he was about to fall. Then the prophet turned full about, those hawk's eyes peering again into Daniel's soul. Something which might have been a smile flickered, ghostlike, across his lips. "That scroll is not yet ready for you, Daniel-Belteshazzar," Ezekiel whispered. "When it is time, you shall have it."

With that, Ezekiel wheeled about and returned to his seat, dismissing Daniel with a wave of his hand.

Daniel threw open the door, gratefully soaking up the comforting reality of the outside world, despite its hot torrents of yellow sunlight. Quickly he distanced himself from the house of Ezekiel the prophet.

◆ ◆ ◆

KURASH STROKED THE HORSE'S NECK, slightly comforted in his anger by the familiar sounds of the animal's chewing, and by the rich, salty aroma of the gelding's hide. Not for the first time, he quietly chanted his grievance to his bodyguard. "They have no right, Gobhruz. No right to treat a king's son this way. I am not their valet nor their stable lackey."

Gobhruz, seated behind his young charge, carefully cleared his throat. "My prince, your father warned you: 'Do not expect special treatment from the patrol leader.' Surely you knew how it might be."

Kurash wheeled upon Gobhruz. "In Anshan I am a prince! Is my father any less a king when we ride beyond its borders? Even outside the valley of my father's vassalage, the clans of the Parsis know how to treat a person of royal birth! And my mother was a daughter of the house of their cursed king himself!" Choking on the potent wine of youthful anger, he turned again to the horse. Hiding his tear-stung eyes from his bodyguard, he reached up to twine his fingers in the coarse hairs of the beast's mane. "I tell you, Gobhruz, Indravash mocks me! He snickers behind his hand each time he orders me to fetch and carry for him, because he knows I am helpless, so far from my own people. If we were within a day's ride of Anshan..." Kurash left the rest of the threat unuttered, but Gobhruz, familiar with the prince's temperament, was in little doubt of its tenor or intention.

"My prince," said the older man, seeking to placate the boy, "you must not allow your impatience—"

Kurash made a sound like the snorting of a charger.

"—your impatience with the leader of this mission to blind you to the chance to learn. Look about you!" Gobhruz waved his arm broadly. "We are in Babylon, one of the oldest cities in the world! When our ancestors were still trekking across the grasslands of the north, men were already building huge monuments to the gods of this place. Babylon has much to teach, my prince. See that you take advantage of the opportunity. Perhaps," the bodyguard continued in a lower voice, his eyes carefully averted from the prince's, "it was for this reason that your father allowed you to persuade his permission for this journey..."

Kurash stared hard at Gobhruz for several long breaths. Picking up a saddle cloth, he clambered up onto a hayrack standing beside the feeding animal and began rubbing the horse's back. "I'll tell you this, Gobhruz," the boy muttered as he scoured the crusted salt from the animal's hide, "the next time I come to Babylon, it won't be as saddle drudge to some arrogant Medean horse-captain. Your cousins may insult me with impunity now, but they had best look to themselves."

Gobhruz knew better than to laugh.

♦   ♦   ♦

EVENING GATHERED as Daniel trudged homeward from the palace. The day had been long and his emotions were a ragged tangle of apprehension and faith. He felt Ezekiel's troubling, hopeful words dragging at the heels of his mind. "An agent of renewal," the prophet had called him. Daniel worried at the fabric of his uncertainties, tugging this way and that. He tried vainly to surmise what might lie behind the enigmatic veil of the future.

Turning the corner onto his home street, he sidestepped a swine that was rooting greedily through a pile of refuse. Hundreds of the semi-wild beasts roved the streets of Babylon, scavenging for offal and trying to avoid capture by hungry beggars searching for a free meal. Daniel aimed a kick at the flank of the pig, which scuttled squealing into the purple shadows of twilight.

Night fell, but the heat of midsummer lingered on like an unwelcome guest. Daniel reached his doorway, longing for a drink of cool water from the courtyard urn. As he passed through the portal, he saw lamplight flickering in the doorway of the main room.

Mishael, Azariah, and Hananiah huddled there, their faces drawn and creased. They looked up when Daniel entered. His eyes widened in anxiety, and he involuntarily took half a step backward, so great was the distress traced upon the features of his friends. "What? Is something wrong?" he asked, as the heavy feet of dread pounded up the stairways of his breast.

Azariah stood, his shoulders slumped as if he had just received a public flogging. "The emperor has called for the armies," Azariah announced in a voice of mourning. "Within the month they will depart on a campaign..."—he wavered on his feet, then went on—"to Judah."

Daniel's eyes searched the face of his friend. "Is it as you feared, then?" Dismay clamped its talons about his throat as he remembered Ezekiel's words concerning the Temple and the hearts of the people of Judah.

Slowly, Azariah nodded. Unable to meet Daniel's gaze, he covered his face with a hand. His answer came in a voice scarcely audible, a threadbare rasp of grief.

"The end has come," he said. Then he turned and walked away.

8

THE DAY WAS CLEAR and warm—though without the debilitating scorch of summer. It was late autumn in Babylon, and though the days still became hot, the nights brought refreshing coolness to soothe and comfort the residents of the imperial city.

Most of those residents were gathered along the great street Aibur Shabu—and on the rooftops nearby. Today was the day of the emperor's triumphal procession, his victorious return from the military campaign in the west, along the shores of the Great Sea. The foolish rebellion of the tiny vassal state of Judah had been put down, and the armies of Egypt's Hophra had been taught a stern lesson as well.

The city buzzed with excitement. Necks craned all along the wide thoroughfare, each vying to glimpse the pomp and pageantry of the conquering Nebuchadrezzar. His glory was Babylon's glory, and today Babylon was an eager mirror, reflecting the regal image of her conquering lord. Jugglers, conjurers, and not a few prostitutes—official and otherwise—feverishly worked the throngs on either side of the avenue. Confectioners and bakers vended their wares with loud cries, and children ran laughing to and fro among the legs of smiling, indulgent parents.

On the roof of the citadel stood Daniel and Azariah, looking out over the Processional Way. Their faces and bearing were in marked contrast to the melee of celebration taking place below them. An invisible, impenetrable wall of gloom separated the two friends from the general merrymaking. Lost on them was the carnival atmosphere, the joy and pride of the city for her lord and his conquest. For they knew that below

them would soon pass—displayed for public humiliation—
Zedekiah, last king of the lineage of David. Today, for all to see,
the pride of Judah would be ground into dust under the heel of
Nebuchadrezzar.

The two years of the emperor's campaign had been a cruel
time for the Hebrews of Babylon. Not only was there dire uncertainty for the fate of kinsmen still in Judah, and the dread of
the inevitable slaughter which would surely be precipitated by
the emperor's vengeance—but there was also the stigma of
being blood-kin to a rebellious people. The transplanted Hebrews had not been long in Babylon, and had had neither time
nor inclination to meld with the general populace. Indeed, one
of their queerest traits, in the view of many citizens of the empire, was their separatism, their pathetic, arrogant resistance to
intermarriage, even with the most desirable of Chaldean families. Many of the more stringent Hebrews had come in for severe ostracism for this insolent peculiarity. The name of the
land of their birth, *Yehudah*, had metamorphosed into a com-
monly employed term of derision. In the variant pronunciation
of the Aramaic language, they were called *Iudd*—Jews. In the
mouths of their detractors, the syllable sounded like a curse.

Now the disgrace of their nation would be complete. The
winnowing fork of Nebuchadrezzar had all but depopulated
the land of Judah, leaving behind only such poor souls as could
evade his net or were beneath notice. An entire nation was
being ripped from the territory it had held since the time of
Joshua. Its people were being driven like cattle before the prods
of Nebuchadrezzar's spearmen, and deposited on the banks of
the Euphrates like so much dilapidated baggage.

Not all children of Judah were objects of scorn, however.
Despite his frequent wish for a return to the relative obscurity
he had known before his now famous dream-reading, Daniel
had slowly but surely ascended into the small, closely guarded
circles of the near-great in Babylon. No one to whom the all-
powerful Nebuchadrezzar had done such public honor could
be easily excluded from the councils of leadership. Indeed, in

his dispatches from the campaign the emperor had frequently made specific inquiry as to Belteshazzar's opinion on this or that matter. The shimmering aura of the emperor's sponsorship had placed him on a dizzying pedestal. Without his desiring it, Daniel's words began to have a weight and import far beyond that expected of one so young. In the intricate, mercilessly efficient marketplace of the palace, where the only recognized currency was the favor and regard of Nebuchadrezzar, Belteshazzar daily gained greater credit in the eyes of his peers —to the pleasure of some, the vague unease of others, and the jealous spite of a few.

With a brazen shout, ranks of trumpeters brayed the beginning of the triumphal procession. As they marched through the dragon-frescoed Ishtar Gate, followed by the drummers, a great shout went up from the multitudes lining Aibur Shabu. Sunlight flashed from the polished brass of the trumpets as they sang their harsh, warlike anthem. As if animated by a single spirit, the drummers pounded out the steady, martial beat, sternly insistent in its hypnotic regularity. Soon, even the heartbeats of the crowds along the way seemed to thump in unison with the pulsing tempo of the marching feet.

Behind the trumpet and drum ranks marched the infantry battalions, their lances polished and honed to a dangerous gleam, the tip of each spear singing a glittering paean to Marduk—and to Nebuchadrezzar, his earthly regent. Carrying their lances proudly, perfectly upright, they resembled a parade of straight-pointed, deadly saplings. The foot soldiers of Babylon displayed the strict pride of the victorious host; their eyes were fixed as rigidly ahead as their spears were braced toward the skies.

A detachment of Scythian cavalry came next, in immediate juxtaposition to the severe discipline of the Chaldean infantry. The ponies of the steppe-dwellers capered haphazardly, skittish of the sound into which their riders forced them. Each Scythian carried a recurved bow of carved horn slung across his back, and a short scimitar at his side. The half-wild mercenaries, dressed in their individual, garish notions of martial finery, stared about them in fascination. Many of them had never actually seen the fabled city of Babylon whose battles they had fought so ably.

There was a gap then, a space to allow the adoring multitudes to catch their breath for what came next.

Through the gate came a band of harpists and singers, all dressed in faultless white linen garments. In unison they sang and strummed a praise ode to the Mighty King Nebuchadrezzar. Daniel and Azariah traded a glance. Mishael and Hananiah surely paced among the band below, singing and playing for the glory of the emperor—paying musical tribute to Nebuchadrezzar from a throat raw with weeping, and with fingers numb with shame for the fate of Jerusalem. Far above them, on the roof of the citadel, Daniel and Azariah's hearts went silently toward their friends. They knew each phrase and each plucked note must have been like a dagger thrust into the musicians' souls.

Behind the musicians came a mob of children, dressed alike in blindingly white tunics. The youths scattered lotus petals in the avenue as the noise of the crowds built to a thundering crescendo of anticipation for the imminent appearance of the emperor.

Nebuchadrezzar burst through the Ishtar Gate in a golden chariot drawn by three white, snorting chargers. The Regent of Marduk wore a white linen robe, interwoven with filaments of the finest gold. On his head was the imperial coronet of Babylon, clustered with precious gems of every type imaginable. The sunlight sparkled from the emperor's raiment and diadem as if Marduk, passing high overhead in his own golden chariot, rained benediction upon his blessed one.

Like a god, he received the adoration of his city. Bowls of flower petals had been placed on the rooftops along the Processional Way; the spectators around Daniel and Azariah now eagerly grasped handfuls of the petals and tossed them outward to flutter down in a perfumed cascade on the heads and shoulders of those below. Dutifully, Daniel took up a handful of the petals, dropping them limply over the parapet of the citadel. Without joy, he watched them fall—like the hopes of Zion—at the feet of his emperor.

Oxcarts trundled through the gate: brightly painted wains heaped to overflowing with the plunder of Judah. Daniel gagged in distress, and felt Azariah's fingers digging into his forearm as they watched the sacred golden utensils of the Temple tumble to and fro in the spoil-wagons. Like so much common loot, the censers and urns, the tapers and candlesticks— some fashioned as long ago as the days of Solomon—rode on their way to the storage bins of Marduk's temple. The enormity of such sacrilege was lost on the cheering multitudes along Aibur Shabu. They were completely insensible to the fact that unclean fingers had pawed through that which was sanctified to the Almighty Lord, holy treasure meant to be handled only by the reverent hands of the consecrated sons of Levi. Nebuchadrezzar might just as well have paraded the mothers of Judah, decorated as temple harlots, through the streets of Babylon. But the indignity of the looted Temple treasures was surpassed by what came next.

Tied by a neck-chain to the rearmost wagon, a pitiful, unclothed wretch stumbled through the gate; a pathetic, mocking coda to the sumptuous splendor which had preceded him. His eye-sockets were a pinkish webwork of scar tissue, and his hands waved weakly before him to ward off the unseen obstacles in his path. Zedekiah, last king of Judah, was displayed as a half-starved, naked, dirt-caked object of contempt.

Daniel's eyes followed Zedekiah in horrified fascination, remembering the fair young prince he had so admired as a Judean youth. That which now limped along behind the wagon was a mere wraith, a deplorable echo of that memory. Daniel heard the jeering, and watched with tortured vision as filth and rotten fruit pelted down upon the helpless Zedekiah, replacing the flower petals which had greeted Nebuchadrezzar.

He could not cry aloud, could not release the black wail of anguish which swelled like a stormcloud in his breast, for that would be a mark of disrespect toward the emperor who had justly punished this rebellious fool. The only words he might be permitted were taunts, to be flung like stones at the disgraced enemy of the emperor. So he stood, trembling and silent, gripping the stones of the parapet so tightly that the pads of his fingers bled from the abrasion of the rough surface. Unheeded, Daniel's blood stained the walls of Babylon while Zedekiah, the Blind King of Jerusalem, the Nakedness of David receiving his tribute of ridicule, made his final, misshapen way along Aibur Shabu.

Just down the wall from Belteshazzar, Adad-ibni's eyes followed the pained gaze of the emperor's favored one. *So. The fool weeps for his disgraced kinsman, does he?* A surly smile smeared the mage's face. *So much the better,* he thought. He looked down to study the comic figure of the disgraced king, then slyly peered back to the wounded face of Belteshazzar. If this upstart boy still harbored such strong feelings toward his rebellious homeland, perhaps some use could be made of it. Adad-ibni's mind began to spin, weaving a dark tapestry of swift return to the emperor's good graces—and Belteshazzar's downfall.

◆　◆　◆

IN THE SPACE—perhaps ten paces broad—between the river's edge and the steep outer wall of the imperial residence, a small garden grew…a green island of exuberance afloat between the fluid brown of the river and the fixed brown of the palace. Here, along the white-pebbled paths that wandered among the exotic plants tended by the emperor's gardeners, Daniel walked, searching for Mishael. He quietly parted the fronds of a young palm tree, peering toward the edge of the palace garden, where it bordered the turgid waters of the Euphrates.

Beside the river sat Mishael, gazing across the expanse of brown water. Then he etched a few marks in a clay tablet he held in his lap. He studied what he had written, then stared again across the river, toward the tan walls of the New City. The look on his friend's face—of pained remembering, of helpless, heartbroken longing—speared Daniel's heart with a poignant thrust, wrenching a soft gasp involuntarily from his lips.

Mishael jerked around, then relaxed, recognizing his friend. "So you have found me," he said, smiling guiltily.

"The council meets at midday," said Daniel, glancing at the sun's position. "I need your presence; decisions will have to be made..."

"Yes, I suppose so," sighed the singer. "And yet, Daniel..." He paused and looked away. "I am honored by the trust you place in me, and I am sure the others feel the same way, but..." The shadow of regret flickered across his face before he continued. "But I scarcely have time to sing anymore..." Where words ceased, silence and expression completed Mishael's thoughts.

Several replies died, unuttered, on Daniel's lips. Walking out into the clearing beside the river, he seated himself beside his friend. Nodding at the clay tablet, Daniel asked, "What are you working on?"

"Oh...this." Mishael glanced at the tablet, then away. "It's not much. A few lines, the suggestion of a tune which came to me. Undeveloped, as yet."

"May I hear what you've done?" asked Daniel.

Mishael looked at Daniel. "Oh, it's not that much. Perhaps, when I'm finished with it." His face hid something; Daniel decided to press him.

"Please, Mishael. I'd like to hear what you've done. Just a little?" Daniel gave the eunuch a playful shove on the shoulder. "Why so reluctant? I remember when Azariah would have to threaten you so you'd pipe down long enough for the rest of us to go to sleep."

Mishael smiled at the memory, then looked down at the ground. Sighing deeply, he took up the clay tablet, glanced at it, then placed it beside him on the sand. For a long moment the only sound was the soft lapping of the river's wavelets on the shore. Then Mishael began to sing.

By the waters of Babylon we sat and wept
when we remembered Zion.
There on the poplars we hung our harps,
for there our captors asked us for songs;
our tormentors demanded songs of joy.
They said, "Sing us one of the songs of Zion!"

How can we sing the songs of the Lord
while in a foreign land?
If I forget you, O Jerusalem,
may my right hand forget its skill.
May my tongue cling to the roof of my mouth
if I do not remember you,
if I do not consider Jerusalem my highest joy…

The melody's long, lilting currents flowed past Daniel. Laden with the silt of a nation's grief, it was slow, like a procession of mourning women, and as plaintive as the cry of an abandoned child. It lifted and sank, it swirled and rose, and Daniel heard within it all the soul-deep, death-moaning sadness of a burned city, a desolated land, a broken covenant, a rootless people.

Unbeckoned, the image of blind, naked Zedekiah reared up before his mind's eye: The broken shamble of a dying king now stood as the true image of all that Jerusalem and Zion had become. The bottomless anguish of his bereft people, and their deep yearning for home which could never again be satisfied— all this surged into Daniel's throat like a clot of ancient blood.

When he could speak, he whispered to Mishael, who held his face in his hands. "It will not always be thus, my friend. The Almighty has surely not forgotten us, even here in this strange place."

Mishael raised his tear-streaked face to Daniel's. "And to what should we return?" he asked. "What is left that draws us back, Daniel? Zion is a charred stump, and the hills of Judah are barren with shame." He laughed a short, scornful laugh. "Jacob's seed is come to this, my friend: His line is preserved by eunuchs, vagabonds, and beggars."

Now it was Daniel who stared blindly across the Euphrates. Slowly he shook his head. "I'm... I'm not sure, Mishael," he said finally. "But I feel it here..."—his hand clasped his heart —"that the Lord is not yet done with the children of Abraham. Some purpose, some future promise..." He wrestled vainly with the vague, unutterable wisps of premonition in his mind.

Mishael stood, briskly rubbing his face with both hands as he took several deep breaths. "Enough talk. We should go, should we not? What will the counselors do without their prophet to consult?" he asked playfully.

Daniel smiled weakly, reaching a hand to Mishael for assistance in rising. "Not a prophet," he demurred. "Not yet, anyway."

◆　◆　◆

THEY ENTERED THE COUNCIL CHAMBER and found the other members already seated, staring at them. If they were impatient at being kept waiting, they deemed it unwise to let the emperor's latest favorite see their feelings in their faces. Nearest them as they entered, Azariah cleared his throat, glancing from Adad-ibni, seated across from him, to Daniel.

"Belteshazzar, Lord Adad-ibni has just come from the emperor. He has made a suggestion, accepted by the emperor, that—"

"Perhaps I should inform Lord Belteshazzar of the emperor's wishes in this matter," interrupted the mage, smugly. "Lord Belteshazzar, will you not be seated?" Adad-ibni gestured toward an empty cushion.

Daniel was under no illusions about the solicitous tone of the chief mage's voice. Whatever Adad-ibni was about to say, Daniel doubted its portent was favorable to himself. Slowly, never taking his eyes off the seer's smirking face, Daniel lowered himself into a seat.

9

THE DAY WAS OVERCAST—rare enough for the Chaldean plains. A cool breeze swirled about the great assembly gathered nervously in the plain of Dura at the command of the emperor. On the northwestern horizon the ziggurats and towers of Babylon reared above the flat sweep of the plain. Countless eyes glanced anxiously back toward the city. Many participants silently wished to be back within the comforting walls of their normal routines, rather than standing in the open expanse of Dura, chilled by the winds of winter.

Only Adad-ibni had the look of unmitigated satisfaction plastered across his pudgy features. He cast another glance over the assembled nobles, officials, commanders, and advisers: Everything was proceeding smoothly. The last few stragglers were arriving—to be absent when the emperor came would be tantamount to a death sentence. The chief seer chuckled inwardly with satisfaction, remembering the ashen looks on the faces of Nebuchadrezzar's Hebrew lap-dogs when he'd described his "vision" of this ceremony.

It was simple in concept. He had appealed to the emperor's basic vanity, coupled with his impatience at the series of nettlesome revolts staged by this or that petty monarch or tribal leader. He had described "seeing" such a nascent rebellion about to take place, and "hearing" the instruction of no less an authority than Marduk himself explaining how such trouble might be avoided. The god had "told" Adad-ibni to cause to be erected an image of himself—here, on the plain of Dura. Nor was it lost on the emperor that the seer had described a figure amazingly similar to that of Nebuchadrezzar himself, endowed with a godly aura befitting the earthly regent of the King of Heaven.

Once the emperor had seen the logic of such a plan, had tasted the gratification of ordering such a public display of loyalty to the god of the state—and to himself—the rest of the arrangements were a foregone conclusion. The necessary decrees were drafted, the artisans and musicians commissioned, and the entire enterprise presented to the Privy Council as a plan complete in every detail. By the time Belteshazzar and his Jews knew anything of the little party on the plain, it already had the force of an imperial decree.

Adad-ibni well knew what this meant to the Hebrews and their precious notions of their invisible hill-god. How often he had noticed their reticence to lend support to any enterprise which depended upon the advice of the seers and astrologers. How frequently they managed to be absent from the court on the high-days of the gods. And—most irksome of all to Adad-ibni—how difficult it proved to find them when the offerings for the temples were collected. Because of Daniel's beginner's luck in the matter of the emperor's dream, Adad-ibni had been powerless to redress these grievances—until today.

The image towered above the uncomfortable crowd, soaring sixty cubits into the gray sky. During its construction two workmen had fallen to their deaths from the scaffolding about its shoulders and head—a small enough price to pay. The statue was of wood, with thin sheets of gold hammered to an intimate fit with each carefully carved feature. But the edgy glances of the crowd shifted from the imposing image of Marduk-Nebuchadrezzar to another new construction, one less pleasing to the eye; some fifty paces to the east it rumbled with ominous interior fervor. Even from this distance the heat from the kiln could be felt, teasing the skins of the crowd with its intimations of warmth as if cajoling them, wooing them to seek refuge from the cold within its fiery embrace.

The decree called for the swearing of a loyalty oath and obeisance before the image. The penalty for failure to comply was consignment to the blast-furnace constructed here simultaneously with the statue. This, too, Adad-ibni had "seen." None of the Chaldean nobles and officials could imagine anyone being so idiotic as to defy the emperor's edict. None, that is, but Adad-ibni, and a certain group of decidedly uncomfortable Hebrews standing yonder.

The chief seer smiled at the thought of their dilemma: Either deny Nebuchadrezzar and die instantly and horribly, in public disgrace—confirming the truth of Adad-ibni's "vision" —or deny their god, the private totem of their queer race. Either way, Adad-ibni knew, this day would see the humbling of that troublesome young pup, Belteshazzar. Surreptitiously, the chief seer flicked a look toward the Jews—and felt his eyes bulge with consternation. Belteshazzar was absent! Teeth grinding in frenzy, the mage stared about the crowd, wondering madly at the absence of the very rival for whom this whole set-piece was staged. The emperor's train was nearing the site —where was Belteshazzar the Jew?

♦ ♦ ♦

DANIEL SAT SLUMPED upon his couch, his insides a miserable, churning broth of shame and fear. For the hundredth time he rose and paced to the grille in his east wall, peering uselessly through its thin gaps toward the southeast. There, beyond the walls of the city, his three friends faced dishonor and death. In cowardice, he had abandoned them.

He had rapidly grasped the intent of Adad-ibni's subterfuge. As he sat in the council chamber and listened to the seer unfolding the details of his thinly guised oracle, he had immediately apprehended the choice Adad-ibni intended to force upon him: Yahweh, or Nebuchadrezzar. The Lord of heaven, or the lord of Babylon. Adad-ibni had carefully crafted the trap so that no concealment of convictions, no compromises, no alternatives were possible.

Faced with such a terrifying prospect, his mind rushed to and fro within his skull, like a trapped beast making ceaseless, futile rounds of its cage. During the weeks that the image and the furnace were being built, he had frantically sought the Lord, hour upon hour. He had scanned the scrolls of the prophets given him by Ezekiel, and had earnestly sought the council of the brittle-faced prophet himself—all to no avail. Adonai, the scrolls, and the prophet, alike and equally, stared blankly back in the face of his impassioned pleas, as if to say: Yes, this is what you must choose. And what, O Daniel-Beltes-hazzar, will be your decision? From all his prayers, all his frenzied reading, all his anguished questionings, he gained no comfort, only confrontation. No deliverance; only dread. It became clear to him that his future lay between two stark, uncompromising options. Unable to withstand the dire, gray hopelessness which oppressed him, he had lied.

He had resorted to trickery even more base than that of Adad-ibni. Two nights ago, shamed into seeking the cover of darkness for his deed, he had slinked into a certain sidestreet, sought out a certain apothecary. Silver changed hands.

In the morning, a worried Azariah had sought out the emperor's chamberlain. Belteshazzar, it seemed, lay sick abed, his face a ghastly hue, his breathing labored, vomiting great dry gouts of nothing from bowels twisted like serpents into writhing knots of pain. Surely the lord Nebuchadrezzar did not expect his faithful servant Belteshazzar to attend the ceremony on the plain of Dura, lying, as he did, at death's very doorstep?

An official had been dispatched, an examination made. It was concluded that Belteshazzar indeed would be unable to attend the loyalty-swearing. The emperor, well-apprised of the longstanding faithfulness of Belteshazzar, would gladly exempt him from the edict; indeed, he would send his own physicians to care for the highly regarded Belteshazzar.

Daniel had watched his friends leave this morning, with many a backward glimpse at him—perhaps as fearful for his condition as they were for their own difficulties.

The effects of the drug abating, Daniel lay on his bed, alternately burning with shame and cringing in fear. What had he done? Why had he allowed his friends to walk toward judgment on the Dura plain without him? His lip curled in disgust. He knew at this moment the irony of his dual identity. He was Daniel—"God-is-Judge"—and he was Belteshazzar—"Bel-protects." Would the lie he had practiced upon his master and friends protect him from the final judgment of Him Who Sees? He hid his head in his arms in an agony of inner torment, suspended between his names over the chasm of his guilt.

◆ ◆ ◆

NEBUCHADREZZAR STEPPED from his palanquin, amid the prostrated figures of his nobles and officials. He peered out over the scene, nodding to himself. Yes, this all appeared quite satisfactory. Then he looked at the image he had constructed.

The dream! The same gray blankness of the sky, the same featureless, flat terrain as in the night vision which had tormented him not so many months past. Involuntarily his face tightened, his shoulders knotted. He expected at any moment to hear the threatening rumble of the overpowering, unearthly stone. Fear prickled along his spine in a rush of unreasoning panic, and his nostrils flared in a sudden flashfire of alarm.

Just as he felt he must leap back into his palanquin and order his servants to return him to his fortress, he managed to gain some measure of control over the runaway horses stampeding through his mind. He looked about: His people, his subjects, prostrated themselves in acknowledgment of his power. The statue stood as open endorsement of the blessing of Marduk on himself and his reign. Drawing several deep breaths, he willed himself into possession of his emotions. When he could do so, he strode firmly to the ceremonial seat prepared for him at the front of the assembly, at the very feet of the glittering gold image.

As he seated himself, the crowd rose, on cue. A herald faced the throng, unrolling a sheet of parchment. Clearing his throat, the announcer read into the expectant silence:

"In the name of Marduk the great and powerful, and of Nebuchadrezzar, his son and heir, most beneficent emperor and father of our land:

"Let all who approach this day swear undying loyalty to Marduk and to Nebuchadrezzar, his regent on earth. Let the sound of the pipes and tabors be heard, the stringed lyre and the voice of the singers. Let a song of praise for Marduk and for Nebuchadrezzar his son be heard, and at that song let all those faithfully gathered here fall down at the feet of Marduk and Nebuchadrezzar his son and do reverence to them. So be it, that the peace of the land may be preserved, and that Marduk the great and powerful may grant long life and clear vision to Nebuchadrezzar, his son and regent. Now let all the faithful give ear to the song, and let the name of Marduk and Nebuchadrezzar be praised upon all lips and in all hearts."

The herald rolled up the parchment with a crisp snapping sound, and marched back to the front ranks of the assembly.

For a moment, the only sound was the muted roaring of the flames inside the nearby furnace. Then a chorus of musicians struck into the praise ode to Marduk/Nebuchadrezzar that had been specially composed for this ceremony.

As one, all the assembly fell to the ground, worshiping Marduk and his prince Nebuchadrezzar, who sat, regal and serene, on the seat at the base of the imposing image.

All except for Mishael, Azariah, and Hananiah. The three stood, abject yet unbowed, a blunt, upright, defenseless promontory among the sea of prone figures. When the emperor's eyes fell upon them, he vaulted from the seat, his voice a sudden, heart-stopping roar. "Stop!"

The knife-edge of his command silenced the musicians as abruptly as the snuffing of a lamp. Once again, the only sound was the avid, hungry growling of the flames in the furnace.

Into the awe-struck silence of the assembly crawled the sniveling sound of Adad-ibni's voice, accusing the Hebrews in mean, pleased tones. Mercilessly delighted by the success of his stratagem, his desire to gloat overcame his abashment before the emperor's anger. He could not resist the temptation to smirk over the snare he had constructed for the friends of the hated Belteshazzar.

"My lord, these three did not worship your image as the decree commanded!" he accused needlessly. "These infidels have inserted themselves into your most trusted councils, yet they have no loyalty toward you or toward the gods of your royal house! These three, Shadrach, Meshach, and Abed-Nabu, friends of Belteshazzar..."—he paused, for effect—"landless aliens whom you have sheltered in your own house, are plotting evil toward you, O great Nebuchadrezzar. Surely it is this treachery which my vision warns against!"

A low mumble of amazement and approval endorsed the mage's words. Feeling quite pleased with himself, Adad-ibni bowed toward the emperor, the very picture of humble, faithful service. He could almost forget, in this moment of triumph and vindication, that he had failed to capture Belteshazzar. Besides, there was plenty of time to attend to the last of the despised foursome, now that a wedge of suspicion had been firmly inserted between the emperor and his Jews.

The emperor's eyes were glowing coals. "Bring them to me," he snarled. Uruk, waiting behind Nebuchadrezzar's left shoulder, made a small signal. Three burly bodyguards strode toward the Hebrews, yanking them forward by their tunics. Unresisting, the three were pushed and shoved toward the waiting Nebuchadrezzar.

Nebuzaradan, commander of the host of Babylon, watched through narrowed eyes to see what would happen. Again the Hebrews brought trouble on themselves by their indiscreet zeal. Though the three did not show themselves violent, they would not yield. He had seen this seemingly suicidal behavior before, in Judah—in the oddly proud words of a starving noble-turned-deserter...and in the burning eyes of an old man, a prophet...

Kneeling before the enraged king, Abed-Nabu's eyes sought out those of Nabu-Naid, his master. The prime minister waited quietly at his place on the emperor's right. His bird-black eyes glimmered toward his most able and trusted servant, reflecting a look as stony, as vacant as if he beheld a complete stranger. Abed-Nabu turned away. Nabu-Naid would not intercede for him this day.

Then the emperor was speaking. "Again I find you before me," he hissed in a voice as quiet and menacing as the sound of a lion unsheathing its claws. "And again you, in your stubborn Hebrew way, refuse to give honor and respect to your king! Though you were children of my own body, I would be forced to punish you for this, this..."—his teeth gnashed as he searched for a word—"this outrage! Have you anything to say before I pronounce your doom before this assembly?"

The three looked at each other, their eyes pulsing with fear. By tacit agreement, Mishael the eunuch, singer, and word-crafter, opened his mouth to reply.

"My king," he said in a near-whisper, unable to raise his head, "we have no defense to offer. If you cast us into the furnace..." Speech failed him for a moment; he swallowed dryly several times before he could continue. "Our God is able to rescue us from your hand, my king. But even if He does not see fit to do so..."—more dry swallows, and visible trembling— "you must know, my king, that we cannot bow before your god or worship this image." There was a long pause. "It...it would be sacrilege."

"Enough!" thundered Nebuchadrezzar, no longer able to contain his fury. "I will hear no more of such idiocy! Yonder is real fire, fools!" he raged, his eyes flashing as he glared at their bowed backs. "I, your king, stand here before you now, with real power and real authority! Do you imagine this—this god of yours will save you from me? Where is it, this god?" The word was a sneer. "Let it show itself, if indeed it has any power!"

Nebuzaradan winced, glancing upward involuntarily.

Lancing an arm toward the furnace attendants, the emperor shouted, "Fan the flames! I want a fire as hot as the very sun-chariot of Marduk!" The servants began raising and lowering the huge bellows devices, forcing air into the bottom of the furnace. With each stroke the inferno inside roared more angrily. Soon hungry tongues of fire could be seen spurting from the cracks about the heavy baked-clay doors. Here and there among the seams between the cubit-thick tiles, bits of melted mortar ran in rivulets down the sides of the furnace.

The emperor turned to his bodyguards. "Truss them up like birds for roasting! I will not permit such traitors to die with the dignity of men!" Guards wrapped thongs of rawhide about the limbs of the three, pulling them so tight that blood could be seen oozing through the folds of their clothing, seeping from the cruelly creased flesh of their arms and legs. Two guards then picked up each condemned man, carrying them like sacks of grain toward the waiting embrace of the death-kiln. Even Adad-ibni cowered before the tempest of Nebuchadrezzar's wrath, while watching in morbid fascination to see the fate of his enemies.

The doors of the kiln stood at the head of a small landing, reached by four ascending steps. Two slaves stood on the ground on either side of the platform, holding long poles by which to pull back the doors. As the guards reached the top step, the doors opened. A searing blast of superheated air rushed out, instantly roasting the lungs of the soldiers carrying the Hebrews. They fell limply, toppling the bound Hebrews to the platform like man-sized cocoons shaken from the low limbs of a tree. Even those on the farthest edge of the assembly felt the greedy heat of the furnace—the cold wind of Dura Plain suddenly seemed less an enemy.

With the long poles, the slaves poked and prodded the three prisoners roughly through the blazing doorway into the furnace, then slammed the thick hatchway closed.

No screaming was heard, no last gasps of agony. The three had been alive before being thrust inside, for all had seen them moving helplessly about as the slaves shoved them into the kiln.

Nebuchadrezzar paced slowly to the furnace, ascending the landing. A thick block of Phoenician glass was set in one of the doors, and the emperor now approached this viewing-port, wincing from the heat coming through the massive doors. He peered intently inside until the temperature drove him back.

Staggering down the steps, he held out his hand to receive the skin of water from the attendant who rushed toward him. When he had soothed his face and neck with the water, he stared toward the commander of his bodyguard. "Uruk! Come here!"

Quickly the commander strode to Nebuchadrezzar's side. The emperor asked in an urgent, low voice, "Three? That's how many there were?"

The commander, puzzled, studied the alarmed face of his king. Had the heat addled the emperor? "Yes," he answered hesitantly. "Of course there were three of them, my lord. Why—"

"Go and look!" whispered Nebuchadrezzar, pointing a shaking finger toward the door of the furnace. Taken aback, Uruk stared at the contorted visage of the emperor.

"I said go and look!" Nebuchadrezzar shouted, gripping the front of Uruk's clothing and all but hurling him toward the steps of the landing.

Uruk felt the waves of smothering heat striking him with physical force as he cringed toward the hatchway. Blinking rapidly, his eyes pouring water, he peered through the glass.

The interior of the kiln looked like the abode of Pazuzu, lord of demons. It was a blinding frenzy of white-hot flames. Uruk squinted into the interior, the sweat pouring from him in sheets in his body's futile effort to cool his flesh. Then he saw, and a chill ran down his spine, despite the terrific heat from within.

The king was not mad after all! There were the three Hebrews—impossibly alive! Their cords burned off, they knelt in the midst of the chamber, bowing before a figure whose brightness made the kiln's flames fade into impotence. The figure seemed to be giving some sort of benediction to the three, who now rose and started toward the door. Uruk felt the eyes—or, more properly, the *knowing*—of the bright figure upon him.

And then his mind snapped.

Adad-ibni gasped with the others when the commander of the guard staggered back from the door of the furnace, his hands across his face. He fell backward down the steps and rolled about on the ground, gibbering and writhing as if possessed. Making the sign against the evil eye, Adad-ibni nevertheless felt cold dread slicing into the very marrow of his bones. Something other than the heat had smitten Uruk. Something incalculably more potent.

"Open the doors!" commanded the king.

As the slaves hooked their rods into the door-handles, the crowd began to back away from the furnace—and not for fear of the flames. The attendants pulled, and the thick-tiled doors swung heavily on their pivots.

The three Hebrews stepped forth to the entrance. Their clothing was not so much as singed by the crucible they had entered, their faces not even reddened by the heat! Spontaneously, every knee bent before this fearsome, utterly inexplicable, unlooked-for conclusion to the ceremony on the Dura Plain. The three, who had refused to bow the knee before, now received the awed respect of the highest and mightiest of Babylon.

Nebuchadrezzar, his face in the dirt, recognized at once the resonance within his panting breast. The dream—it lived! All his carefully cultivated and strictly enforced control crumbled into ashes before his very eyes. Perhaps the statue still rose behind him, but its self-important grandeur was made pointless as wind-blown dust by the unimagined, unassailable miracle he and his entire court had just witnessed. He, the King of Lands, might order his entire populace into the furnace—but how could such paltry, transitory dominion compare with the power to preserve life where life could not exist? Any common bandit could take a life—only an Almighty One could give it.

With the dream-fear rising in his throat, he cried, his face still bowed to the ground, "Come out! Come out, you who are servants of—" His mind stalled. What should he call this

Almighty One? Nebuchadrezzar could think of no title worthy of such overcoming, absolute power. Not for nothing was He nameless among the Hebrews! "Servants of *El Illai*, the Most High God, come forth!"

The three, their faces glowing not with the temperature of the kiln but with the lingering glory of the One who had saved them, approached the king and knelt before him who knelt before them.

To Mishael's mind came, almost unbidden, a psalm from the days of David the King:

> *For You, O God, tested us;*
> *You refined us like silver...*
> *We went through fire and water,*
> *but You brought us to a place of abundance...*

The throng made its cautious way, by ones and twos, toward the Hebrews, fingers longing to verify the unbelievable evidence of eyes. Adad-ibni inched to the rear of the crowd. He turned, alone and unnoticed, to retreat to his house—cursing this day by the name of every demon he knew, even as his teeth chattered in fear.

◆ ◆ ◆

AN ICY BLADE stabbed Daniel's heart when he heard the sound. *Tap-tap...tap-tap.* The beggar's cane!

He vaulted to his feet, standing in the middle of his chamber, eyes stretched taut on the rack of his nerves. He knew in his soul why the blind man sought him out. The stench of his disapproval was in Daniel's nostrils. He who had once chosen Daniel to speak to the king now came to reproach—or worse!

Tap-tap...tap-tap. Again! It was not his fevered imagination; the sound was real. Daniel remembered the sightless perception, the careful way the blind man had peered inside him that night on Aibur Shabu. The sense of being summoned, considered, and ratified by the nod of the beggar's head—all these feelings came back to Daniel in a rush, with the sound of wood tapping stone.

Shuffling steps could be heard just outside the door. Daniel wanted to hide, but somehow knew the stain of his faithless cowardice would be as a scent to a tracking hound, leading the ancient messenger directly to his place of concealment.

A shadow fell across his threshold.

"Young master, is there anything I can—What is wrong?" Caleb had halted in mid-stride, just inside the doorway, his face wide with alarmed concern for the strange expression on Daniel's countenance. He held a stick in his hand, one end bloodied. Seeing Daniel staring at the strange implement, he explained, "Oh...this. There was a rat in the scullery—I killed it." Caleb held up the weapon, smiling hopefully. "I came to see if I could bring you something—some broth perhaps, or a cold cloth?"

Daniel passed a hand over his eyes, sighing deeply with guilt-laced relief. "I'm sorry Caleb, to behave so. You frightened me. I thought you...Never mind, Father Caleb," he finished, a weak smile fluttering along his lips. "You were kind to attend me, but I don't need anything just now, thank you."

He gave Caleb what he hoped was a convincing smile, and returned shakily to his couch. The old man shrugged and turned to leave, but not before Daniel heard him mutter, "Not so sure about that."

When Caleb's steps had turned the corner into the main room, Daniel leaned his head upon his arms. Caleb was right. There was indeed something he very much needed just now.

"Have mercy on me, O God, according to Your unfailing love..." He quoted the ancient words of David's confession, the words springing from his heart as if fresh-minted there. "For I know my transgressions, and my sin is always before me..."

PART II

Visions

10

PRINCE KURASH STOOD BESIDE the tenant farmer's field, near the place where the *qanat* surfaced, bringing life-giving water from springs in the faraway mountains. Again he pulled in his faraway thoughts, trying valiantly to listen carefully to the old man's rambling complaint.

"And so you see, my prince, that my crops cannot thrive as in the past, as long as those thieves farther up the *qanat* steal more water than they need. I know my levies have been less of late, but I hope you will tell your gracious father, the king—may the *fravashi* preserve him—that my loyalty and my skill are as great as ever, but I cannot feed my herds dust, which is all I shall have in a few years if those dog-sons up the *qanat* don't change their sorry ways..."

An impressively tall man now and fully bearded, Kurash nodded thoughtfully, even as his awareness resumed its prodigal wanderings, following the direction of his gaze toward the far horizon.

He realized presently that the old farmer's voice had stopped. His eyes met those of the farmer, who waited, plainly expecting some answer to his grievance. Kurash rubbed his beard, studying the craggy, wind-worn face of this man of the earth. Presently he turned to his bodyguard. "Gobhruz, have you made note of this man's predicament?"

"I have, my prince," answered the older man dutifully.

"Very well," the young lord pronounced decisively. Turning away from the farmer, he swung himself up into his saddle. Looking down upon his subject with what he hoped was a benevolent, wise smile, he said, "Ulaig, your problem will be brought before the king. Justice will be done."

The farmer turned away, apparently satisfied for now—or, if not, afraid to say more.

Kurash and Gobhruz reined their horses away from the place, the prince sighing pensively.

"Do these squabbles among the people never end, Gobhruz?" he complained as they rode away. "Is this all a king has to do: arbitrate controversies over water rights, stolen goats, and whether the horse was lame before or after the trade?"

"My prince," shrugged Gobhruz, "the affairs of state are beyond me. But I have observed," he continued, "that a ruler who spends more of his time assuring full bellies for his people usually spends less of his time protecting his neck."

Kurash glanced sidelong at his mentor, grinning from ear to ear. "So the affairs of state are beyond you, are they?"

Gobhruz again shrugged, the tiny smile on his lips hidden by his great bush of graying beard.

They rode into the outskirts of Parsagard, yard fowl and dogs scattering before the hooves of their horses. Those who chanced to glance up long enough to see the prince passing made the small, deferential bow of respect. Kurash had long since become inured to the display; not since childhood had he felt the small tingle of pride when his elders bowed before him.

"Don't you find it odd, Gobhruz," Kurash asked as the horses slowed to a short, choppy trot, "that Parsagard, the capital city of the Parsis, has no walls? The Medes erected great walls around Ecbatana and Shushan—not to mention the huge, thick walls which the Chaldeans built around Babylon and the cities of the plain. I have heard it said," he continued, "that two teams of horses can be driven abreast along the top of Babylon's walls! Can you imagine such a thing, Gobhruz?"

"The mountains of Parsis are our walls, my prince," replied Gobhruz after some thought. "When the Medes began to enter greatly into the affairs of the world, only then did they begin to build walls. That is what greed does to a people—creates the need for walls."

"You speak harshly of your own kin," observed the prince quietly.

"Aye," nodded Gobhruz. "That is why for these many years I have cast my lot with your father and the clans of the Parsis, why I chose to live in Parsagard—the Camp of the Parsis. The tongues of the Medes and Persians may be much the same, but their hearts are not. As long as our peoples wandered together—with the sky of the world as our roof, its grasses our carpet—the need for armies and taxes was not so great. A man with a sound-winded horse was rich. An antelope taken in the chase was a banquet.

"But then," mused the older man as the horses walked through the streets of Parsagard, their hooves kicking up dry spurts of dust in the late summer morning, "the Medes settled in the plain, beside the rivers of Elam. Their eyes began to desire more—and then more still."

Gobhruz's voice fell silent as they reached the stable. The two men dismounted, handing their reins to the attendants who rushed to serve them. Walking along the path toward the gabled-roofed house of the king, Gobhruz mumbled, more to himself than to Kurash, "Uvakhshatra learned well from the Chaldeans. To build, and to burn. To fortify, and to hoard. To write down what is said so that one need not face his opponent, need not remember a man's face nor the sound of his words—only the dry mud-tracks of the words themselves. Uvakhshatra learned well, indeed. His son Asturagash has inherited all his father's greed, but none of his imagination."

Suddenly Gobhruz stopped walking and glared hard at the prince. "Thus it is with those who build empires," he growled into Kurash's startled eyes. "No matter how grand, how noble the original dream, rarely does it outlive the son of the dreamer. Kings are but men, my prince—mark it well."

Scowling at the ground, thinking he had perhaps said too much, the Medean pushed open the heavy wood-plank door of the great hall of Parsagard. Kurash stared thoughtfully at the lowered head of his servant and friend. Then he stepped across the threshold into the house of his father, the king.

Kanbujiya sat upon the throne of his hall—or, rather, within the throne, as if it were a chalice to gather and hold his frail, wasting body. The aged ruler's life flickered like a candle guttering in a breeze. Sometimes Kurash believed his father's face was becoming transparent, as if he might eventually disappear. The frail carpet of flesh covering his tired old bones grew more and more worn and threadbare, though the eyes of the ruler of Anshan were as keen and piercing as ever.

Kurash approached and knelt, kissing the hand of his father.

"My son," came the tired, husky voice, "what will you do now?"

Kurash tilted his head quizzically toward Kanbujiya's wrinkled face, the king's clear amber eyes lancing him with a query he did not understand. "What do you wish me to do, my lord?" the son asked. "I have just come from inspecting the fields and hearing the petitions of your faithful subjects. If you wish," Kurash went on, "I will present the cases for your judgment. Or, if the king is too tired, I will—"

With a feeble wave of his hand and a turning of his head, Kanbujiya cut short his son's speech. With his eyes closed and his head leaning against the back of the throne, Kanbujiya wheezed, "It is far too late in the day to waste breath on humoring a dying old man, my son."

"Father!" protested Kurash. "Do not speak so! Let me get something for you."

"No," whispered the king. "Nothing you can bring will benefit me now, boy." Kurash winced at the last word, but said nothing.

"I know you have been rendering judgments in my name for several months," continued Kanbujiya, his breath coming in shallow, jagged draughts. "What else is to be done, when the king must use all his strength to hold his head upright?"

"No, Father—"

"But what will you do, my son," Kanbujiya persisted, again locking his son's eyes with that stern gaze, so disturbing for its unexpected strength, "when your time soon comes to sit in this seat and command in your own name? What will become of this valley of Anshan? What will happen to the peaceful way we have lived for the years of my stewardship?" As the eyes of his father bored in on him, Kurash dropped his head upon his chest.

"I know what courses in your blood, boy," said the dying king. "I know how poorly tranquility sets with you. And I know, as surely as I hear the beating wings of the *fravashi* who come to bear me to the Undying Flame, that you dream of glory, and of power, and of conquest. This valley of Anshan can no more contain your ambition than a wicker basket can hold live coals. I have seen it in your face since the day they brought you to me for naming."

For several moments the only sound in the hall was the ragged sound of the old man's breathing. Then he roused himself once more. "Kurash—'Shepherd'—is what you are called, my son. Never forget that you are the shepherd of this flock, this house, this land. Be careful where you lead them. Be careful of other pastures, other herds. Be careful…"

A long silence followed, punctuated by the distant outside sounds of children, birds, dogs—of life in Parsagard. When at last he could raise his eyes, Kurash looked again at the face of his father.

The keen eyes of the king were fixed in an unblinking stare toward the raftered ceiling, a glassy, translucent sheen gathering slowly on their drying amber surfaces. Kurash knew. Tenderly he reached up and pressed his father's eyelids closed. Turning to Gobhruz, kneeling silently by the door through which they had entered, he said in the tongue of his homeland, "*Shah mat*—the king is dead."

◆   ◆   ◆

IT WAS THE WEEK of the New Year Festival in Babylon, and the streets of the capital thrummed with the frenetic jubilation of her two hundred thousand residents as they celebrated the most important high day of the year. Many merchants' shops were closed in observance of the feast. Young sons of noblemen and wealthy merchants, emancipated from the strict lessons of their tutors, ran giddy beside the canals and along the avenues, drunk on the freedom that accompanied the celebration. Even the riverside Karum district—its docks, quays, and exchanges usually bustling with commerce until late at night—was largely abandoned during these days. In the month of Nisan, as the sun crossed the midpoint of his journey back from his southern winter quarters, Babylon gave herself wholly to celebrating Marduk's homecoming.

Today was the climactic day of the festival. With great pomp and ceremony, the image of Marduk would parade down the Processional Way, from the Temple of the New Year Festival just outside the Ishtar Gate to the huge temple complex of Esagila. For several days now the god had been sequestered outside the walls of the city in the closely guarded temple, as secret rites were performed to consecrate the city and thank Marduk, Lord of the Sun, for his rebirth and return. Today, with fanfare and flourish, the glittering image, dressed in regal purple linens and resplendent with flower garlands, would proceed along Aibur Shabu while the people showered their praises and adoration upon him. His palanquin would be heaped with grain offerings and the choicest fruits, and a host of brilliantly clad priests would solemnly accompany him to his sanctuary in Esagila.

But this was not the end. Once Marduk was ensconced in his seat of power, the emperor, dressed in the drab costume of a supplicant, would come out of his palace, humbly traveling afoot—with no crown, no gold-threaded linens, no gaudy display of rank or power. The crowds along the way would watch in somber, hushed reverence, in stark contrast to the earlier loud celebration for the passing of Marduk. With only a handful of bodyguards surrounding him, Nebuchadrezzar would make his annual pilgrimage, tracing the god's route along

Aibur Shabu to the judgment seat of Marduk. Here he would prostrate himself before the Father of All, as was proper for the earthly regent of Marduk.

After making the prescribed obeisance and taking part in the sacrifice of a sacred white bull, Nebuchadrezzar would grasp the outstretched hands of the god, and a representative of Marduk would bestow upon the god's earthly prince a scepter, the badge of his favor and authority.

Having thus received his charter to rule for another year, Nebuchadrezzar would throw off his drab cloak to reveal beneath it the splendor befitting the chosen regent of Marduk. A crown of gold would be placed on his head, and a torque of silver about his neck.

By then the late evening shadows would be falling across the broad boulevards of the capital city, but not a soul would stir toward home. They would be crammed as a solid mass into the huge plazas of Esagila and along every approach to the temple complex. Breathlessly, all Babylon would watch as the emperor, no longer displayed as supplicant of Marduk but as his earthly manifestation, passed the portal of the god-house and promenaded toward the ziggurat of Etemenanki, the Foundation of Heaven and Earth. He would ascend the steps to the very topmost platform. To the gaping masses the emperor seemed to climb, like a glittering god, to the roof of heaven itself. There, perhaps two hundred dizzying cubits above the heads of the eagerly waiting masses, Nebuchadrezzar would raise the scepter in a salute to the setting autumn sun.

This was the signal for the revelry to begin in earnest.

◆ ◆ ◆

IN THE DECLINING SUNLIGHT outside the city walls, beneath a grove of palm trees on the river's eastern bank, a few dozen devout Hebrews gathered in a small huddle. This sunset would also mark the day of *shabbat*, although scant few inside the walls of the city would have known or cared. These few under the palm trees did know and care, however, and chose to be here rather than partaking in the merrymaking of the New Year Festival.

A few groups like this one were now clustered in other meeting places—beside a remote stretch of canal, or at an unfrequented section of the riverbank. The Hebrew faithful sought such unobtrusive places for their weekly gatherings because of the unofficial censure and private rancor of much of Babylon's populace. No one, however, dared open hostility toward the Jews; the emperor's edict in favor of the odd religion of Vizier Belteshazzar and his fireproof friends had been in place for almost a score of years.

Despite the resentful mutterings toward the Jews of Babylon, many of them clung tenaciously to these weekly gatherings as the only available means to retain a grip on their identity. The destruction of Jerusalem and the Temple had caused a profound shift in the way these Chosen Ones saw themselves and their God.

How was it possible, they asked, that the covenant God made with Abraham and Jacob, and reiterated to David and Solomon, could be so disastrously and completely revoked? That the Holy One could prove false was unthinkable. Therefore the fault must lie within His people.

This line of reasoning spurred them into meticulous compilation and assiduous study of the Books of the Law and the Prophets. The warnings and pleadings of Isaiah and Jeremiah came to have a retrospective meaning they had never before apprehended. The codes handed down during the Exodus gradually became the measure of faith and practice for a generation of exiles learning to see with new eyes.

As the glowing disc of the sun touched the featureless rim of the western horizon, the middle-aged Levite who presided over this assembly rose to his feet before the group. With eyes closed, swaying to the rhythm of the ancient language of Judah, he led the congregation in the singing of the *Shema*:

> *Hear, O Israel:*
> *The Lord our God, the Lord is One.*

And thou shalt love the Lord thy God
with all thy heart,
and all thy soul,
and all thy strength,
and all thy mind...

As the last tones of the age-old hymn faded in the gloaming, the teacher took up a scroll. Unrolling it to the place he sought, he began reading.

All who make idols are nothing,
and the things they treasure are worthless.
Those who would speak up for them are blind;
they are ignorant, to their own shame...

The blacksmith takes a tool
and works it in the coals;
He shapes an idol with hammers,
he forges it with the might of his arm...

The carpenter measures with a line
and makes an outline with a marker;
He roughs it out with chisels
and marks it with compasses.
He shapes it in the form of a man,
of man in all his glory,
that it may dwell in a shrine...

Far behind him, a great shout went up from Etemenanki and its environs as Nebuchadrezzar's ritual salute to the sinking sun released the tightly wound anticipation of Babylon's celebrants. The heads of the teacher's listeners shifted toward the huge sound, plainly audible even here. For a moment, just outside the walls and a world away, they pondered the vast difference between the quiet, reflective mood in the grove and the raucous, pagan spirit which possessed the vast majority of the empire's citizens on this day. Then their eyes returned to the reader's lips as he went on:

Half of the wood he burns in the fire;
over it he prepares his meal.
He roasts his meat and eats his fill.
He also warms himself and says,
"Ah! I am warm; I see the fire."
From the rest he makes a god, his idol.
He bows down to it and worships,
He prays to it and says,
"Save me — you are my god."
They know nothing, they understand nothing.
Their eyes are plastered over so they cannot see,
and their minds closed so they cannot understand...

Remember these things, O Jacob,
for you are My servant, O Israel!
I have made you; you are My servant.
O, Israel, I will not forget you.
I have swept away your offenses like a cloud,
your sins like the morning mist.
Return to Me, for I have redeemed you...

Carefully the teacher placed the scroll aside, his eyes lowered in reflection for several heartbeats before he faced his audience.

"On this day of all days, my brothers, these words of the blessed prophet Isaiah should remind us that we dwell here, like latter-day sons of Moses, as strangers in a strange land. This place is not our place, and it was not for nothing that the Eternal called our most ancient father Abraham out of this same land, with its false gods and innumerable idols.

"Remember the Lord, my people," he said, his eyes punctuating his words with quiet fervor. "Do not forsake His ways. Keep yourselves according to the covenant He gave us at Mount Sinai. Because our kings and people broke faith with Him when we lived in Judah, He has allowed these calamities to befall us; we are captives here because of the iniquity of the past.

"But the past is not the present, nor the future," the preacher insisted, a faint hope blushing in his cheeks. "The Almighty One is faithful, and He will remember His people. We, for our part, must be faithful to Him."

The rabbi sat down, inviting comment or discussion of the reading. In the lull, the sounds of flutes and tabors, of clapping hands and dancing floated above the walls of the city and down to them on the wind.

One of the younger men rose to speak. "What you say is true, Ezra ben-Seraiah. The people of this place, even its king, do not revere the One. My employer, Jacob the son of Uriah—whose people once knew the Lord—even he does not do righteousness. Babylon has turned aside Jacob's face from the Lord, just as Babylon seeks to do to us all—just as it has done to people of all places for ages beyond remembering. Why then, Teacher, must we continue to pray for the welfare of this place?" The speaker looked about him for support, and saw several heads nodding. Even beyond, in the circle of women and children who sat apart, yet within hearing, his words found acceptance.

He went on: "Like you, Brother Ezra, I am of the tribe and lineage of Levi. I was born in Babylon, and my son is now almost old enough to receive the Law. From the time I can remember anything, I have gathered with the faithful, *shabbat* after *shabbat*, to hear the Law and receive its instruction. Is this all my son may look forward to—an uneasy truce with a king and people who do not know the Living God? How long must we wait for the fulfillment of the word of the Lord, according to His servant Jeremiah? When will the time of return come?"

The young man sat down, having aggravated in each heart present the constant, unspoken question pondered by every Jew in Babylon: *Will it be too late? Will we, or our children's children, be subsumed by the dragging, ever-present seduction of the glittering culture surrounding us? When the Lord calls, will anyone still desire to listen?*

Ezra stared at the ground, unable to frame the words for a

reply. How many times had he asked himself the same thing? How often had he felt the pull, the desire to surrender to the easy blandishments of life within the majority? His own unease tied his tongue, preventing him from giving the quick denial he knew his listeners wanted to hear.

He heard the rustle of robes—someone else standing to speak. Raising his eyes, he saw Daniel looking carefully around the circle of faces. A deeper silence fell as the respected, powerful noble gathered his thoughts.

"Brother Jozadak," he began, addressing the man who had just spoken, "you have well said that this kingdom and its king do not worship the Lord. Who can know this better than I?"

This was accepted silently, each hearer rehearsing his own memories of the career of Daniel-Belteshazzar—interpreter of dreams and confidant of the emperor. Sometimes quietly, often openly, he had interceded on behalf of the people of Israel. What Hebrew did not rest easier at night knowing Daniel sat at Nebuchadrezzar's right hand?

Daniel, for his part, had other memories: of the abandonment of friends and the embracing of falsehood...of the rapping of a beggar's cane, and an inward, certain choosing...of the sickly sweet taste of a lie, and the nausea of guilt. As recently as today, he had fought the old fight with fear—it was not an easy thing for such a highly ranked one as himself to be absent from the New Year Festival.

Taking a deep breath, Daniel went on. "And yet, I believe Adonai has a purpose for this place—perhaps even a love for its people."

Jozadak's expression plainly advertised his skepticism.

"Don't you see, my brothers and sisters?" Daniel asked, his arms spread wide, taking them all within his embrace. "He is the Creator of the whole world, of every living thing, every rock and river. Marduk did not build Babylon! Nabu didn't trace the path for the Tigris and Euphrates! The One God, *El Shaddai*—it is He who has made this and all other places, and who has brought His people here for a season, for purposes of His own."

A few more faces seemed to be listening, turning over these words, strange-sounding though they were.

"Don't you remember," said Daniel, leaning firmly into his plea, "what was spoken by the Lord through the blessed prophet Jeremiah? *'I made the earth and its people and the animals that are on it, and I give it to anyone I please. Now I will hand all your countries over to My servant, Nebuchadrezzar...'"* Daniel allowed the last three words to hang in the air, allowed the silence to shout it in their ears again and again: *My servant, Nebuchadrezzar...*

"A time is coming, my people," said Daniel, "when God shall kindle a light to be seen by all the nations." Something ignited in his voice with those words; a deep, strong radiance spread within him, wafted him upward, giving bright tongue to a beacon-glow better known by the heart than the eyes.

"He shall draw unto himself a holy people called out from every tribe and tongue under heaven," intoned Daniel, his voice like a father's comfort. "And every king, every prince, every power shall serve Him, just as this very day the emperor of Babylon serves Adonai's purpose, though he knows it not."

A few heartbeats longer Daniel stood, staring avidly up through the gently swaying leaves of the palm trees, wrapped deep within the potency of his vision. He remembered the turbulence of words he had uttered on another day, a day when a young man stood in the court of the emperor and spoke of things taught him by a Source beyond. *Has it really been so long ago?* he wondered.

Passing a hand over his eyes, he sat down.

A reflective silence softly enfolded the congregation beneath the palms. As the last gold-and-rose streaks of evening ebbed past the threshold of the west, Ezra picked up his scroll and read softly Isaiah's comforting words of Judah's future, with their mysterious reference to a chosen one called *Kurus* in the Hebrew tongue:

"I am the LORD,
    who has made all things,
who alone stretched out the heavens,
    who spread the earth out by Myself…
who says of Jerusalem, 'It shall be inhabited,'
    of the towns of Judah, 'They shall be built,'
    and of their ruins, 'I will restore them…'
who says of *Kurus*, 'He is My shepherd,
    and will accomplish all that I please…'"

11

THE COUNSELOR'S VOICE droned drily on, drearily reciting statistics gleaned from the tablet he carried, his finger carefully tracing the mud-baked characters as if they were a lifeline, a tether to a cherished reality. His hand cradling his chin, Babylon's Crown Prince Awil-Marduk leaned his elbow wearily on the table in the council chamber, making no effort to hide his boredom.

With the fingers of his other hand he drummed on the tabletop, barely enduring the arid matters of state to which his title had chained him. Far better, he thought, to be on patrol along the Lydian frontier, breathing the crisp mountain air of the Cilician highlands. Or perhaps in the harem, enjoying the music, the incense, the languid eyes and accommodating bodies of the perfumed courtesans. Anywhere but here, listening to this insufferable talk of wheat harvests and droughts, of river traffic and military levies.

Nebuchadrezzar watched his son, bridling with frustration at the boy's complete disregard of his responsibilities. No doubt he would prefer to be gambling on some foot race or trying the latest vintage from Syria. Never mind that he was the designated heir to a domain bestriding not just one, but two of the greatest rivers in the world—and enfolding the great seaports of Phoenicia besides. It was an empire comprising scores of peoples and languages, and commanding wealth beyond the wildest dreams of ordinary mortals. This was Babylon, the repository and treasury of the most ancient civilizations of man —and all her future king could think of was his next dalliance with some sloe-eyed concubine.

Nebuchadrezzar was infuriated. He thought of the dangers and uncertainties which he and his father, Nabopolassar, had overcome to raise Babylon again to her just place among the kingdoms of the earth. Painstakingly they had forged the alliance with Cyaxeres the Mede and his Aryan horsemen. Cautiously—it was years in the planning!—they built their organization, courting the favor of this or that diplomat, soothing with flattery the resentment of this or that disaffected governor. Only when the time was right had they sounded the war cry. And Marduk had granted them victory. The hated Assyrians had been destroyed, their capital ransacked. For fifty years now Nineveh had been an abandoned, haunted ruin, while the bounty of the world flowed into Babylon. But what did Awil-Marduk know of this? There he sat, for all the world like a truant schoolboy being force-fed his lessons!

Though having grown up in the imperial court, the boy's attention had ever tended away from the convoluted affairs of government and politics. Nebuchadrezzar wondered if his son had managed, for all his years of luxurious upbringing, to actually avoid the thought of taking responsibility for that which provided the bounty he thoughtlessly enjoyed. The burden of leadership—grimly earned at great risk and with absolute dedication—seemed repugnant to Awil-Marduk. As well might the plow harness be offered to a wild ass of the plains. Did his son think, unconsciously perhaps, that there might be some way of avoiding the mantle being readied for him?

Nebuchadrezzar rose from the table, able to stomach no more. Hastily the courtiers in the council chamber fell from their seats, making obeisance. Out of the corner of his eye, the emperor saw his son rise to leave with him. Whirling, he thrust his finger in Awil-Marduk's face. "You will stay," he grated through clenched teeth, "and discharge your duty as crown prince. Even I will not live forever, boy, and I did not build this kingdom as your personal plaything. Sit, listen—and by the gods' teeth, learn to be a *king!*" His eyes lashed Awil-Marduk as the crown prince sullenly returned to his place. Still glaring at his recalcitrant son, the emperor spoke to one of the kneeling advisers. "Belteshazzar, do what you can with him. As he is, he is unfit to lead children, much less a kingdom. Perhaps your Hebrew god can open his ears. Apparently I can't."

Daniel's face was burning, as much with embarrassment for such public humiliation of the crown prince as with fear of the wrath of Nebuchadrezzar. Along with the rest of the prostrate courtiers he remained as still as death until the sound of the king's rapid, heavy footsteps had faded into the distant reaches of the palace. Carefully they all resumed their places about the table. Daniel looked up without expression at the crown prince, and remained silent.

Finding his place on the tablet, the counselor resumed his droning report.

Seated at the far end of the table, Prime Minister Nabu-Naid carefully sifted through the scene just ended. Shifting, replacing, recalculating. Pieces of the puzzle clicked into place.

♦　♦　♦

NEBUCHADREZZAR STALKED THROUGH the palace, meeting not a single soul in his angry march—as if his ire plumed out before him like the bow wave of a Phoenician trading vessel, warning all in his path to hide and avoid contact with him. He strode to a courtyard giving access to the huge staged garden he had built so many years before—still the wonder of all who saw it. Passing quickly into the foliage, he climbed to his place of refuge, the place he sought in times like this, when the burden of empire became insufferable.

Sometimes he found it odd: He had commissioned the construction of this extravagant sky-garden to please his earliest wife, a maiden from the hill country of Medea—in fact, the mother of Awil-Marduk, the very son whose intractable lack of vision had driven him here. Weary of the unrelenting flatness of the river-lands, she had wished for some small reminder of her homeland. So he had built this artificial mountain for her, and planted its terraces with all manner of trees and bushes. And yet, he found its green, lofty isolation comforted him more than it did the wife for whom it was intended.

Now he ascended to its highest point, where, from the shade of carefully tended palm trees and tamarisk saplings, he could gaze out over his city—the crown jewel of his empire.

It comforted him to come here and remember all that had been accomplished. He liked the early mornings best, when the city was yet dewy with the repose of the night. But any time was acceptable—especially now, as he heard the rustling leaves whisper solace in his ears, and felt the cool shade caress away the heat of his frustration with Awil-Marduk. By degrees he allowed the seething in his breast to recede, exhaling the stale breath of irritation as he inhaled the calming, cool-scented air of the garden. Picking a handful of ripe dates from one of the miniature palms planted nearby, he chewed the sticky-sweet fruit and contemplated his Babylon.

Surely all this could not be wiped out easily. Yet such was his greatest fear—that all he had so painstakingly forged would be forgotten, and his name be swept aside by the winds of time like dust in the waste places. This—although he could admit it to no man—was the true source of his impatience with his son, his adamant insistence upon the boy's assumption of responsibility.

With each passing year, the shadows in the corners of the king's consciousness testified to the encroachment of his mortality. During the early years, the time of building, he had been too busy to attend to the messages murmuring in the silences of the night. The din of battle and the exhilaration of victory had drowned out the quiet, insistent doubts which waited, cat-like and self-contained, in the undusted corners of his mind.

In these days, however, those soundless voices kept up an incessant din within the chambers of his soul. However he might crave permanence, regardless of the magnificence of his monuments, the voices inexorably reminded him of the ruins of ancient kings, of their stone-carved decrees—fragments of which lay like so much rubble in the study of Nabu-Naid, his prime minister. Lately Nebuchadrezzar had begun having his stone-carvers and masons inscribe his statues and obelisks in the archaic Old Babylonian tongue. Perhaps by evoking the ghosts of history and bygone glories he might somehow create a connection, a bridge of perpetuity, between the forgotten dust of the past and the undreamed-of aspirations of tomorrow.

But the voices still chittered in his ear, mocking his vain, temporary efforts at staving off the inevitable. Here, at the summit of his garden, he could almost forget the voices. How could this vast metropolis, this seething network of diverse tongues and customs held together by his authority and governance, vanish into the sands of time? How could the world forget Babylon? Such was not possible—was it?

Popping another date into his mouth, he chewed as noisily as he could, praying to the the rustling leaves and their green shade to again give him soothing enchantment.

◆　◆　◆

EGIBI SAT IN THE VAULT of his counting-house, once more tallying the day's take. Rubbing his snow-white beard in satisfaction, he reached for his bowl and swallowed a cool draught of beer. He wiped his mouth on the sleeve of his linen robe, nodding slowly to himself.

Two hundred *mana* of silver lay before him. The flickering lamplight reflected softly from its lambent surface. Astyages had been as good as his word—not that Egibi had to rely on the Medean king's word overmuch. Astyages had at least as much reason to desire Egibi's discretion as Egibi had to want the interest on his principal. After all, if it became known in certain quarters that the lord of the Medes pawned his household gods to finance his army's rationing and wages, there would surely be trouble for the son of Cyaxeres. Egibi smiled to himself. How would Nebuchadrezzar like it, he wondered, knowing that a banker within his own capital supported the lifestyle of the Medean monarch?

He took another swallow of beer, allowing his mind to roam along the path of possibility. He had lived a long life, and had seen kingdoms come and go. He recognized the signs: Astyages had allowed his desire for personal comfort and lavish living to overwhelm his judgment. And now he must hock the most cherished totems of his house to prevent disaffection within the ranks of his host.

The banker wondered: How long could Astyages maintain the charade? Already one heard rumblings of change in the east: Generals entertained notions of empire, vassal kings plotted revolt. What was the name of that Parsi cousin or nephew of Astyages? Kyrus, perhaps, or Kurash, was it? Yes, traders talked. One heard things.

And yet… Egibi's fingers caressed the strips of silver stacked in orderly piles next to his scales, a small frown dragging at the corners of his mouth. Through the years he had gained handsomely from Astyages' inability to deny himself. He would regret to see the Mede overthrown. Where would he find another customer as profitable?

A knock on the door interrupted his rumination. The head of his servant Jozadak appeared in the opening. Egibi's eyes sent a silent query toward his overseer.

"Master, the accounts are tabulated and the valuables secured," Jozadak announced. "Is there anything else you require before the doors are locked for the night?"

Egibi squinted at the ceiling a moment, mentally running through the nightly checklist which over the years had become as ingrained in him as the routine by which he dressed himself in the morning. He glanced back at his overseer, about to shake his head in dismissal, when his eye, as acute as ever, discerned some indefinable something in Jozadak's manner; an evaluating, almost unapproving look which gave Egibi pause.

Seeing Egibi's eyes lock with his own, Jozadak looked downward quickly, but too late.

Egibi studied his manager more carefully. Jozadak, conscious of being captured in the act of assessing his employer, stared fixedly at the floor, the color rising in his cheeks. The silence between the two men swelled huge within the small chamber.

"Close the door and sit down, Jozadak," said Egibi quietly. The manager complied. A moment more the older man regarded his overseer, then said, "The way you look at me, Jozadak—as if you don't quite approve of what you see. I have noticed this before."

"I'm sorry, master—"

"You are a fine employee, Jozadak," cut in Egibi. "You have been with me since your youth. What is it in me that you find objectionable? Do I treat you unfairly?"

"No, master," said Jozadak, after an uncomfortable pause, his hands furiously kneading a fold of his robe. "Your employment is agreeable, and I hope my service has been—"

"Exemplary," Egibi finished for him. For several moments he allowed the quiet to gather force. His insight into human nature had not diminished with his years, and he was perceptive enough as a businessman to realize Jozadak's worth to him: The overseer's honesty and industry made him a prized commodity in the firm of Egibi and Sons. Besides, he genuinely liked the man who sat across from him, sweating profusely in the cool vault. And after all, were they not distantly related kinsmen, if the legends were true—the stories about the tribes around Samaria and Jerusalem having once been a single, glorious kingdom?

Finally Egibi's voice pierced the pregnant hush. "Jozadak, I hire scribes and bookkeepers to read my accounts and tell me what I must know, so I do not concern myself much with scrolls and tablets. Instead I have learned in my long life to read people—as carefully as ever you examine the tallies each evening. What I see in your eyes—in those moments when you believe I'm not watching—disturbs me. I am disturbed precisely because I value you. I am not sure whether you perceive something in me which compromises your respect, or are merely analyzing your chances of stealing from me. In either case, I must warn—"

"No, master! It's nothing like that. You must believe me!"

Egibi was taken aback by Jozadak's interruption. After peering at the younger man's insistent face a few surprised moments, he asked quietly, "Then what?"

Once more Jozadak's eyes dropped, his fingers wrapping themselves tightly within the wrinkled creases of his robe. "It's …I can't help thinking…" Chest heaving, Jozadak looked up at Egibi, then away. "Once your people, like my own, knew the Lord of Hosts," he said, unable to look directly at the older man. "Once the people of Israel and Judah were alike in their devotion to the Eternal. But now…" Jozadak gestured helplessly, unable to finish. Wishing he had veiled his feelings more carefully, berating himself for giving occasion to this wretched conversation, he fell miserably silent, waiting for Egibi to dismiss him from his presence, and probably his employ.

"Ah…I see," came Egibi's soft response, after he reflected a moment on Jozadak's words. "I do not care what gods a man prays to if he keeps his word. I have never concerned myself with the religion of my patrons—or my servants, for that matters. As long as—"

"But it makes a difference!" blurted the overseer. "It matters very much, master! A man can be no better and rise no higher than the gods he serves." Jozadak, seeing his employer's puzzled, surprised look, groped for a way to clarify his assertion. "These gods of stone and wood and metal—they are only thinly disguised versions of the desires and grievances of their makers!"

Egibi stared into the intense gleam of Jozadak's eyes. Despite his sophistication and—he had supposed—his indifference to such intangible ideas as gods or the lack of them, he felt something stirring inside him. He was drawn in despite himself by the almost embarrassing candor of the younger man across from him.

"When men pray to Shamash," Jozadak went on, "they really bow to notions of their own strength and radiance. When they worship Ishtar, it is only their own lusts and covetousness which they adore. All these gods are made only by men themselves, and they consist of no more than the fancies, fears, and aspirations of their creators. Men use lifeless images of molded clay and hammered gold as an excuse to applaud themselves."

Egibi shifted uncomfortably. He did not much like the tenor of Jozadak's remarks. They seemed, if not sacrilegious, at least disloyal. He thought of the New Year Festival just concluded and of his own participation in the celebration, along with that of all the most respected merchants and tradesmen in the city. Like the vast majority of the wealthy citizens of Babylon, he had allowed his servants and employees much free time during the festival days in honor of Marduk's homecoming.

"But the Lord God," pressed Jozadak, his face glowing with the earnest heat of conviction, "is above all such limitations. He is above all understanding. He alone is the true God! And He calls His people to be holy, set apart from this city's trappings and its false gods and its—"

"Enough," pronounced Egibi, standing abruptly. "Jozadak, I have heard you. I suggest you keep your opinions about the religions of Babylon to yourself. I do not wish to be without your services, but if your scruples will not allow you to work for me, I will give you high recommendation to others whose employ you find less distasteful. In the meantime, we may consider this interview concluded."

Jozadak, brought up short, made a small bow toward Egibi. "Master, I…I do not wish to leave your service. But I…" Observing Egibi's stern look, he swallowed the words on his tongue. "I will see that the doors are secured," he finished quietly, turning to leave.

"Thank you," said Egibi. "And Jozadak?"

The overseer paused, his hand on the latch of the vault door. His shoulders tensed, as if in anticipation of a blow.

"In the morning," said Egibi, "make sure we have adequate stores of oil on hand. I have heard some of the traders say there may be a shortage soon."

"Yes, master. I will see to it." Then he was gone.

12

THE NIGHT WAS CLEAR, the moon so full and brilliant that Nabu-Naid felt he might almost hear the singing of Sin as he passed overhead in his pearl-white chariot. The prime minister paced along the wall of the citadel overlooking Aibur Shabu, where only weeks before Marduk had ridden in his victorious processional and the emperor had made his annual penitent passage.

But the moon god Sin, not Babylon's Marduk, was the patron deity of the prime minister. His mother was a priestess of Sin in Haran, the northern city now under sway of the barely civilized Medes. Even now, with the temple of her god in shambles, the ancient matron clung tenaciously to life. Perhaps it was only the stubborn will of this shriveled, defiant old woman which maintained one stone of the moon-lord's temple upon another. It grated upon Nabu-Naid to remember the temple of Sin in Haran, and the indignities heaped upon it. In better days the moon-lord had been revered and widely respected —unlike now, when blatant Marduk held his brassy sway over the hearts and minds of the people. It galled Nabu-Naid that Nebuchadrezzar could not be troubled to redress the injustice done to Sin. In these, the emperor's waning days, he could not be bothered by so trivial a matter as the liberation of the disgraced temple of Nabu-Naid's mother and the moon god she served so faithfully.

It would not always be so, the prime minister promised himself. Hearing footsteps, he turned, smiling and opening his arms to greet the one whom he had come here to consult.

"Greetings, most excellent Nergal-Sharezer," the prime minister gushed, gripping the forearms of the emperor's son-in-law as he made a small bow.

Nergal-Sharezer gave a curt nod, returning the salutation. "And health to you, honored Nabu-Naid," clipped the younger man. "You wished to speak with me—somewhere private, you said?" The prince gestured about him. "We are alone, as you can see. What did you wish to say?"

"The young lord says so much in so few words," said Nabu-Naid admiringly. "Certainly, your humble servant is grateful for the prince allowing such an imposition as this meeting."

Nergal-Sharezer looked away, bored, tapping his fingers on his crossed arms.

"If the prince will permit me," hurried Nabu-Naid, "I will speak more directly. Although…in such matters as we must discuss this night, one would be wise to tread carefully." The prime minister allowed the phrase to hang in the air, glistening invitingly in the moonlight.

"Careful of whom?" said the prince finally, unable, despite his air of affected *ennui,* to endure the suspense.

Smiling inwardly, Nabu-Naid leaned toward the prince. "Of those who wish the downfall of Babylon."

Nergal-Sharezer's nostrils flared, his eyes widened. "Is there rebellion afoot?" he demanded.

"Oh, no, no, my lord," assured Nabu-Naid, "nothing... quite so—obvious." The prime minister, knowing the fish was now hooked, caused the inflection of his denial to belie the surety of its words.

"Well, man? What, then?" queried the prince, his voice rising in impatience.

"There are those," answered Nabu-Naid, "who would like nothing better than to see one seated on the Dragon Throne who would be, shall we say, less than vigorous in his prosecution of the affairs of the kingdom. Those, perhaps, who would benefit from the..."—Nabu-Naid affected a look of careful consideration—"the distraction of him who wears the mantle of Nebuchadrezzar. Those, for example, who might stand to gain from the encroachment of the Medes."

Nergal-Sharezer stepped away from the prime minister, thoughtfully rubbing his beard as he gazed out over the city, silvered by the lustrous moon. Slowly he nodded. "Since you have broached the subject, good Nabu-Naid...I too have sometimes thought the crown prince did not have the necessary... discernment for the task of governance. And it is true that Astyages the Mede creeps ever closer to the heart of the empire. Today Haran—tomorrow, who knows?"

"My lord's eyes are truly keen," oozed the prime minister. "A pity that one with such penetrating vision should not inherit the crown—especially with the vital interest my lord has, as prince consort, in the ongoing prosperity of this great empire..."

"Perhaps," agreed Nergal-Sharezer, turning again to face

the older man. "But the honored prime minister knows that our father the emperor has already decreed—"

"Yes, yes," groaned Nabu-Naid, shaking his head in saddened resignation. "A pity, that." For several moments the two men stood silent, contemplating the unfortunate, apparently insurmountable difficulties of the situation. "Still," intoned Nabu-Naid finally, stroking his cheek in deep study, "perhaps..." He allowed a long hush.

"Well? What now?" asked Nergal-Sharezer, his eagerness pathetically obvious in his voice. Again the prime minister sternly suppressed a chuckle.

"I was just thinking," muttered Nabu-Naid, outwardly lost in thought. "There are a few wiser heads among the court—men who might be persuaded to see reason..." He allowed the sentence to ramble into silence. He fancied he could hear Nergal-Sharezer panting with anticipation.

"Yes," Nabu-Naid went on, whispering reflectively, "it is just possible..."

"What should I do?" prompted the prince at last.

Nabu-Naid started as if he had forgotten he was not alone. "Oh, my lord prince," he stuttered, "forgive me. When an old man gets lost inside his own head—"

"Never mind that," urged Nergal-Sharezer. "What is to be done?"

"Nothing for now," cautioned Nabu-Naid. "One must not forget that while our father Nebuchadrezzar lives..." He watched as the prince finished the thought for himself.

"True," conceded Nergal-Sharezer. Peering directly into the older man's eyes, he said, "I am grateful to you, honored Nabu-Naid. It cheers the heart to know there are minds as wise as yours in this city. It gives one hope."

Nabu-Naid bowed humbly. "I am your obedient servant. My only wish is the good of Babylon."

"I must go now," said the prince. "Shall we speak more of this later?"

Nabu-Naid nodded serenely. "In the fullness of time, my prince."

He watched Nergal-Sharezer whirl about, striding across the roof and down the stairway. Then Nabu-Naid gazed upward into the gray-white orb of the full moon.

"Like you, my lord Sin," he said, smiling, "I shine brightest when most men are asleep." Chuckling to himself, he followed the prince toward the stairway.

♦　♦　♦

A SWORD-BRIGHT SWATH of moonlight fell through the window and across Nebuchadrezzar as he tossed on his bed, moaning and muttering. His eyelids fluttered, his fingers twitched as he chased night-phantoms through the dark halls of the dreamworld.

He stood beside the Euphrates, the sky above him the exultant blue of summer. A huge tree rose up before him, the mightiest and most magnificent tree ever seen—a king of trees. Its branches spread wide as if to embrace the entire world. Even the splendid cedars of Lebanon could not compare with this leviathan, the girth of its trunk as great as the base of the Etemenanki ziggurat itself.

As he looked up into its branches, every bough was a chorus of birdsong, every leaf a hymn of joy. He laughed with delight at the beauty of the fruit hanging in profusion from its limbs—so abundant that it seemed this tree, of itself, could feed the whole earth. Beasts of the field and forest lay down in its shade, lulled into peace by the cool tranquility of its overarching shelter.

Even before he looked up into the sky, he felt the heat of holiness raising the hair on the nape of his neck. Afraid to raise his eyes, yet unable to avoid doing so, he looked into the sky to see one coming down from the blue vault whose brightness made the midsummer day darken to twilight by comparison. Beholding the frightful messenger's descent, the emperor had no doubt of his source: He came from the awful presence of the gods themselves—or beyond. Then the holy one spoke in a voice like thunder and storm.

"Cut down the tree and hack off his branches! Strip his foliage and scatter his fruit! Let the beasts flee, and let the birds in the

branches scatter to the four winds! Leave him only a stump and the dead roots in the ground, bound with iron and brass.

"Let the dew of heaven drench him, and let the beasts of the field be his companions. Let his mind leave him, and let the consciousness of an animal be given to him. The holy ones have declared this verdict: 'This shall come to pass, so that all living beings may know that El Illai, the Most High, is sovereign, that His hand extends over all the kingdoms of men from the utmost ends of the earth, and He makes such disposition of them as pleases Him. He sets over them such as He wills, and exalts even the lowliest of men...'"

Nebuchadrezzar's eyes snapped open, staring blindly into the darkness of his bedchamber. His hands, stretched on corpse-rigid arms to either side of him, gripped the fabric of his couch like the throat of an enemy—or a lifeline.

◆　◆　◆

AT THE OTHER END of the palace, Daniel shifted uneasily in his sleep. A voice not heard since—when?—called out to his spirit. Groaning in his slumber, with a knowledge beyond sleep or waking, he recognized the voice of his summoner.

Then he slept on, perhaps realizing he would need all his strength to bear the burden of the vision being placed within him.

◆　◆　◆

A HAGGARD, DROWSY GROUP of astrologers and mages shambled into the council chamber of the emperor. Outside, the cocks still slept, yet these men had been roused from their predawn beds to assemble here at Nebuchadrezzar's command. Mutterings about the emperor's irrational behavior and his possible dotage ceased abruptly when Nebuchadrezzar himself hobbled into the room.

Even allowing for his advancing age, the emperor looked feeble. His appearance was that of a man aging swiftly, beyond the bounds of time's normal passage. The drooping skin under his eyes told the tale of sleeplessness; the harried, haunted glimmer within the eyes told of something else. The wizards and seers genuflected, each wondering what new terror stalked the emperor's soul.

"I have suffered great fear from a dream I have had," the emperor began.

Adad-ibni stiffened. To the wizened mage, this had the unpleasant ring of familiarity.

◆　◆　◆

DANIEL PASSED THROUGH the portal of the house on Adad Street, nodding to the gatekeeper. As he entered the courtyard, he saw Ephratah, the wife of Azariah, gathering water for the morning meal from one of the standing urns along the far wall. As she straightened and turned, he bowed respectfully toward her.

"Peace to this house, and to its mistress," he said.

"And peace to you, friend of my husband," she returned, smiling in greeting. "Azariah is with the children, washing for the meal. Will you break your fast with us, Daniel?"

Grateful to hear his infrequently used Hebrew name spoken aloud, Daniel made a small gesture of appreciation. "Nothing would please me more."

Azariah, though well-advanced in the imperial service and thus entitled to quarters in the palace complex, insisted instead on living in this house in the New City where he had spent so much time. When Azariah took Ephratah to wife, Hananiah— like Daniel, a confirmed bachelor—continued living in the house at Azariah's invitation. He had become like an uncle to Azariah's two sons and daughter, a beloved member of the household. Mishael lived at the palace, as Daniel did, but the four friends maintained close contact, frequently gathering in this house which they had shared as younger men.

This morning Daniel felt a vague sense of foreboding, as if some task faced him for which he had no stomach. He craved laughter, familiar faces, and the warm glow of shared memories as antidotes to the nagging premonition which tapped at his shoulder like an unwelcome guest.

Passing into the family's common room, he passed Caleb— ancient, gnarled, impossibly still alive. The aged servant squatted by the doorway of the common room, awaiting the arrival of the family and the food. Though Azariah and his wife begged him to rest, the dried-up old one—deaf and devoted and stubborn—insisted on continuing to serve the patrons of this house. He shrugged off their entreaties with no more notice than a dumb beast, persisting in the duties which had framed the daily rhythm of his life for more years than anyone else in the house could calculate. It was as if he himself were part of the furnishings of the place; as long as the house lived and functioned, so would he.

Daniel leaned near Caleb's face—in his great age, the old man's vision had begun to fail, even as his hearing had long ago. "Good day, Father Caleb," Daniel shouted, touching a bony shoulder in greeting. "Why don't you return to your couch? Azariah's children can manage the serving duties."

Caleb's eyes, their rheumy orbs enfolded within a face as wrinkled and creased as ancient parchment, flickered over Daniel's face. "Good morning, young master," croaked Caleb. "Please make yourself comfortable. I will bring you food."

Daniel smiled and shook his head. He straightened and turned about just as Azariah entered the room, one hand steadying his daughter on a hip, the other interlocked with that of his youngest son. Seeing the familiar figure standing beside Caleb, Milcah fought free of her father's grasp. She raced across the floor, holding out her hands in a plea for Daniel to pick her up.

Laughing as the little girl toyed with the graying hair about his temples, Daniel hefted Milcah playfully. "Oof," he grunted, "you are too heavy for such games, young maiden."

In response, Milcah twined her arms about Daniel's neck, pressing her cheek against his beard. "It tickles," she smiled.

A young servant bore in a large board, heaped with freshly baked wheat cakes, honey, dates, and soft white goat's cheese. Ephratah came in, carrying a clay jar filled with water. Joel, Azariah's older son, entered from the direction of the sleeping quarters, still rubbing his eyes blearily despite the vigorous scrubbing his father had administered to his face. Dragging cushions and straw mats into place about the board, Daniel and the family of Azariah gathered for the morning meal.

Before anyone touched food, all eyes turned to Azariah, the master of the house. Closing his eyes and raising his hands palm upward in supplication, he intoned, "Blessed art Thou, Eternal God, King of Creation, who has blessed us and given us the fruit of the earth to eat…"

The benediction concluded, each person helped himself to the foodstuffs on the board. Caleb hobbled to his place behind Azariah's left shoulder, ready to fetch and carry or render such assistance as might be needed. The servant who had carried in the food retired unobtrusively to a nearby position where he might see Azariah's discreet hand signals, unobserved by the revered yet feeble Caleb.

"So then, Vizier Belteshazzar," began Azariah in a teasing, pompous tone, "to what do we owe the unexpected delight of your presence at this, our humble house?" Licking the honey from his fingers, he waited, eyes twinkling, for Daniel's reply.

"Why, to this excellent bread, of course," rejoined Daniel. "If the bakers in the Avenue of Enlil knew of its existence, they would kill one another to possess the secret of its making."

Ephratah smiled, rolling her eyes wearily. "Lord Belteshazzar jests, I fear," she said. "Is there no bread in the royal house, that he should be driven so far from his quarters in the palace of the king to this poor board?"

Daniel smiled, a hint of melancholy tugging at the corners of his eyes. "Alas, good mistress, it is distance from the palace I seek this morning. Distance, and the companionship of good friends. The rich foods and veiled hostilities of the imperial court are an inauspicious combination for a settled stomach."

"What is wrong in the court?" asked Azariah, his tone sombered by the dour tone of Daniel's response. "Is the emperor so near death?"

Daniel sighed, toying with his food. "No, it isn't that. In fact, it's nothing I can name. Only a feeling; a sense that something is—about to happen." His eyes locked with those of Azariah, a meaningful communication passing wordlessly between them.

Azariah knew the concerned, burdened, knowing look in Daniel's eyes. He had seen it before, in their youth—in the court of a humiliated, powerless king in Jerusalem, when they were summoned to appear before the cold, evaluating eye of a foreign conqueror's official. He had seen it again when, as frightened boys in this strange new city, they were told they must consume a diet not compatible with their religious scruples; and again, a few years later, when an angry emperor made threats against seers powerless to interpret a troubling dream; and once more, when a decree had gone out concerning a ceremony, an image, and a furnace...

"My friend," said Azariah, "don't borrow trouble. Perhaps you worry about nothing. Let events unfold as they will—there will be time enough then to deal with them." Even as the words left his lips, Azariah knew he spoke nonsense as far as Daniel was concerned.

"What's going to happen, Uncle?" queried Joel, the oldest child. His eyes were wide, his face advertising absolute acceptance of Daniel's intuition. *From the lips of a child,* Azariah thought to himself, looking down at his son.

Daniel smiled, ruffling the hair of the round-eyed boy. "Perhaps nothing, Joel, as your father says. Perhaps I allow the cares and problems of the court to intrude upon me too much." Daniel looked away, over the heads of those seated at the table, his manner far louder than his words.

"Daniel, don't think too much about...the other time," ventured Azariah into the uneasy silence, as the pain of a festering memory clouded his friend's countenance. "A man does what he must, and none of us may reach backward in time to undo what has been done."

Daniel's eyes narrowed, but he said nothing.

"Leave the past in the past," insisted Azariah, sallying once more into the breach of his friend's remorse. "This is a new season, and the mistakes of yesterday need not burden today."

At last Daniel looked at Azariah, a smile of gratitude testing the surface of his lips. "Thank you, old friend," Daniel said. "My heart is warmed by your concern." Looking about him at the other quietly anxious faces at the table, he went on. "In truth, this is what brought me to your house this morning, not the taste of your excellent bread."

Ephratah smiled demurely, inclining her head toward Daniel. "Our home is always open to you," she said. Milcah, seated beside her mother, nodded vigorously.

A low, rasping snore was heard. The eyes of everyone went to Caleb, still seated at his station behind Azariah. The ancient servant had fallen asleep where he sat, his head lolling on his chest. Through his open mouth he sucked noisy draughts of air. The children giggled, covering their mouths to avoid waking the beloved old man. Amid broad smiles, the family resumed its meal.

13

AT MIDMORNING Daniel returned to the palace. As he passed over the bridge spanning the Zababa Canal and on through the wide, guarded gateway of the imperial residence, his eyes met with those of a messenger who was nervously scanning each face which entered or left the palace grounds. Seeing Daniel, he hurried toward the vizier, a relieved expression becalming his troubled face.

"Lord Belteshazzar, you must hurry! I am commanded to take you straightway to the emperor!"

Foreboding balled Daniel's stomach into a cold fist. Nodding, he said to the page, "Lead on." Quickly they passed into a nearby corridor.

♦   ♦   ♦

NEBUCHADREZZAR SAT by a high window overlooking the clustered buildings and the wide, straight thoroughfares of his Babylon. In the middle distance, directly in his line of sight, soared Etemenanki, within the walls of the Esagila complex. But the emperor saw none of this.

His chin rested in his hand as he sat by a small lacquered table, the fingers of his other hand mindlessly sifting leaves of aloe, dried and crushed, from a small carved-ivory bowl. The rich aroma of the spice leaves failed to penetrate his consciousness any more than the sight of his city's energy stimulated his eyesight. Blindly he stared out the window, his vision turned darkly inward. Restlessly, vainly, he pondered the enigma of this latest omen which had invaded his sleep.

Behind him a door opened and closed. Gradually, he became conscious of another presence in the chamber, and turned to look behind him.

Belteshazzar was there, kneeling by the doorway, his eyes fixed in a sad, knowing gaze on the face of his emperor. For as many as thirty heartbeats, the two men beheld each other. The emperor sensed it was not necessary to tell Belteshazzar why he had been summoned: The vizier's eyes exhibited comprehension, pity—and perhaps too much knowledge. It was only needful to fill in certain details. Nebuchadrezzar opened his mouth to speak.

"They could not help me." Nebuchadrezzar's tone was neither angry nor resentful. The emperor was not accusing, not condemning. He was pleading.

Daniel's chest pounded. As He had to Joseph in the most ancient chronicles, the Eternal had given into his hand the secrets of another man's innermost passions. It seemed indecent to know such intensely private things as another man's dreams —let alone an emperor's! Even now, before hearing Nebuchadrezzar's words, Daniel felt the Lord's message burning within him like a white-hot key eager to find its lock. He did not want to hear what would come next, yet knew it could not be avoided. The burden lay before him like the blazing summons of Moses. He could not walk away.

Daniel sighed deeply. "Tell me, my king."

He did.

By the time the emperor had finished speaking, his vizier was trembling visibly. Seeing Belteshazzar's ashen face, his dry swallows, Nebuchadrezzar demanded, "What's wrong? Speak, Belteshazzar! Do not spare my emotions, for I have walked in nothing but fear since this night-specter came to me."

Still Belteshazzar could not speak. His mouth moved, but his voice was mute, swathed in the gauze bindings of dismay.

"Surely knowledge cannot be worse than this dreadful uncertainty!" said Nebuchadrezzar, his voice rising in alarm. *"Speak!"*

But it was not the emperor's apprehension which clamped Daniel's jaws in a vise of panic. He knew the words he must utter, and a chaotic fright gripped him in its cold, ruthless fist— a fear for the wrath he knew his interpretation of the king's dream must engender.

Again he stood divided within himself, as if still young and alone and half-mad with anguish, helplessly pondering two untenable alternatives. Once more the rending agony of choice tore him screaming asunder—Adonai's axe cleanly clove him body from soul, husk from center. This day no apothecary, no cleverly concocted ruse could save him. The heartbreaking loyalty of his deceived friends would not avail now. He balanced on the diamond-sharp point of a sword, and all steps led to doom.

Through the thick, cloying fog of his dismay, he heard the imperative voice of the king: "Speak, Belteshazzar!" In this moment, he fancied Nebuchadrezzar's voice echoing Adonai's command: "Speak!" Looking at the aging monarch, his eyes began to betray him. No longer did Nebuchadrezzar sit in the chair, staring urgently at him. Now his place was taken by an old, blind beggar, peering intently into the abject, quivering center of Daniel's torment, shouting with a silent, deafening voice: "Speak!"

Falling on his face, he heard his words tumbling out in a blubbering rush. "My king, I would to God that the interpretation was directed at your enemies! I beg you, my lord: Consider your ways, and turn, lest the things the Lord has shown me come true!"

Nebuchadrezzar sat absolutely still. His voice came in a low, inflectionless murmur. "What things?"

Blindly Daniel rushed over the precipice of his panic. "The tree, O my king—the tree represents yourself. Your power is great, your rule vast. Many nations and peoples rest in your shade, O Nebuchadrezzar, and your dominion nourishes the whole earth…"

Nebuchadrezzar did not move or speak. His eyes narrowed to slits as he waited wordlessly for Belteshazzar to continue.

"The holy one you saw, my lord, and the command he gave concerning the tree—" A fear-induced palsy clasped Daniel's throat. After several moments of ragged panting, he was able to go on. "This word means that you will be brought down, my king."

Nebuchadrezzar stiffened in his chair. Without looking up from the floor, Daniel felt the icy blast of the king's indignation prickling the nape of his neck. Rushing helplessly forward, he said, "You will live like a beast of the field. The dew of heaven will drench you and your mind will become like that of an animal, until seven times pass. When you acknowledge that the Eternal, and He alone, is sovereign over all creation, then your kingdom and your mind will be restored. This is why the stump and the roots of the tree remain in the ground."

The emperor felt stabbed to the very heart by the graceless words of his vizier. He had humbled himself before Belteshazzar—practically begged! In return he had hoped for the slightest comfort, the smallest crumb of assuagement. Instead, at his most vulnerable moment, Belteshazzar chose to humiliate him with this simpering polemic, wheezing the same tired theme: the power of his nameless god, the sad state of the "chosen" Hebrews. *Here* sat his king, real and alive and in the room—in need of balm. But did Belteshazzar bring words of healing? No! He moaned and whined about his Almighty!

"So," growled Nebuchadrezzar, "the stump remains, does it? How benevolent."

"My king, I beg you," sobbed Daniel, his face mashed into the cold oaken planking of the floor. "Take heed! Consider the error of your ways and turn, that the wrath of the Almighty might be avoided! Lift up the weak, and do justice to the oppressed, and perhaps—"

"*Enough!*" hissed the emperor, thrusting himself angrily from his seat and pacing to the window. He spoke without turning his head. "I protected you. I shielded you from the jealousy and wrath of those who could not allow themselves to see your worth." He snarled over his shoulder toward the cowering vizier: "I brought you into my own house, elevating you above those who had served me far longer. I trusted you, Belteshazzar—and this is how you repay me?"

Galvanized by his wrath, Nebuchadrezzar stood spear-straight, his eyes flashing sparks as he flung verbal coals upon the humped back of Belteshazzar. "Why is simple loyalty so difficult for you Hebrews? Why must your every profession of allegiance be offered alongside the galling, high-handed demands of your invisible Almighty? With one hand you offer service, and with the other you slap the king's dignity in the face!

"Well?" he demanded, wheeling suddenly. "Have you nothing to say, no defense to give?"

Daniel, prone and trembling on the floor, made no response.

"Get out of my sight, and out of my palace," gnashed Nebuchadrezzar in contempt. "For the sake of your past service I will spare your life. But I will not tolerate two-minded advisers in my presence. Leave me at once."

Turning back to the window, he heard the rustle of clothing as Belteshazzar limped forlornly out of the chamber. The door closed, and he was alone with his anger.

◆ ◆ ◆

KURASH ALLOWED the Nisayan gelding to pick its way slowly among the loose stones of the steep trail. The way to the shrine was serpentine, twisting back and forth across the mountainside like water seeking the easiest path to the sea.

The early morning sun splashed crimson and gold along the craggy heights of the Zagrash range. Across the jagged gorge, four peaks reared their heads above their brethren. Kurash studied the scene, appreciating the quadrilateral symmetry which was such an integral part of Parsi symbology: the four winds of earth, the four legs of the horse, the four walls of a house. *Perhaps one day I shall rule four kingdoms*, he thought with a smile.

Turning his head slightly, Kurash asked, "What did you learn in your latest foray among your plain-dwelling brethren, Gobhruz?"

The Mede, his mount carefully following behind that of his liege, thought long before replying. "There is much discontent in Shushan, and elsewhere in the Medean kingdom," the older man said finally. For some moments the only sound was the squeak of polished tack, the clacking of hoof against stone, and the snorting of the horses. "In Ecbatana, of course, King Asturagash maintains iron-fisted control. His profligacies are not much commented upon, as long as the nobles have enough new territory to divide among themselves. Elsewhere…" The unfinished sentence shrugged with possibilities, with conjecture. Gobhruz knew Kurash too well to suppose the inflection would go unnoticed.

Glancing at the peaks above them, rearing saw-toothed against the azure sky of the Parsis, Kurash spoke thoughtfully: "The walls of the clans of Hakhamanish. For long years his children have desired no other fortification. They have dwelt in relative peace and security among their high valleys, content to send their horses and their sons to fight the fights of the Medes, their cousins.

"What will they think," the king of Anshan asked, more of himself than Gobhruz, "of the wide world beyond these mountains, the world of which they know so little? What will they think of the one who leads them forth from this tiny realm into the broad lands of the earth?"

He turned his gaze to the path climbing ahead. "Will they go gladly forth and take their place among the kingdoms of men? Or will they hate the one who invites such an irrevocable birthing?"

◆ ◆ ◆

HEARING THE APPROACH of the two horses, the priest glanced up from his contemplation of the flame on the altar. Assuring himself the fire had sufficient fuel to burn for some time, he rose, dusting off his tunic and woolen breeches.

He bowed as Kurash dismounted, receiving in return the salute of the king of Anshan.

"Greetings, Diravarnya," called Kurash. "And may Ahura Mazda preserve your life."

Bowing toward the fire on the altar, the priest replied, "May the Divine Flame preserve us all to the Day of Testing."

"Do the worshipers provide adequate sustenance for your needs?" asked the young king, handing the reins of his horse to Gobhruz.

"Well enough, my king," replied the priest, his gray eyes never wavering from the face of Kurash. "I am sustained by my service to the Wise Lord. I do not require much."

For several moments the only sound was the sighing of the wind through the desolate crags round about. Kurash and Diravarnya locked gazes in measured silence. Finally the young king tore his eyes away from the calm, unmoving stare of the holy man.

Clearing his throat a trifle too loudly, Kurash said, "I wish to make a gift to the shrine—in the name of my father." In a ruffled, jerky manner, Kurash fumbled in his saddle pouch, fishing out a wallet. From inside it came the muffled clinking of silver. Avoiding the priest's cool gray eyes, he held out the offering. "In the memory of King Kanbujiya, my sire and your protector."

Slowly reaching out to take it, Diravarnya said quietly, "I accept your gift, King Kurash, with thanks, and I am grateful for your memory of me. But my protector is Ahura Mazda, the One Lord, whose flame I guard. As long as it is his will, I shall live; when he wishes it, I will die. So it must be."

With difficulty, Kurash again raised his face to peer at the holy man. After a false start, he stammered, "Diravarnya, I...I would ask a blessing..."

The priest inclined his head, silently waiting for the king's next words. His expression was an odd mixture of curiosity and cognizance—as if he knew what Kurash would say, and only wondered in what words the request would be couched.

The detached, self-possessed manner of Diravarnya the priest rattled Kurash. He was not accustomed to eyes with such long, beyond-seeking focus. Unnerved, he struggled for words to make his petition. "I...I have certain...plans," stuttered Kurash. "Ambitions. Dreams. Will you...could you beseech Ahura Mazda on my—on our behalf?"

A tiny smile pursed Diravarnya's lips. He nodded slightly, as if Kurash's words had merely confirmed what he already suspected. He turned his head to peer into the heart of the flame on the altar.

Turning back to the waiting monarch, he said, "Before our ancestors ever came to this place—indeed, since the beginning of all things—the Wise Lord, Ahura Mazda, taught men to worship him. In fire, sky, and water—in the stars and in the clouds of heaven—in all life and all creation, his hand can be traced. Few are those who hear his voice, Lord Kurash. Fewer still are those who follow.

"All the times and fates of men are in the hands of Ahura Mazda, and have been forever. It is he who raises up kings, and he who abases them. It is he who places song in the heart of the victor, and he who silences the tongue of the vanquished."

Looking carefully into the widened eyes of the young ruler, the holy man continued: "Your days are in his hands, King Kurash, whether you acknowledge him or not. He has already determined your course according to his own designs, and these are the paths you shall surely tread. I believe he calls you forth from Anshan for a purpose—though my poor vision does not extend so far as to see its end. I am not so great a seer as others have been..." The priest looked away wistfully, over the heads of Kurash and his bodyguard, then back again. "If in these words you can find some comfort, Lord Kurash, it is well. Further counsel I cannot give."

Turning away from the king, the holy man went back to his place by the altar. Carefully he added fuel, his attention absorbed by the service he rendered to the flame. He did not glance up when Kurash and Gobhruz remounted, leaving the way they had come.

◆　◆　◆

ADAD-IBNI RUBBED HIS PALMS together in delight, an oily cackle issuing from between his smirking lips.

News of Belteshazzar's disgrace had trickled down from the highest levels of Chaldean society to the lowest, but it was especially here in the palace that its import was felt. The void created by his dismissal brought quick adjustments in the convoluted web of loyalties and alliances by which the courtiers of Babylon lived and died. Spaces were filled, modifications made. Some who thought themselves well-placed experienced a sudden, unwelcome reversal in their prospects; others on the periphery suddenly discovered themselves closer than ever to the dizzying centers of influence. Belteshazzar's great misfortune set off a whole series of sympathetic misfortunes or happy chances, depending on one's prior allegiances.

Adad-ibni himself was one of the primary beneficiaries of Belteshazzar's unexpected humiliation. The mage sat now in his chamber congratulating himself on his good fortune, and glanced up as a knock came on his door. Motioning with his eyes toward his servant, he watched as the slave went to the entryway.

A page entered the room and bowed, holding out a small scrap of parchment. The servant took it and brought it to Adad-ibni.

Quickly the seer scanned the note. It was autographed with the sign of Lord Nabu-Naid. Showing no reaction, the mage dismissed the courier. As the door closed, his eyes narrowed in calculation. He rapidly sifted back and forth through the probabilities created by the invitation he held in his hand. Arriving at a decision, he stood.

"Fetch my robe of office," he ordered his servant. "I must pay an official visit to the emperor."

14

THE LAMP FLAME SPUTTERED unsteadily, signifying a lack of oil in the reservoir. For the third time that night, Azariah rose to fetch additional fuel.

Daniel, Hananiah, and Mishael, gathered in a worried knot around the table on which the lamp sat, watched Azariah leave. The four friends had been huddled in a corner of the main room of the house on Adad Street. Ephratah and the children had long since retired for the night. Indeed, the moon had risen and half-traversed the night sky since the apprehensive discussion had begun. But for these four, sleep fled.

Agitated anxiety shouted in quiet desperation from Daniel's eyes, dancing in nervous twitches along his face. He looked about at his lifelong friends as Azariah returned with the oil and carefully poured it into the lamp's basin. "I tell you, brothers, my fear is less for myself—it's too late for that anyway—than for what may happen to this city if the emperor listens to the wrong advisers. If those whom I suspect gain his ears..." A long, brooding silence followed.

"Adad-ibni cloaks himself in a new smugness these past weeks," agreed Azariah. "Even my own master, the prime minister, is changed in his demeanor toward the emperor. Like you, Daniel, I believe dark work is underfoot in the court. I cannot see the direction of the tide, but I feel the pull of the current."

"When a king asks counsel from one who knows nothing," muttered Mishael gloomily, "it is usually safest to tell the king what he wishes to hear."

"Precisely!" agreed Daniel vehemently. "What benefit are advisers who only parrot the opinions already in the emperor's head? He will hear nothing save his own thoughts, parlayed back to him in words calculated to please his palate. And I— when I was with him and had the chance…" Shamed by the memory of the paralyzing terror that had seized him when he was closeted with the emperor, Daniel fell silent.

"It accomplishes nothing to blame yourself," insisted Azariah, seeing the chagrin on his friend's face. "Who knows whether, given your burden, any of us would have done any better?"

Daniel looked up at him, the slow tread of an accusing memory crossing the careworn track of his face. Azariah looked down, shaking his head. *Still he has not forgiven himself,* he thought.

"Is Nebuchadrezzar's memory so short that he has no fear at all?" asked Mishael. The eunuch shifted uncomfortably, then went on. "How many omens and signs must the Eternal send before the emperor learns to heed such warnings?"

Glancing sharply at his friend, Hananiah softly hummed the opening phrase of a psalm. The two musicians' eyes locked, then Mishael smiled and nodded.

Azariah stared from the round, smooth-cheeked face of Mishael to the withdrawn, ascetic features and shadowed eyes of Hananiah. "What passes between you two?" he demanded a trifle testily.

"Hananiah reminds me of the song of the prophet Hosea," replied Mishael. "The Lord says,

> *When Israel was a child I loved him,*
> *and out of Egypt I called My son.*
> *But the more I called Israel,*
> *the further they went from Me…"*

Azariah contemplated these words a moment, then looked up again at Mishael, puzzlement still creasing his brow. "Unravel your riddle for me, Mishael. I haven't the mind of a poet —I cannot fathom your meaning."

Again Mishael smiled, looking at Hananiah. Patiently he

explained. "I believe Hananiah means this: If the Almighty One, after so many generations of teachers and prophets and plagues and blessings, could not cause Israel and the kings of Samaria to heed His voice, how can we expect Nebuchadrezzar to be mindful of Him after two mere dreams?"

Azariah nodded appreciatively at Hananiah. Looking at the quiet musician, he said, "He who speaks fewest words strikes the most telling blows." After a few moments' reflection, he continued soberly, "The burned ruins of Jerusalem give eloquent testimony to the stubbornness of hearts which should have known better."

As Daniel nodded in agreement, the shadows of trepidation deepened across his visage. His forehead furrowed with the weight of the burden in him, and he stared darkly into the steadily burning lamp flame. "There you have it, my brothers," he said. "I know, as surely as I breathe this moment, that the Unnamed One shall again send His shafts toward the soul of Nebuchadrezzar. If the Eternal did not spare even the House of His Name, what dire consequences may attend the awakening of the emperor of Babylon? And when that happens, what may become of the rest of us?"

His worried glance took them in, each in turn. Failing of any fit answer, the three dropped their eyes to the table top, where the lamp flame flickered, a tiny light lost in the great darkness of the night and the city.

◆　◆　◆

SNIFFING IN DISDAIN, Gaudatra, governor of the Medean province of Elam, looked down the main street of Parsagard. It was not a street really—more a dirt path. Simple, gable-roofed houses of wood and rough-cut stone cluttered randomly about the haphazard, unpretentious village, the Camp of the Parsis, as if the herdsmen led by this Kurash person had simply allowed their stick-and-hide tents to ossify where they sat in this small valley among the Zagrash highlands.

Accustomed to the grandiose scale and permanence of the walled cities of Medea, Gaudatra found himself wondering:

Could this disorganized hamlet—without walls or planning or architecture, and with yard fowl, dogs, and urchins chasing each other noisily between the unpainted dwellings—could this really be the capital of the great leader he had been hearing so much about?

He arrived in front of another of the tent-shaped houses, distinct from the others only for its size. That, and the contingent of armed Parsis guarding the bronze-sheathed oaken doors, were the only hint that Gaudatra had reached the palace —if such a dignified term might serve—of Kurash, King of Anshan and of the Clans of Parsis. Of course, since these highland cousins of the Medes were illiterate, no legend or motto endorsed the emissary's supposition. Shaking his head in disgust, he stepped from his palanquin.

His bodyguard parted to make way for him, their mounts tossing their heads and rattling the bits in their mouths. Striding to the leader of the guards, he said in a bored voice, "Announce me to your master. I am Gaudatra, lord of the province of Elam and servant of the emperor Asturagash, monarch of the Medes."

Without glancing at the finely dressed emissary, the commander replied tersely, "My lord Kurash is in council. He may not be disturbed at this time. When he commands me, I shall be pleased to escort you into his presence."

Astounded by such arrogant, unjustified audacity, Gaudatra was speechless. He stood gulping air like a beached fish, uncertain where to begin in berating this bumpkin for such presumption.

A day and a half of tedious, wearying travel—most of it uphill—had been required to reach this insignificant, outcountry settlement. They had wound through tortuous mountain passes, along narrow, twisting trails hardly suited to comfortable passage. A few times he had been obliged to descend from his sedan and walk along the flinty, rough-hewn paths, so crude was their fashioning. He was tired, annoyed at being so far from his comfortable home, and thoroughly nettled at the prospect of such rude accommodations as this pathetic mountain village must surely offer. And now this insolent minor functionary of some mountain-goat pretender to royalty had the cheek to ask him to wait, like a common peasant, on the pleasure of the ruler of this horse-kingdom!

Just as he was about to lash the guard with his wrath, the twin doors were flung open upon their stone-socketed hinges. The guard bowed, gesturing Gaudatra toward the opening into the hall of the mountain king.

The Medean noble crossed the threshold, indignation still smoldering in his breast. He paced the length of the high-raftered hall, four great wooden pilasters supporting the central beam of the roof. His eyes were drawn toward the end of the large, airy chamber, to a skylit dais where some person—presumably the king—waited. Gaudatra's eyes were still unaccustomed to the dimmer light offered by the high, narrow openings in the walls of the chamber, and he stepped a bit uncertainly toward the throne.

Arriving at the foot of the dais, he made a proper bow—more than the upstart deserved, he thought—toward the youngish man seated on the ceremonial seat. Gaudatra's vision had finally adjusted to the interior lighting, and he took in the scene: Kurash's startling amber eyes were fastened on him in a measuring gaze the more disconcerting for its frankness. The king of Anshan sat on a carved mahogany chair covered with the pelt of a lion. The beast's mane hung off the back of the throne; its forelegs—claws still attached—draped off the arms of the chair on which rested the hands of the monarch of this place.

Kurash wore little jewelry. A plain silver circlet nestled amid the straight, straw-colored locks of his head. His clothing, though well-fitted and finely wrought, was of spun wool and tanned leather. He wore the breeches of a horseman rather than the robes and gowns of the more sedentary nobles of the plains.

Hanging behind him on the wall of the throne room was a

woven tapestry depicting a lion slaying a gold-hoofed bull. This ancient heraldry of their shared Aryan heritage, little-remembered by the Medes, proclaimed the differences between their related peoples. The Medes had gone on to greater pursuits, reflected Gaudatra, using more sophisticated means to achieve their ends. The Parsis, meanwhile, still lived in backward recapitulation of their more-recent nomadic past. In Gaudatra's opinion, they longed for the nonexistent splendor of days better forgotten.

"Be welcomed, Lord Gaudatra," pronounced Kurash finally. "I trust your journey from Elam was smooth and unhindered?"

Gaudatra glanced at the king sharply. Did he detect a wisp of irony glinting within those amber eyes? Without replying verbally, he made another small bow.

"I believe you may know my adviser and bodyguard, Lord Gobhruz?" The king gestured to an older man seated below his right shoulder.

Gaudatra scanned his memory. Ah, yes; this fellow had at one time lived in Shushan. He had been a military commander, if Gaudatra's memory served. His odd manner and old-fashioned notions had gradually alienated him. No one was sorry when he emigrated from Medea. The emissary gave Gobhruz a bow which stopped just short of being derisive.

"If the king will permit me," began Gaudatra in a patronizing voice, "the king should consider directing some of his subjects to construct a wall around his…city. Surely in these wild parts one would sleep better behind a strong fortification. And, might I say with all due respect"—realizing the irony of his last words, the Mede could not suppress a tiny smirk—"that one who is so late in sending the emperor's tribute of horses should spend less time conferring with expatriates"—he sneered at Gobhruz—"and more time considering the security of his own future." Gaudatra made a sardonic bow.

To his surprise, when he looked up Kurash was smiling at him. Those brass-colored eyes again gripped him in a cool, appraising gaze. Gaudatra had the uncomfortable sense that the expression on this man's face had less kinship with a smile than with the bared fangs of a crouched beast of prey. Somewhat concerned, he thought of his bodyguard, waiting outside the now-bolted doors of this chamber. He was not afraid—not yet. After all, he was the protected envoy of Asturagash, the overlord of these parts. Kurash realized this—did he not?

"Asturagash will not be receiving horses from the Parsis this year, or any other," announced Kurash in a voice as flat and dangerous as the blade of a sword. He sat very still, apparently waiting for Gaudatra to reply. Swallowing drily, the lord of Elam carefully considered both the tone and wording of his rejoinder.

"My...my lord surely realizes the...the gravity of the situation? For many years the Parsis have sent to their kindred and protectors, the Medes, a levy of the Nisayan chargers for which these lands are famous. To withhold from the king what he has every right to expect... My lord cannot be seriously considering such a course." Despite his best intentions, Gaudatra could not avoid a weak, interrogative inflection in his words.

Kurash made no answer. There was only that smiling, perilous amber stare, the same shade as the lion's hide, relentless as a stalking cat.

Choking on the apprehension rising rapidly in his throat, Gaudatra stammered, "My lord Kurash leaves me no choice... but to report such words to his king and mine, the Emperor Asturagash—"

"As you made your way here," cut in Kurash, "I hope the mountain passes gave you no difficulty. I instructed the lookouts in my outlying territories to watch most carefully for you." Kurash allowed the import of his words to absorb slowly into Gaudatra's consciousness. "I gave them most specific instructions," the king continued, "about the description and numbers of your entourage. So often in the ravines and narrow trails of the Zagrash mountains, rock slides can block the path, boulders can break loose and slide down into the restricted gorges through which one must travel…" The silence stretched to the breaking point.

"You dare not!" breathed Gaudatra in horror. "I am a protected envoy of—"

"And then there are the avalanches," continued Kurash smoothly. "In these mountains one must constantly be watchful."

The lord of Elam could not speak. His chest rose and fell in great spasms of fear. Once he made as if to sprint toward the locked door of the chamber, to beat upon it and call for his guards to break in and save him from this madman. But when Gobhruz slid his hand along the hilt of his throwing-knife, the Mede thought better of any such attempt.

"Good Gaudatra, you seem overwrought," observed Kurash drily. "You will sleep in my house tonight, and perhaps the weariness of the road will be abated somewhat. Tomorrow, when you are rested, we will discuss these matters further. I believe you will see," he finished, peering carefully into Gaudatra's widened eyes, "that I have more to offer than a few horses."

◆   ◆   ◆

"AND SO, MY LORD," finished Adad-ibni, "the portents signify the need for caution." The mage glanced surreptitiously toward Nabu-Naid, who was seated at Nebuchadrezzar's side. Seeing the prime minister's tacit approval, Adad-ibni went on. "The lion is in the house of Marduk, which is all to the good, but the moon drifts between Nergal and Ishtar. Lord Sin the moon god requires placation just now. It would be better to give him no reason for anger."

Nebuchadrezzar shifted in his seat, now cupping his chin in his hand, now drumming his fingers on the table beside him. He grew impatient with Adad-ibni's long-winded circumlocutions. After all this time, he thought, surely Adad-ibni did not think his rumblings about signs and portents frightened his emperor. Let him state what he wanted and why, and save all this self-justifying blather for the more easily impressed. Nebuchadrezzar was old; he didn't have time for such nonsense.

Nabu-Naid could see the the emperor's pensive expression. "What my lord the High Mage seems to be pointing toward," he interjected, "is that the great temple of Sin, the House of the Moon Lord in Haran, still lies in disrepair and disrespect. Surely something can be done."

Nebuchadrezzar glared at his prime minister. "Again, Nabu-Naid? Still you bait me about the wrong done to your family, and ask me to risk the anger of our respected ally, King Astyages of the Medes. That's the point of all this..."—he searched for a suitable word—"all this astrological *gossip*, isn't it?" He gave a scoffing laugh, shifting his scowl to Adad-ibni. The shaven-headed seer dropped his eyes, fumbling awkwardly with the hem of his robe.

"You two are quite a pair," scolded the emperor. "When hints and importuning don't get a result, you bring the gods into the fray—don't you, Nabu-Naid?"

The prime minister made no reply.

"Such advisers I have!" moaned the aged king. "Such counselors! Who cares a fig about the empire? Who troubles himself about the benefit of the provinces and their affairs? No one!" Nebuchadrezzar rose from his chair, hobbling angrily back and forth before the two abashed courtiers. "Every sniveling one of you in this court cares only about his own advancement, his own wants!"

Whirling upon them, he shouted, "There are no men of vision left in Babylon—only men of appetites!"

His shoulders slumped as the stiffening anger leaked from him. "You are all leeches—good for nothing but sucking the life out of an old, tired man," he muttered. "Leave me, both of you! I'm bored by the sound and sight of you!"

When the door closed, the emperor stood, leaning against the arm of his chair, panting with exertion and annoyance. In these graying, dimming days, he became ever more aware of the niggling voices at the back of his skull—wheedling, teasing, accusing. They mocked him, baited him. And now the voices were beginning to speak to him, the voices of Adad-ibni, Nabu-Naid, and the others. It wasn't *him* they spoke to; only the idea he represented for them, only the potential benefits he might bestow. That was what they curried favor with, made obeisance to. Not him. No one cared for Nebuchadrezzar the man. Only Nebuchadrezzar the ruler.

He felt a familiar, stifling panic rising within him. *Out!* He must go out somewhere. He must breathe freer air, hear cleaner, less stagnant sounds. To the garden—yes, he would go to the sky-garden. He would see more clearly there. Finding a favorite cane, he hobbled as quickly as he could from the chamber.

Soon he was climbing laboriously toward the pinnacle of his handmade mountain. A gentle spring breeze rustled the leaves of the miniature fig trees. Gratefully he breathed the green, growing life-smells.

Even now, at night, he could feel the eternal energy of the plant life around him. Standing here in the peaceful evening he could even imagine this as a real tree-clad mountain: It was possible to forget about the slaves down below, hidden by layer upon layer of earth and stone and archway, endlessly turning the mechanism which lifted water from the Euphrates to the artfully hidden irrigation ditches cross-hatching the sky-garden. He could fancy this his own forest—brought here as if by incantation from the lush lands of the north—where he might find solace from the nagging importunates of his court.

At last he neared the highest point. He stood beneath the date palms, not yet in their fruit-bearing season. The dark, flat expanse of the city stretched at his feet like a shadow-woven carpet. Here and there a light glowed. He could sense the resting, steady pulse of this metropolis he had called forth from Assyrian dominion. Babylon slept; but even in repose she was mighty indeed. Even at rest Babylon was a matchless monument to the things he had done correctly, an incontrovertible endorsement of the power of his vision and his dominion.

And then the voices spoke. No, not the voices, but a Voice —a distillation of an infinite majesty, a Reality which cast this paltry village of streets and canals into such insignificance that Nebuchadrezzar's soul cowered in the farthest corner of his mind. He could not escape this Voice, nor hide from it, though he were to climb to the top of the world's tallest mountain.

Thundering into his shivering consciousness with undeniable authority, with world-shattering immediacy, the Voice uttered words like crushing tablets of stone.

This is decreed concerning you, Nebuchadrezzar of Babylon…

Hearing his own name uttered by the Voice, he quaked all the more. He was known! Known to the very core—to the naked center!

Your kingship is stripped from you. You will be driven away from people, and will live with the beasts of the field. You will eat grass like the cattle eat. Seven times shall pass, and you shall be as a dumb animal until you acknowledge that the Most High is sovereign over the kingdoms of men, and gives them to whomever He pleases.

Like some furtive night-thing, the emperor of Babylon crouched down to the ground. His panicked mind darted into a cleft hidden deep, deep within him. On all fours, he crawled into the bushes of the night garden, to hide from the hostile, all-seeing eyes of the bewildering, tiny world he now inhabited.

15

STEPPING SOFTLY into the royal chamber, the emperor's morning servant moved quietly to avoid prematurely disturbing the sleeping Nebuchadrezzar. Though it was his daily task to assist the ruler in waking and performing his morning toilet, the eunuch was careful not to rouse his imperial master until he had completed all the preparations.

Since the spring nights were still somewhat cool, he had brought warm water, heated in the kitchens, to pour into the alabaster wash basin the king used to rinse the cobwebs of sleep from his face. This he now did, managing the flow carefully, so that scant sound of splashing could be detected.

Next he set the emperor's chamber pot beside the royal couch, so that his master might not encounter the inconvenience of walking across the room to relieve himself. When the emperor was fully dressed and had left, the eunuch's task would be to lug the foul-smelling vessel down to the river, emptying it in a private place.

Finally he laid out the emperor's toilet articles: the finely tooled gold comb, the myrrh-impregnated oil for his beard and skin, the flawless linen under-robe with vivid purple stitching. When all was done, he turned his steps to the couch, to softly grasp the shoulder of his master and summon him to the day at hand.

Still three paces from the gold-and-ebony bedstead, the slave stopped, puzzled. The couch was vacant and undisturbed. Odd, that. In his waning days the emperor did not much avail himself of the concubines who took their turns sleeping in the adjoining suite, available to provide companionship if wanted. The slave shrugged, smiling. Even among the old, could the desire not make itself felt? Since his own neutering, the servant of course could not feel such things himself; but doubtless the king could—and apparently had.

He silently drew aside the silk veil which partitioned the imperial bedchamber from that of the concubine. Again his forehead wrinkled in confusion. There lay the concubine, fast asleep—and alone. The king was not here either.

Could he have risen early, and be already up and about? Such had never happened in all his long years of service, but the eunuch knew no other explanation. He went to the sleeping girl, shaking her rudely awake.

"Where is the king, you?" he demanded. "Tell me his whereabouts, and quickly. I must see that he lacks nothing for his morning preparations."

The sleep-drugged girl raised herself on one elbow and blinked blearily at the fat old body-slave. "How should I know where he is?" she asked petulantly. "I haven't seen him."

He stared at her. "What do you mean? Wasn't he sleeping with you last night?"

Sleepily, she shook her head. "I was here by sundown," she said, rubbing her face. "But he never came in." Looking out through the drawn veil, she commented, "It appears he didn't sleep there either."

The eunuch felt the first beginnings of panic. He had attended Nebuchadrezzar since his youth. Always the emperor's routine upon awakening had been the same. Instinctively the servant knew something was amiss.

Leaving the concubine to drift back into sleep, he paced quickly out of the suite.

♦ ♦ ♦

HE SQUATTED in the shadows, eagerly gnawing at the handful of roots and grass he had plucked from the moist soil. His clothing was torn and dirty from sleeping on the ground in the garden. As he chewed, his head darted this way and that in mindless, instinctive fear of what might be lurking about him.

Hearing footsteps, he scrambled back among the low

shrubbery which had concealed him during the night. Peering through the gaps in the foliage, he saw the feet and legs of one who made strange, incomprehensible sounds as he walked along the path. With the dumb skill of a wild thing, he made no sound, no movement as the threat moved toward him, then past and away. Long after the meaningless cries and the sounds of breathing and walking had receded down the side of the incline, he stayed in his den, fearful of discovery.

◆ ◆ ◆

"YOUR MAJESTY! Where are you? Please, you are frightening your humble servants! My lord Nebuchadrezzar?"

His voice growing hoarse from the repetitive calling, Azariah trod wearily down the steep side of the sky-garden. For a moment, near the top, he had sensed—something. But he had seen and heard nothing. Where was the emperor? With a chill, he remembered the troubled words of Daniel. What would happen if they could not find him? Worse yet—what would happen if they did?

◆ ◆ ◆

"AND I SAY we must take action!" insisted Nabu-Naid with quiet emphasis. "For six days now we have combed every chamber, every closet, every corner of the palace grounds—yet we cannot find him anywhere! How much longer can we afford to let the empire stumble along, headless and groping? If our enemies knew—"

"But perhaps they do know!" hissed Awil-Marduk. "Perhaps it is they who have created this confusion! Have you considered that possibility, my lord prime minister?"

With barely veiled anger, Nabu-Naid grated, "My lord prince knows we have thought of nothing else these six days past! But how much longer do you think we can hide such a state of affairs from the people of this city? How much better to make a decision, to take affirmative steps, to make an open proclamation! Better far than this, this…futile effort to hide from a serious problem." His glaring eyes roved the circle of the Privy Council, daring anyone to contradict him.

All eyes shifted to the prince-regent, crumpled into a chair at the farthest remove from the head of the table, openly miserable at the thought of such immense accountability being thrust upon him. Where a more ambitious man would be exultant, Awil-Marduk wished only to hide. But it was too late for that now.

Nabu-Naid knew well the anguish with which the crown prince regarded his prospects: It suited the prime minister's purpose to intensify and accelerate the hapless prince's discomfiture with his destiny. What better way to cause the nobility to recognize Awil-Marduk's unfitness for leadership than by allowing him—no, forcing him—to assume it? And when certain matters took their course, and the nobility and populace cried out for stability, for vision...

"And when does the prime minister suppose such an announcement should be made?" queried another of the council members.

"One more day," pronounced Nabu-Naid decisively. "If he —or his body—is not found...then we shall move."

◆ ◆ ◆

IT WAS DAYBREAK. His eyes fluttered open, squinting against the rays of sunrise which sought him out in his lair. Before he made any overt motions, his nostrils tested the air, his eyes flickered this way and that, seeking any indication of hostile presences. Satisfied, he sat up, wincing with the cramps his body invited by sleeping in the cool night air.

His belly was empty. Crawling through the underbrush, he found the place he sought. Digging through the loose soil, he found more of the roots and tubers on which he subsisted. He crammed a dirty clump of these into his mouth and chewed, all the while scanning the narrow horizons of his habitat for signs of danger.

As the last stringy, half-chewed clump of vegetation slid down his throat, his mind peered forth, wide-eyed and wondering, from the cavern in which it had hidden these last several days. Suddenly he awoke, staring without memory or comprehension at the grimy, scarred hands in his lap, his fingernails filthy black crescents of dirt. He looked down at his torn, soiled raiment. Where was his purple robe? Why did his hair hang in straggling, unkempt clumps? Why was his beard torn and ragged, matted with filth? Why did he sit here in his sky-garden like some animal?

Like an animal. With the force of a thunderclap, he remembered. The Voice…the dream…and Belteshazzar!

♦ ♦ ♦

"VERY WELL. It's decided, then," said Nabu-Naid, black eyes glittering from his wrinkled face at each somber countenance gathered in the chamber. "We shall make a public announcement of the emperor's death, simultaneously acclaiming Prince Awil-Marduk's succession to his father's place."

Gravely, the other heads in the room nodded slowly. Awil-Marduk's face was drawn and ashen—he looked very unlike an emperor.

"Scribe, take down these words," commanded the prime minister. The clerk, moistened tablet in hand, took up his stylus and waited attentively.

"By the order of Awil-Marduk, rightful heir to the throne of Babylon, the chosen Crown Prince of his father the Emperor Nebuchadrezzar; and with the concurrence of the Privy Council: Be it hereby made manifest…"

A gasp, as if each occupant of the chamber breathed through a single throat, prompted Nabu-Naid to pause in his dictation. The widened eyes and gaping mouths of the others caused him to look over his shoulder, toward the entryway.

There stood an apparition which might have been the emperor back from the dead. Indeed, he appeared to have clawed his way out of a shallow grave: His face and hands were caked with dirt, his hair and beard flying wild as wind-tossed branches. His clothing had the look of a beggar's rags, though the tatters which hung from him were of the finest linens and silks. But the most shocking feature of his appearance, the magnet to which every gaze in the room was finally drawn, were his eyes.

They shone like lamps of heaven. His face, though grimy and stained, reflected their glow with the radiance of a seraph. His was the face of one who has seen the gods.

Perhaps fifteen heartbeats passed before anyone thought to make obeisance. Then the counselors scrambled frantically to their knees, as eager to avoid the hypnotic luster of the emperor's eyes as to demonstrate their loyalty to one whom, moments ago, they had agreed to pronounce dead.

For an eternity no sound was heard, save the thud of pulses and the half-suppressed panting of awed courtiers. Then the emperor spoke, with the voice of a man who has returned from a journey of incalculable length:

"Bring to me Belteshazzar."

♦   ♦   ♦

DANIEL WALKED into the emperor's chamber, his face stiff with apprehension. The summons had reached him at Azariah's house, the runner breathless and white-eyed with the urgency of the message. Since learning he was to appear alone before Nebuchadrezzar, Daniel had scarcely drawn an even breath. He took two paces into the room, then a third.

Then he saw the emperor.

The tangled, matted hair, the filthy, ragged appearance—at once Daniel knew the reason. He had seen it all in his mind's eye, when with fear-choked breath he had given Nebuchadrezzar the implications of his dream. Falling to his knees, he could hardly speak. "My lord," he murmured finally, hardly knowing whether he addressed the visible emperor, or the invisible Presence.

At length, Nebuchadrezzar spoke. Daniel had never heard the emperor's voice sound so aged, so tired—as if this last ordeal had sapped the last reserves of the vitality and decisiveness which had driven and sustained him all these years.

"Belteshazzar...you...you spoke and saw truly."

A thrill of fear shot through Daniel's chest, a racing of his already rapid pulse. He remained silent.

"The Voice...my sanity...all just as you said." The sound of his words was faded, threadbare; the speech of a man who had been finally, irrevocably humbled. Slowly Daniel raised his eyes until he was looking at his king. Nebuchadrezzar leaned weakly against a wall, staring out a window.

The silence stretched so long that Daniel thought perhaps he should venture some word, some summons to recall the emperor from the distant place of his inner vision.

"What do you see, my king?" asked Daniel softly.

Nebuchadrezzar sighed. "Only a city, Belteshazzar. A city I once ruled."

"But my lord is yet the emperor! No one would dare say—"

"No, Belteshazzar," said the emperor, shaking his head. "In my time...my time away...I learned the identity of the true Ruler of Babylon." He raised his eyes, and the light shone in them. Daniel felt his own face widen with wonder at the brilliance of Nebuchadrezzar's certainty.

"I can never again believe that I reign in this place," asserted the emperor, a wistful smile drifting across his features. "Now that I know..."

An immense silence draped the room as each man bowed within the temple of his own mind, each in his own manner reflecting, remembering, wondering, worshiping.

"My king, you have never been greater in my eyes than at this moment," Daniel breathed softly.

Nebuchadrezzar peered quietly at Daniel. "Thank you, Belteshazzar...my friend. Perhaps at the end of a life of conquest and dominion, I begin at last to learn the way of true greatness." Another reflective hush stretched between them for a moment. Then the emperor said, "I wonder if you might fetch a tablet. I would like to create a record of this revelation, and I believe you should be the one who inscribes it."

When Daniel had returned with the tablet, Nebuchadrezzar began:

"Nebuchadrezzar, Emperor of Babylon; to all peoples, nations, and men of every language, who live in all the world. May you prosper greatly!

"It is my pleasure to tell you about the miraculous signs and wonders that the Most High God has performed for me..."

◆　◆　◆

THOUGHTFULLY, GAUDATRA SHIFTED the baked-clay goblet in small circles before him. Squinting through one eye at his host, the governor asked, "So, then: In return for my allegiance and assistance, you are prepared to extend my authority throughout central Medea, and northward along the eastern shore of the Tigris?"

Kurash nodded, calmly.

"But what prevents me from making my own arrangements with Asturagash, perhaps returning here at the head of a punitive army? Why might I not keep what I already have, and add your territories to my suzerainty?"

Kurash made no reply other than a crafty smile.

"Ah, yes..." mused Gaudatra. "Your mountain passes, and those unpredictable rock slides..."

"That, and the unquestioning loyalty of all the clans of Persis," added Kurash. "After your difficulty in coming here, you would find a large host of very warlike horsemen ready to defend their homeland to the last drop of blood."

Gaudatra toyed with the gold braids in his beard. Again he aimed a question at the young, smiling king of Anshan. "But why me? Why approach the governor of the richest province of Medea? How could you think, Kurash, that I would be easy to persuade to your cause?"

"That's *Lord* Kurash," growled Gobhruz in warning, from his seat in the corner. Kurash waved a calming hand toward his mentor.

"Because you *are* the governor of the richest province of Medea," Kurash answered the query. "You have far less reason than any other noble in Medea to tolerate the wasteful ways of your sire. How long has Elam been the very breadbasket of Ecbatana? How long has she filled the gluttonous bellies of the lords of the Medes? And how long can she continue to send the best fruits of her fields and rivers north to Ecbatana, when so little flows back south to her?" Kurash carefully watched the face of the governor as his words struck home. "You and I know, Gaudatra: Asturagash is not the equal of his father. Uvakhshatra, vicious and vindictive though he was, at least understood the economies of empire. Were one of his stature astride the throne in Ecbatana, one such as myself would have no more chance than a marmot in an eagle's nest. But Uvakhshatra is dead these long years past, and his son understands little save his own cravings. Look within yourself and see if it is not as I say."

Gaudatra contemplated these words for several moments. Outside, the sound of children and dogs at play could be heard. The governor ladled another dollop of goat's-milk yogurt into his mouth. Swallowing slowly, he posed a final question.

"Granting all that you say, *Lord* Kurash," he began, "what, other than the eventual annexation of the territories you mentioned, does the province of Elam stand to gain from a Parsi monarchy? And why come toward Medea? Do not easier pickings lie to the east?"

Kurash rose from the table, smiling and stroking his beard as he slowly circled the table where Gaudatra sat. "As to what Elam may gain from my kingship: If the imperial capital of my realm were located at Shushan, rather than Ecbatana, would this not benefit the people of Elam—and their governor?" He glanced sidelong at Gaudatra, whose calculating face told Kurash all he needed to know.

"As to your second question..." Kurash paused, remembering the frustration of a young boy, the son and grandson of kings. He recollected a dusty, humiliating ride to Babylon, a city whose walls were so wide that two chariots might be driven abreast along their tops. He recalled a promise he had made to himself, and to his lifelong friend and protector seated so quietly in the corner. "Let us simply say, Gaudatra," he said softly, turning to grip the envoy with his perilous amber eyes, "that I have undertaken a quest whose goal lies west, not east."

16

THE CHORUS of professional mourners paced slowly past, each singer swathed in identical white mourning garments, each cheek cleanly, evenly gashed with the official badge of grief. As they trod past the silent crowds thronging either side of Aibur Shabu, they sang a carefully rehearsed funeral ode to Nebuchadrezzar, whose embalmed and decorated corpse followed along behind, atop its shimmering golden bier.

For a final time, the populace of Babylon lined the Processional Way to watch in somber fascination as the body of Nebuchadrezzar, the only ruler all but the oldest Babylonians had ever known, promenaded past on its way to Esagila. There it would receive its final consecration by the priests of Marduk.

Awil-Marduk strode solemnly behind his father's bier, striving with every fiber of his being to appear kingly. Behind the dutiful, sober facade, however, a frightened child screamed silently for rescue. The new king already felt entrapped, hemmed in by the stifling confines, the onus of his inherited, unavoidable obligation. *Why?* he shouted silently to the dead ears of his father. *Why have you done this to me?*

In step just behind and to the side of Awil-Marduk, Nergal-Sharezer cut his eyes unobtrusively toward his brother-in-law and new king. Unbidden, a smirk curled his lip as he studied the profile of the one about to embark upon the rule of Babylon without a single qualification other than the accident of birth. *But that might be remedied*, the prince told himself, remembering his conversation with the prime minister. Awil-Marduk might inherit the mantle, but it remained to be seen how long it would remain on his shoulders...

Daniel followed closely behind the bier and the emperor's family, at the front of the nobles and court officials whose duty prescribed their attendance at the emperor's last procession. As he walked, he thought of the closing days of this king who had brought him to this city so long ago, who had raised him to the inner councils of empire, then lowered him, and finally raised him again in the waning rays of his life's sunset.

Something had left the king after his experience in the sky-garden—and something had been added. From that day forth, Nebuchadrezzar seemed to relinquish his grip on the fabric of this world. To Daniel he appeared to lose interest in maintaining his mortal life, putting in its place a type of anticipation of something yet unseen—as if craning his neck to spy what might await him beyond.

The fire, the urgency, the spark of command—the attributes which had made him the lodestone of the empire for decades—all these were gone, shuffled off as suddenly as one discards a cloak no longer needed. In his last days, Nebuchadrezzar had exhibited instead a sort of amused detachment from the matters of state—a weary, knowing uncoupling from the harness in which he had placed himself upon the death of his own father, so many years before. He had ceased to be a king, and had become instead a tired old man ready to accept death...and even to embrace it.

Daniel wondered: What had the Eternal whispered into the ears of the one whose body now lay on the bier ahead? How had that terrifying encounter with the Holy One altered Nebuchadrezzar, that he could so suddenly shift his gaze from the glittering, fortified habits of a lifetime to the dark vulnerabilities of Sheol?

And what now lay in store for the empire, and for the Chosen? For all but a few years of Daniel's life, Nebuchadrezzar had been the pivotal fact of daily existence—the adversary to be feared or the patron to be served. Now he was gone. Who might the Lord of heaven be raising up to assume the place Nebuchadrezzar had vacated?

Nabu-Naid trod along in his place within the ranks of courtiers, his mournful face masking the eager anticipation hammering in his breast. Since the first wavering wail of the priests had announced the emperor's death, the prime minister had tasted the intoxicating draught of a carefully laid scheme ripe for implementation. With the powerful Nebuchadrezzar out of the way, he felt his time had come at last.

He did not fear overmuch for his ultimate success. He had spent too much time and made his preparations too sure to overestimate his chances of fulfillment. With the crafty certainty of years of cunning, he knew the pieces were falling into place.

Glancing to his left, he noticed the profile of Belteshazzar. Nabu-Naid was slightly puzzled by this fellow. In all the prime minister's years of tangled maneuverings within the court, he had never found this Belteshazzar involved in any intrigue whatsoever. And yet he maintained his position and standing with the emperor—even returning from disgrace to march in the front ranks of the nobility! What was it about the Hebrew that enabled him to enjoy such effortless immunity from the vicissitudes of fortune? Nabu-Naid decided to keep Belteshazzar near him. A leader had need of good luck—perhaps proximity to Belteshazzar would grant it...

Peering ahead, Adad-ibni burned with indignation each time his glance lit upon Belteshazzar, who occupied a place of great honor near the bier of the emperor. How was it possible? Why did the gods jest with him so, taunting him with this Jew who could never be finally disposed of?

Adad-ibni had barely averted a disaster, even as the final preparations of the king's corpse were being completed. It seemed that Nebuchadrezzar had dictated to this hated Jew a tablet alluding to his bizarre seven-day disappearance as a visitation by Belteshazzar's god! As if having Belteshazzar back in the good graces of the court were not enough, having a public proclamation of the power of his god become a part of the public records of Nebuchadrezzar's reign—the thought of it caused the chief mage to shudder even now. Fortunately he had been able to find and destroy all the tablets copied from the original, and he had managed to "store" the original with the priests of Marduk. He had no doubt that their self-interest would dictate the damning tablet's ultimate fate.

But still, there walked Belteshazzar—not two shoulder-widths away from Nabu-Naid himself! And Adad-ibni had thought the prime minister his ally. Fuming silently, the seer walked on...

Daniel's fingers slipped beneath his mourning robes as he walked, fingering the small, rustling packet secreted away in his girdle. He smiled inwardly. The parchment copy of the king's narrative, carried in his belt, gave him comfort on this day of uncertainties. Regardless of the hostility of Adad-ibni and the others, Daniel's fingers, tracing the outlines of the parchment, reassured him that a God existed who raised and abased kings, who remembered promises made—and who could preserve His people.

♦ ♦ ♦

DISMOUNTING HIS HORSE, Commander Indravash of the Medean army grunted with the effort of levering his old, unpliant body down from the stirrup. Hobbling with saddle-stiffness, he approached the door of Egibi and Sons.

The slave attending the door looked him up and down, a cool appraising manner in his stare. Indravash, who had come so often to this door on missions of the same sort, felt himself bridling with resentment. In these last years he did not receive the unctuous welcome of former days. No longer did Egibi dispatch a boy to the cellar to fetch a cooling draught of beer. No longer was their business conducted behind a latched, private door, under Egibi's personal supervision. Nowadays the treatment accorded the envoy of King Asturagash stopped barely short of perfunctory.

Indravash, though unwilling to admit it openly, knew the reason. Asturagash was losing his grip on the far-flung empire built by his father. What was it about kings, wondered the old commander, that so often inhibited their children from receiving the vigor of their sires? Horseflesh could be improved and strengthened with breeding—why not men?

The slave at the door had returned with some minor clerk of Egibi's establishment. "Follow me, please," the employee announced in a dull voice, striding away within the house, not bothering himself to ascertain whether Indravash followed. Grumbling under his breath, the old Mede limped behind, carrying the package Asturagash had sent for pawning.

The servant motioned for Indravash to be seated on a palmwood bench just outside the main counting-room door, then strode off to other duties.

Indravash looked about him: Apparently Egibi was as prosperous as ever. Slaves and scribes hurried in and out the chamber, some carrying deeds to loaned property or transaction documents, some toting bags of silver, bales of spices, and sundry other goods. No one glanced in the direction of the dusty, tired old man holding the worn leather pouch. Indravash slumped wearily on the bench, with no choice but to wait.

Presently Egibi's youngest son strode out of the counting-room, busily dusting his hands together. Briskly he approached Indravash, smiling a businesslike smile. "Greetings, Lord Indravash. I hope you have not been waiting too long. Let me see what you have brought us this time." Expectantly he studied the bag in Indravash's lap.

Slowly the Mede reached into the bag, gingerly drawing forth a piece of statuary. From the dull yellowish color and the straining of Indravash's sinews as he hefted the piece, Egibi's son could tell it was of solid-cast gold—heavy and quite costly. It was the figure of a horse. Its eyes were of tiny emeralds, its flaring nostrils rubies. The teeth of the beast were fashioned of seed-pearls, set evenly inside the finely worked line of the spread lips. A jewel-encrusted saddle and bridle caparisoned the beast, and it stood with one hoof upraised, as if poised to gallop away when placed on the floor. The banker immediately discerned that the figure was the work of a meticulous crafts-man, and quite valuable—not to mention the worth of the gold alone.

Carefully he took the figurine in his hands, turning it this way and that, studiously examining the piece for flaws, defects, anything which would lessen its value to the collector. There were none. It was an exquisite piece; Egibi's son imagined Asturagash had parted with it only grudgingly.

Setting the figurine gingerly on the low table beside the bench, he pursed his lips as Indravash looked at him expectantly.

The banker cocked an eyebrow at the Mede. "Forty *mana*," he said at last.

Indravash's eyes bulged in disbelief. "Forty *mana?*" he glared, the veins standing out on his forehead. "The gold in this statue alone amounts to nearly a talent! This is an insult!"

Egibi's son shrugged. "Lord Indravash, you are not bound to accept my offer. There are other banking houses—"

"You know cursed well why Asturagash comes to you," grated Indravash. "He cannot very well have the priests of Marduk whispering in the ear of your new king that Medea must auction off the treasures of the royal household to pay her troops!"

The son of Egibi, his face a blank slate, stared coldly at the Mede. "Lord Indravash, this is a banking house. We don't consider it our business to discuss political matters with the patrons—"

"Not your business?" scoffed the Mede, jumping angrily to his feet. "Since when has politics not been your business? In better days, when Asturagash breathed heavily on Nebuchadrezzar's eastern frontier, your father fell over himself lending money to the king—whenever asked, and at terms more generous than he offered to his own people. But now," he growled, "now that Croesus and his Lydians nibble away at our northern frontier, now that this upstart Kurash withholds his levies and makes war-noises on our southeast flank, you offer me forty *mana* for a piece worth more than the miserable hide of every slave in this house!"

The Medean commander stood panting, his teeth bared, while the still-seated banker's gaze was cool, unemotional. Unseen by Indravash, a small circle of armed slaves gathered behind the Mede, poised to intercept any physical threat to their master. Egibi's son allowed several moments to grind awkwardly past, then said quietly, "Lord Indravash, you have heard the offer of Egibi and Sons. It is the only one you will receive. You may stay or go, as you wish."

Making as if to leave, he smiled secretly when he heard the low, defeated voice of the Mede. "Wait," said Indravash, miserably. Veiling his emotions, he again faced the commander, a neutral, interrogative look on his face.

Shoulders slumped in resignation, the Mede gazed long at the precious statuette. Unable to look the banker in the face, he said, "Very well. Weigh out the silver."

Egibi's son made a small gesture to a waiting scribe, who

hurried forward to make the arrangements. "Thank you, Lord Indravash," said the banker, breezily. "I am grateful you allowed us to make an offer. I hope your return journey to Ecbatana is safe and swift." He strode busily away, his mind already moving on to other matters.

Behind him, Indravash watched dejectedly as the scales parceled out the paltry worth of his master's future.

◆   ◆   ◆

AWIL-MARDUK PACED NERVOUSLY to and fro at the end of the council chamber. Those seated around the table glanced nervously from the matters at hand to the king's frenetic gait. The conference had already lasted most of the morning, and several important matters still awaited the king's attention. But the king became progressively more restive as the meeting ground on, until at last he seemed able to pay only the scantiest heed to the discussion. No one knew exactly what to make of this odd behavior.

Nabu-Naid, clearing his throat discreetly, said, "Your majesty will no doubt wish to hear again the summation of this last report? I believe my king was distracted when the ambassador made his statement."

Awil-Marduk halted his pacing, a startled look on his face. He looked at the council for several awkward, expectant heartbeats. It became painfully obvious to everyone in the room that the emperor had no idea what topic was currently under consideration. At last he spoke.

"Belteshazzar?"

"Yes, my king," answered the august, silver-bearded official.

"It strikes me just this moment: I have never considered the prisoners my father impounded. Shouldn't a new king release some captives?"

Embarrassed by the random gyrations of the king's thoughts, Belteshazzar carefully studied the hem of his sleeve. Across the table, Nergal-Sharezer stifled a snicker.

"Yes, my king," answered Belteshazzar finally. "That sort of thing is sometimes done at the outset of a king's reign…as a gesture of goodwill." Another long, tortured silence enveloped the room.

"Very well, then," snapped the distracted young king. "Take me to the prison cells at once."

Belteshazzar, looking quizzically about the table, then back to Awil-Marduk, asked, "Me, my king?"

"Yes, of course," snapped the monarch, with a sharpness engendered by his discomfort. "I wish to see the prisoners. Immediately."

Shrugging at the others, Belteshazzar rose from the table. "As you wish, my king."

◆ ◆ ◆

THE GUARD AT THE BOTTOM of the stairway bowed at their approach, somewhat startled to see the king in this area of the citadel.

"What sort of prisoners are kept in the citadel?" asked Awil-Marduk, as he and Belteshazzar made their way along the dank passageway.

Belteshazzar drew a deep breath before replying. "Most of the captives kept here are of the political sort, my king: persons of royal or noble blood from conquered lands kept here as hostages: defeated generals, vanquished kings—"

"Kings?" asked Awil-Marduk sharply. "Kings in this place?"

Belteshazzar looked carefully into the face of the young man. "Yes, my lord," he answered softly. "Your father conquered many lands, many peoples. And not all of them acquiesced easily to his authority. Sometimes it was necessary to take rather stern measures…" The vizier's voice faded into sad remembrance, then silence.

Awil-Marduk reached out and took hold of the older man's shoulder. "Belteshazzar, I know my father trusted you. I…I must tell you this, for I know no one else to tell…I—I do not know how to be a king, Belteshazzar." The eyes staring at the vizier from beneath the imperial crown were desperate, liquid with worry. "I am not my father, Belteshazzar. I do not delight in this"—he gestured about him—"this subjugation of others, this deciding who shall live and who shall die."

"But, my king—" began Daniel.

"I am *not* a king!" shouted Awil-Marduk. "Others may call me that, but naming a thing does not make it so! I never wanted this, but it sought me out nonetheless. Why doesn't anyone *listen* to me?"

"Here, lad. I will listen."

The king and his vizier looked at each other, startled. The voice had come from one of the dark, barred doorways of the many cells along the torchlit corridor. A morbid fascination drew Awil-Marduk to the opening, and the shadowed, gaunt face waiting there.

"Who are you?" asked the ruler of Babylon, softly.

"I don't know," replied the ghost-voice in the cell. "Once I was was known as Jeconiah, king of Judah. But now...I don't know..."

At the name, Daniel felt a thrill spiking along his spine. The lost king of his people, carried to this place while still a smooth-cheeked youth! Rushing to the bars of the door, he whispered in awe, "Coniah! Is it truly you?"

A long hush fell, broken only by the sibilant sputtering of the torches bracketed along the walls. "How long it has been since anyone called me by that name!" breathed the prisoner. "You must have been in Judah, friend, to have known of me."

"I am Daniel, son of Kemuel," said the vizier, bending near the bars. "I came to Babylon almost at the same time you did, although..."—Daniel paused, glancing self-consciously at Awil-Marduk, standing quietly beside him—"under better circumstances, I fear."

Awil-Marduk spoke. "How long did you reign in Judah, Jeconiah?"

The wretch within the shadows tilted his head, thinking. "So long ago, so long...I was only a boy when my father died, when they made me king..."

Daniel felt Awil-Marduk stiffen beside him as Jeconiah spoke.

"It could not have been more than…three months. Three months, perhaps."

"You… When they made you king," asked Awil-Marduk uncertainly, "were you…afraid?"

A spectral chuckle escaped the dry lips of the prisoner. "Ah, yes," he nodded. "I was a terrified child disguised in the raiment of a king."

Awil-Marduk's fingers twitched at his sides, as if he longed to reach toward this prisoner of his father's ambition, to heal—or to draw sustenance. He wanted to win back from the greedy grasp of unforgiving time the boy who had once been locked into this cell, guilty of no offense other than the accident of his birth. How well he knew the sensation of being trapped by the unasked-for, the unavoidable.

Turning to his vizier, Awil-Marduk made the first confident decision of his reign. "Belteshazzar, summon the guard. I wish to release this prisoner."

17

NABU-NAID CAREFULLY EXAMINED the man seated on the embroidered silk cushions of his private suite. He wore the garb of a horseman, his clothing dusty and rank with sweat from the long time he had spent in the saddle on his journey here. He spoke Aramaic which had something of a Medean accent about it, but with a slight difference. He claimed to be an emissary of this Cyrus—Kurash, they called him in Shushan—who was causing such a stir in the territories east of the Tigris. This envoy had arrived at the gate of the palace accompanied by only one other rider. Both were mounted on handsome Nisayan chargers, the horses bred by the Persians in the high valleys and tablelands of their distant country.

The prime minister was intrigued by the possibilities for this meeting. One of his dearest desires was purging the Medean presence from Haran and its environs. Could Cyrus be used as the lever to loosen Astyages' grasp on the city of his ancestors?

"It is said Cyrus seeks to extend his domain," began Nabu-Naid. "How far does your master believe he can reach?" asked the prime minister, his obsidian eyes closely observing the messenger's reaction to such a direct thrust.

The amber eyes of the envoy never wavered from the prime minister's, his face a relaxed, unreadable mask. "My lord Kurash keeps his own council in such matters," stated the Persian, deftly deflecting the prime minister's question. "My mission to Babylon is to determine the stance of your king on the question of my lord's intention to annex Medea. What will his posture be in this regard?"

Parry and thrust. Nabu-Naid liked the style of this outlander; he gave as good as he got. With new caution, the prime minister pursed his lips before replying. "One might think your master a bit brash in his disdain for the might of Astyages' arm. The Medes have ruled vast territories for longer than you have been alive."

The Persian smiled. Nabu-Naid's eyes widened at such an unexpected response. "My lord's enemies have frequently commented on this brashness of his," the emissary said, "but he has not seen fit to change his practice. Most of those who have found fault with his impetuosity are by now either his vassals, or dead."

Such confidence, reflected Nabu-Naid, was either well-founded or suicidal. Filing this away for later analysis, he framed his next query. "How soon would Cyrus move against Medea?"

"The answer depends," retorted the Persian, "on the disposition of your king. My lord Kurash would be ill-disposed to mount an early offensive without knowing whether he might be forced to face the combined resources of Babylon and Medea."

Again the quick parry. Playing for time, the prime minister asked, "Why does Cyrus believe Babylon might align herself with Medea?"

"You were allies against the Assyrians, were you not?" answered the envoy. "Didn't my own kin ride under the banner of Uvakhshatra, alongside the infantry of Chaldea? The memories of Parsis are not so short that we can easily assume your neutrality in this matter. Today's foes can be tomorrow's advocates, and it is always best, if possible, to know which is which."

So the horseman knew his history, thought Nabu-Naid. If Cyrus commanded the loyalty of many such as this sharp-witted one, his bravado might indeed be well-justified. "I have never spoken to my lord Awil-Marduk on the matter you raise," admitted Nabu-Naid. "But," he went on, seeing the impatient look of the Persian, "I believe I can say that his, ah…his *inattention* can be assured, at the very least."

As the Persian digested this veiled promise, Nabu-Naid smirked inwardly at the joke he had made with himself. Inattention, indeed—to be sure!

"I must caution you," the Persian warned finally, "that my lord Kurash is most intolerant of double-dealing. If I am allowed to take him this word you have just given me, be assured that he will rely on it. If he is disappointed…"

Nabu-Naid kept his face carefully neutral. Inwardly he bridled at being threatened in his own chambers by an outlander errand boy, even if a clever one. "Your master may rely on the words spoken here this night," he said at last, his tone inflectionless.

"Very well," said the Persian decisively, rousing himself quickly from the cushion. "I must be off. My lord Kurash will be most grateful for your frank understanding."

Nabu-Naid allowed his chin to bend toward his chest. When he straightened again, the horse-sweat smell of the Persian's clothing was all of him that remained in the room.

♦   ♦   ♦

AS HIS COMPANION swung astride his steed, Gobhruz asked, "Did you find what you needed to know?"

Grinning, Kurash nodded his head. "There are currents and crosscurrents in this place, Gobhruz. The prime minister is a jackal with the patience of a serpent and the belly of a swine. We have not seen the last of him—yet he may entwine himself in his own trap."

As they reined their mounts out of the citadel courtyard and into Aibur Shabu, Gobhruz mumbled, "Still, I fail to see why you risk your neck on such errands as this. Why not send someone?"

"Some things," replied Kurash as the horses' hoofs clattered over a canal bridge, "one must see first hand."

♦   ♦   ♦

AWIL-MARDUK LAY RESTLESSLY on his couch, waiting impatiently for sleep to come.

Through the open window he could see the vivid disc of the moon, coursing on its stately path among the lustrous stars of the clear Chaldean night.

During these last few weeks, a deep sense of well-being had gradually displaced the nervous apprehension of his early days as heir to his father's throne. With the freeing of Jeconiah, something shifted in the depths of his soul—a calming, a blooming confidence rose up within him, as if knowing he was free to show mercy somehow mitigated the solemn nature of his responsibility. He had found the first traces of his identity as king of Babylon.

This quiet exhilaration was what kept him awake tonight, staring out at the blazing host of the heavens.

The change in Awil-Marduk's nature was noticed in other quarters as well. Outside the king's chamber, in a shadowed corner out of earshot of the bodyguard stationed beside the door, a whispered conference was taking place between two who were not as pleased as the rest of the court with the increasing control exerted by the newly confident young king.

"Are you certain this is required?" asked Nergal-Sharezer nervously. "If we are discovered—"

"How can we be discovered, fool?" hissed Nabu-Naid, allowing his impatience with the prince to pierce his self-control. "As I told you, I have ensured the silence of those who will know what has passed, and taken steps to place the blame far from anyone within these walls." His midnight-dark eyes lashed the fretful prince. "The weaklings who once agreed with our cause are now wavering, because they suppose Awil-Marduk's abilities improve. But you and I know better," he asserted fiercely. "If you would sit on the throne, you must learn to do what is necessary. Because of my love for this city and its kingdom, I am able to face this unpleasant reality. Are you?"

Nergal-Sharezer, perhaps as fearful of the one before him as of the deed afoot, nodded hesitantly, then dropped his eyes.

"Good," grunted Nabu-Naid. "Now go and do what we planned, and I will make certain of the rest." Quietly the two men stole away from the king's chamber.

◆ ◆ ◆

LATER, IN THE DEAD HOURS when even the night creatures have ceased stirring, Nergal-Sharezer, dressed only in a light sleeping-robe, strode toward the king's door, his face agitated with alarm.

"Guard!" he half-whispered to the soldier standing outside the door. "You must hurry! As I lay on my bed, unable to sleep, I heard a sound outside, below the king's window! I fear intruders may be seeking a way to the king's couch from the garden outside! Come with me!"

The guard, his face furrowed with concern, hesitated, glancing from the urgent visage of the prince to the door where duty bound him.

"Come on!" hissed Nergal-Sharezer. "I have summoned another to take your post! You are the night guard—it is your duty! As prince, I command you!"

A man dressed in the livery of the palace guard came hurrying from the shadows down the hall, rubbing his eyes as if just roused from sleep. Seeing this, the bodyguard wavered, then turned toward the prince. "Show me, my lord," he said in a low voice. As they strode off, he turned to the drowsy soldier just arrived. "You guard the king," he warned. "See that you stay awake!"

The replacement sentry nodded, taking his station outside the royal bedchamber.

As the prince and the bodyguard paced swiftly around a bend in the corridor, Nabu-Naid sidled out of the shadows. Going to the king's door, he produced a key from within his robes. Quietly he unlatched the heavy oaken door, while the disguised sentry stood by and drew his dagger. Then Nabu-Naid stepped back to let the weapon-bearer slip noiselessly into the room's darkness. In a moment the prime minister heard a quick rustling of bedclothes, then nothing.

The footsteps came quietly back to the door, where Nabu-Naid waited, holding out a wallet bulging with silver. Reaching eagerly for the wallet, the catspaw failed until too late to see the dagger in the prime minister's hand.

◆　◆　◆

SEATED ON THE DRAGON THRONE, Nergal-Sharezer looked somberly about the hushed gathering in the huge hall. Outside, the fierce heat of late summer broiled the walls and streets of Babylon, where the funeral of the lamented young Awil-Marduk had just been solemnized.

"My people," intoned the newly installed monarch, "the

gods shall not allow the treachery practiced upon my dear brother, your murdered king, to go unavenged. The dagger which took his life bore a Medean device. The criminals shall be punished, though they hide in the very citadel of Astyages himself. As regent of Marduk, who sees and redresses wrongdoing, I swear this to you."

From his place by the king's shoulder, the prime minister smirked inwardly. Indeed. The gods would punish this betrayal. He would see to it personally.

♦ ♦ ♦

A GROUNDSWELL was gathering in Medea, a tempest which battered the walls and watchtowers of the citadel in Ecbatana. The nobles and commanders of the provinces of Astyages' empire, from embattled Armenia and Cappadocia in the north and west to Bakhtrish and Arachosia in the south and east, made pilgrimage in ones and twos to Parsagard in the Zagrash highlands. Following the lead of the clans of the Persian plateau, they sought out one who could supply them with a quality of leadership missing in Astyages' gluttonous tyranny.

At first cautiously, then with a building enthusiasm, they pledged loyalty to the charismatic Kurash, son of Mandane and Kanbujiya. Along with the Parsi's quick intelligence and grasp of the intricacies of empire, they discovered a sensibility and appreciation for the diversity of their ways and cultures which Astyages had always lacked. The old Aryan virtues of independence and open dealing found a refreshing new expression in the court of Kurash of Persia. He was becoming the first people's king. The tide would prove to be irreversible. Kurash would march into Ecbatana all but unopposed, and would take upon himself a new royal name and title: Darius the King of the Medes and the Persians.

♦ ♦ ♦

BABYLON FOUND HERSELF in mourning once again for the untimely death of a king. Nergal-Sharezer had succumbed to a sudden illness brought on, according to the court physicians, by consumption of spoiled pomegranates. The poison had swiftly carried away the prince who promised justice for the slayers of his sister's husband. The prime minister made a stirring oration in the vast courtyard of Esagila on the day of the royal corpse's consecration, lamenting the mysterious workings of fate and circumstance. Weeping uncontrollably through all the proceedings was Labashi-Marduk, the sallow-skinned son of Nergal-Sharezer who was confirmed as king in his father's stead.

He too died—less than one year later.

♦ ♦ ♦

IN A SMALL SEMICIRCLE at the tomb's opening, Daniel, Azariah, Mishael, and Hananiah stood and looked sadly upon the wrapped, spice-sheathed body of Caleb. The ancient, gnarled servant had finally breathed his last, and the friends resolved to do this final service for one who had attended them so faithfully for more years than they could readily reckon. As a gesture of respect, Azariah had insisted the beloved servant's body be encrypted in one of the spaces reserved for the members of his family, here in a small, rocky valley not far from the walls of the city. Azariah's son stood beside him trying to appear brave, but unable to avoid wiping his cheeks and nose with the backs of his hands.

"So much death these days," sighed Mishael, wiping the perspiration from his forehead with a chubby forearm. "From the greatest to the least, all must bow before the scepter of the grave."

Azariah looked at Hananiah. "Have you a *qaddish* for our fallen servant?"

The musician nodded, glancing at Mishael. The eunuch cleared his throat as Hananiah strummed a melancholy phrase on his lyre. The song began.

> *O Lord, the God who saves me,*
> *day and night I cry out before You.*
> *May my prayer come before You;*
> *turn Your ear to my cry.*

For my soul is full of trouble
   and my life draws near to the grave.
I am counted among those who go down to the pit...

I call to You, O Lord, every day;
   I spread out my hands to You.
Do You show Your wonders to the dead?
   Do those who are dead rise up and praise You?
Is Your love declared in the grave,
   Your faithfulness in Destruction?
Are Your wonders known in the place of darkness,
   or Your righteous deeds in the land of oblivion?

As the last strains of the *maskil* wafted away on the cool winter breeze, Azariah looked deeply into the moist eyes of the eunuch. "It always comes to this, doesn't it, my friends? Kings, beggars, prophets—all must come at last to this closing door which never reopens."

"But even worse is to sleep forever in a land not your own," observed Hananiah quietly. "Perhaps, one day..." The taciturn man fell silent.

A distant echo, quiet as the bursting of a lily's bud, caused Daniel to catch his breath. He looked at his friends, a strange hopefulness pressing tentatively against his breastbone. "Perhaps..." he breathed, and could say no more.

Too fleeting to name, too beautiful to trust, the moment passed. The others watched him until he shook his head and rubbed a hand across his eyes. "Forgive me," Daniel shrugged, "I thought... Never mind. Azariah, should we not seal the tomb?"

"Yes," said Azariah, still thoughtfully studying his friend's face. "I suppose so." The four men and the boy placed their shoulders against the large round, flattened stone beside the entryway. As they heaved, the rock rolled grudgingly down the stone channel cut into the valley floor, until it ground into place across the opening of the tomb. Dusting off their hands, and sighing as they looked a final time on the resting place of the one they had known and loved so long, the small party turned to go back to the city.

18

NABU-NAID WAS IN A QUANDARY. The nobility and military were anxious to fill the void created by the disappointing susceptibility of the last three kings to sudden mishap. The prime minister had every intention of stepping into the vacancy, but he could not wrest the Dragon Throne by mere, crude force. Such overt action, though well within his capabilities, offended his sense of tidiness, of destiny. Something further was needed, some validating sign, some endorsing portent —some way to persuade all and sundry of the inevitability of his succession to power.

Scratching his beard in perplexity, he suddenly thought of Belteshazzar. Of course! The Hebrew's interpretations of Nebuchadrezzar's dream-omens had heralded great change before —why not now? Smiling to himself, he summoned a runner.

◆ ◆ ◆

WHEN BELTESHAZZAR ENTERED the suite of the prime minister, he was shocked to see Nabu-Naid crumpled on the floor, heaving great moist sobs into the hands covering his face.

"My lord Prime Minister? What is the matter?"

Nabu-Naid leaned on one elbow long enough to peer past

soggy eyelids at the concerned face of the vizier. "Ah! Beltes-hazzar! Thank the gods, you are here at last! Come," blubbered the aging Nabu-Naid, tugging a cushion into place beside him. "Sit. I must tell you—for you alone can help me."

Still puzzled and slightly alarmed, Daniel edged down beside the prime minister. Hesitantly he asked, "How...may I be of service, my lord?"

A deep, quivering sigh fluttered from Nabu-Naid's breast. Peering into Belteshazzar's eyes, he said solemnly, "I have had a dream, Belteshazzar."

Almost instinctively, Daniel searched within himself for the inner eye, the burning heraldry of the Almighty's summons. He felt nothing, sensed nothing. His forehead creased in confusion. "Can you describe this dream, my lord?"

Good, thought Nabu-Naid. *He will hear me out, then compose a suitable explanation.* Believing his goal well in hand, the prime minister rose from the floor, clasping his hands behind him as he paced pensively to and fro in front of the listening Belteshazzar.

"As I lay on my couch last night, my soul was troubled. In my sleep, a voice called to me, but I could not understand the words..."

Again Daniel tested the inner waters of his spirit, finding not the least ripple of a response. Nabu-Naid continued.

"Again and again the voice called out, but I could not discern what was said. However," the prime minister said as he halted pacing and fixed Belteshazzar with a significant stare, "the tone was familiar to me." Five heartbeats went by, and he resumed his prowling.

"In my dream I asked myself, 'Whose is this voice which sounds so familiar, yet whose words are hidden from me?' And suddenly, I realized!" The prime minister's voice dipped to an awed whisper. "It was the sound of our departed lord—Nebu-chadrezzar's voice!"

Daniel looked askance at the restless figure of the prime

minister. A small doubt had raised its irksome head. Still, he listened on.

"I knew that my dear master was trying to say something to me," the prime minister was saying, his voice beginning to fray with emotion, "but I could not comprehend his meaning. Now and again certain words or phrases would pierce the veil of my cognizance. 'Throne,' he seemed to say once, then 'my son,' and finally, 'my friend.'" Overcome by the memory, Nabu-Naid halted again, daubing his eyes with a linen kerchief concealed in his sleeve.

Daniel's inner voice still told him nothing.

Returning to where the vizier sat, stooping to grasp his forearms in a fervent, beseeching grip, Nabu-Naid begged: "O, Belteshazzar! You were often able to comfort our beloved father Nebuchadrezzar! Can you not again bring balm to his restless spirit, and to mine? Can you not tell me the meaning of this dream?"

Something deep within him whispered to Daniel that he lacked all the parts to this whole. He closed his eyes for a moment, in reflection.

Aha! thought Nabu-Naid. *Here it comes…*

"My lord," said Belteshazzar at last, "I do not see the truth of this dream. It does not lie within me."

Taken aback, the prime minister stared open-mouthed at the vizier. "But…I do not understand—"

"I cannot help you," said the vizier, standing to leave. "This —this dream of yours is not revealed to me. The Almighty has not shown it to me."

Nettled by this unexpected recalcitrance, Nabu-Naid frowned. "How can you not aid me, Belteshazzar? Always before—"

"I had no choice before," interrupted Belteshazzar on his way toward the door. "The word of the Lord burned in me, and I could not hide it, even though…" A regretful memory plucked at the sleeve of his mind. "Even though I wanted to. But know this, my lord," the vizier finished, "some dreams are better left undisturbed. Once their meaning is announced, the dreamer may wish he had remained unroused, uninformed. Sometimes the way forward is harder than the way back." Then he was gone.

Fuming, Nabu-Naid ground his teeth in frustration. He *would* have his omen, if not by Belteshazzar, then by some other. Adad-ibni, perhaps...

◆　◆　◆

"THE MEANING OF THIS DREAM is this, my brothers," intoned Adad-ibni pompously to the assembly of priests and mages. "Our father Nebuchadrezzar speaks from the blessed realm beyond to say to our lord Nabu-Naid—and to us—that a wise and experienced hand is required to steady the tiller of Babylon in this pivotal time."

The smells of sandalwood and myrrh were thick in the great hall of Esagila. The senior priests of all the chief deities were gathered to hear the interpretation of Nabu-Naid's portentous dream. After seven days of fasting and consultation with the sky-charts, after arcane divination ceremonies and rigorous sacrificial procedures, Adad-ibni had convened this council of the topmost echelons of the god-houses to announce his findings.

Not that many were in doubt about the ultimate result. The rise in Adad-ibni's fortunes, and his correspondingly close association with the prime minister these last years, were factors lost on no clear-eyed observer. To some of the priests this reading of omens had about it the odor of a thing done after the fact.

"Our father Nebuchadrezzar," proclaimed the seer, "whose firm and mighty hand lifted Babylon out of bondage to the Ninevite intruders, now speaks to us again, this time from across the chasm of death. He bids us recognize the value of age, of wisdom acquired by years of experience, of steady, sure knowledge gained through long association with the inner workings of the kingdom..."

Seated among the front ranks of the dignitaries, Nabu-Naid

shifted a bit uncomfortably. He had asked the mage to work in some reference to his wisdom, but Adad-ibni made him sound as if he were in his dotage.

"First, our father Nebuchadrezzar says, 'Throne.' What else can this mean but that he wishes to speak to us in our confusion about him who shall sit upon the Dragon Throne itself? Next, he says, 'My son.'" Adad-ibni affected a pained, grieving look, his voice dipping several pitches. "How we have suffered, watching the rending pain to which our royal houses have been subjected! Who has not wept within himself for the sorrow brought on by the untimely passing of three scions of our greatest families?"

Again Nabu-Naid squirmed slightly in his seat. Was the fool trying to eulogize Awil-Marduk and the others? Let him get on with the matter at hand!

"And finally, my brothers," announced the mage self-importantly, "Nebuchadrezzar says, 'My friend.' Who else can he mean than one on whose arm he has leaned, one on whose advice he has depended? One whose patient, capable hands have helped guide and shape the governance of the empire for so many years? One, in fact, to whom our departed lord himself spoke through the mysterious dream-world, to show him the charge he must accept? Nebuchadrezzar, seated among the lords of heaven, has aided us in our hour of need. The man he has chosen to uphold Babylon among the nations is our lord prime minister, Nabu-Naid. This is the meaning of the dream. The gods have spoken."

◆　◆　◆

THE CLAY WAS SCARCELY DRY on the proclamation tablets before Nabu-Naid performed his first official act as emperor, dispatching several divisions of infantry to Haran with his son Belshazzar at their head. Their nominal mission was to defeat the Medean garrison there and reclaim the ancient city between the Tigris and Euphrates for the Babylonian Empire.

Not much resistance was encountered at Haran, since Astyages' dwindling resources were focused on the growing problems on his southeastern flank. Crown Prince Belshazzar and his legions made quick work of the few hapless defenders they met, and soon began the real task Nabu-Naid had set before them: to restore and rebuild the Temple of Sin, which had languished so long under the inattentive Medean hegemony.

In some quarters, grumbling was heard about the folly of sending Chaldean troops so far north for no other purpose than refurbishing the dilapidated shrine of a lesser god. After all, they reasoned, why should the king, the earthly regent of Marduk, concern himself with the faraway temple of the moon god Sin, to the neglect of Babylonian bellies? In recent years the river-fed plantations of Akkad and Sumer had not yielded with the bounty of times past. The waters of the Tigris and Euphrates, carried through a webwork of canals, did not nourish the soil as in the past; fields which once had produced amply now bore less and less—as if the land was fatigued. Even the temples found themselves in the position of being silver-rich and staple-poor. More and more, Babylon had to import her bread—such as was available.

The new emperor could not completely scorn the rumblings in the marketplaces and along the river docks. Perhaps it was inevitable that this son of a priestess should once again look to the heavens, to the signs and omens, for delivery from his dilemma. Nor had he forgotten the quick-witted Persian—and Cyrus, his presumably clever sovereign—who had bandied words with him in his suite. Shrewdly Nabu-Naid found a way to fuse the two needs, forging a double-pronged justification for the Haran gambit.

◆　◆　◆

"THE GODS HAVE LET ME see a dream..." quoted the crier from a clay tablet bearing the imperial seal. A crowd had gathered in the square before Egibi's counting-house, attracted by the gaudy livery of the imperial household, and the strident fanfare of the accompanying trumpeters. At the mention of yet another royal dream-sign, the throng grew quiet, even as it muttered with muted skepticism.

"Marduk, the Great Lord, and Sin, the Light of Heaven and Earth, appeared to me. Marduk said to me, 'Nabu-Naid, king of Babylon, bring bricks on your own horse and chariot and build in Haran the House of Joy for Sin, that he may take up his dwelling there...'

"Then I replied to Marduk, 'But the Medes, the barbarian hordes, have laid siege to the house of Lord Sin.' Marduk said to me, 'These whom you have named—they shall cease to exist!'

"And indeed, Marduk has brought against them Cyrus, king of Anshan, his young servant..."

Egibi, standing in his doorway, stroked his beard as he leaned on his cane. So Nabu-Naid openly admitted his dependence on the Persian's success, did he? Whether the mountain-king was victorious or not, the banker ruminated, the new king's words confirmed certain suspicions about the undergirding of the Babylonian royal house. The merchant began questioning whether the size of the barley shipment he had just taken on consignment was truly adequate. In uncertain times, he thought, a full belly may cost dearer. Wheeling about in decision, he called a runner to him. "Boy, fetch me the latest tablet of accounts," he ordered as he hobbled toward his private vault. "I may wish to make some changes..."

◆ ◆ ◆

"I ASSUME, OF COURSE, that you will wish certain alterations made in the religious observances here in Shushan," began Gaudatra, bowing deeply to his royal host as a slave passed him the bowl of sweetmeats. "Shall I give orders that the shrines and temples be destroyed, or will you merely replace the images and altars with those more suitable to yourself?" Daintily the governor picked through the delicacies presented to him.

Gaudatra dined now as a guest in the fortress of Shushan, which until Kurash's coming had been his own residence. The stronghold was temporarily commandeered by the newly acclaimed lord of Elam until completion of the more grandiose citadel-palace which would be the capital of Kurash's empire. The new ruler's many lavish gifts to Gaudatra had considerably lessened the chagrin of being moved out of his own house.

Looking up from his food, Kurash stared at the governor strangely. He had been in control of Elam for almost a year, and still the oddities of these plains-dwelling city folk shocked him. "Why would I wish the shrines and temples destroyed?" the Persian asked in honest befuddlement. "My fight is not against the gods, but against men."

It was Gaudatra's turn to be confused. "But...my lord," he stammered, a candied almond halfway to his mouth, "thus it is always done by the conqueror. A victory for my lord Kurash is a victory for his god, and a humiliation for the defeated gods. For countless generations it has been this way. Surely my lord sees the sense of this?"

"I do not," stated Kurash flatly. "I care not a fig to whom or what the people pray, as long as they pay their taxes. While I reign in Shushan there shall be no destruction of temples or holy places. The customs of the people of my lands shall be respected, and they shall not be prohibited from worshiping the gods their ancestors worshiped. Is this understood?"

The governor bowed low. "My king's wishes shall be obeyed." As Gaudatra straightened, Kurash thought he detected a lingering crease of doubt or confusion. *Just as well*, he thought. *Let him ponder for a while—perhaps he'll come to see the stupidity of such blind adherence to tradition.*

After the meal, as the governor paced in disciplined steps from the hall, Kurash turned to the ever-present Gobhruz. "Well, old friend? What say you? Shall Ahura Mazda be jealous of the freedom which I grant to my new-found people? On the Day of Testing, shall my spirit be cast into outer darkness with the *devas* and the wicked men?"

The old Mede grunted, shifting his eyes away from those of Kurash. "My lord knows I bother little with such matters," he muttered. "I concern myself with the ways of men, not the ways of gods."

"Well said, Gobhruz," chuckled the new lord of Elam and most of Medea, as well as Persis. "Well said, indeed."

The older man chewed the words he wished to offer next. Kurash, sensing unspoken thoughts rambling about in his mentor's head, finally said, "Out with it, Gobhruz. Your silent thinking is more painful for me to bear than whatever it is you would say."

Glancing at his lord from beneath his graying, bushy eyebrows, the Mede asked, "What next, my lord? After this?"

Kurash leaned back in his chair, staring down at the open palm of his hand. "My informers tell me that Croesus has extended his Lydian clutches along the River Halys to the upper reaches of the Euphrates. Perhaps he thinks that because Asturagash lies gasping in Ecbatana, no one concerns himself with the northern lands of Medea. But I suspect he shall soon learn the error of his suppositions."

Impatiently Gobhruz shook his head. "Not that, my king. I already knew that, or guessed as much."

Kurash's forehead wrinkled with perplexity. Wordlessly, he waited for his most trusted adviser to continue.

"You were bred to rule," explained the Mede, "or to die. No other choice was ever permitted you. From the time of your birth I have known this. Your father knew it too, though he would fain have not." The older man peered carefully at the face of his king, then away. "Do you know the story of your infancy?"

Kurash shook his head, helpless to do anything but listen.

"It is rumored—and for my part, I believe it," said Gobhruz, "that Asturagash, after he had given his daughter Mandane to your father as wife, suffered from a dream. The form of the dream differs from teller to teller, but suffice it to say that the night-vision gave him cause to fear you."

Kurash's eyes widened, his nostrils flared. An echo of the child's anger caused him to clench his teeth. So! The ambivalence toward Medea he had felt as a young boy had been more than infantile pretension! Apparently his grandfather, in the far-off palace at Ecbatana, had felt some intuition of the destiny which had brought them both to this day. Perhaps the old king, through his daughter, felt and feared the birth-pangs of the new.

Gobhruz continued: "It may be these stories were only entertainments for the old women and eunuchs of the palace at Ecbatana. I cannot say. But I do know this…" Again the bodyguard fixed his king with a challenging stare, and this time his eyes did not blink away. "From your first breath, something—be it a god, or a *deva*, or both—has drawn you toward empire, as a moth is drawn to the flame of a lamp. Your feet are set on a path which you can neither change nor understand."

The eyes of the two men sparked with each other, the amber eyes of the king burning hot and quick, the dark gaze of his friend and servant glowing with a more stubborn, grudging warmth. Presently Gobhruz went on.

"What I meant earlier was this: After the throne of Medea is gained, what then? Have you considered this?"

Kurash's face silently asked him to continue.

"Yesterday you ruled Persis. Today and tomorrow, Medea. The day after, Lydia—perhaps the islands of the Hellenes after that. And one day you will stand before the walls of Babylon, and some star-gazing Chaldean king will know what your grandfather Asturagash learned on his bed, in the hush of the night."

Kurash smiled. "Good Gobhruz, I believe you make too simple what is really—"

"But mind this, O Kurash, Shepherd of the People," pressed the older man, "and take it to heart: You cannot conquer any city, lay tribute upon any land, or set satraps over any tribe which has not already been subjugated by some now-forgotten chieftain in some vanished yesterday." The bodyguard's words rained upon the king's shoulders like fate, stabbing Kurash in the hidden places of his soul. "Think of it, Lord Kurash: Tomorrow you shall take the preeminence, but only yesterday it was the Medes, and the day before that the Chaldeans, and before them the Assyrians." Gobhruz paused, continuing in a softer voice. "What you win today," he said, "what your sons after you may hold for a little while, will one day lie under the shadow of another—perhaps a child yet to be born. Each conquest shows the way of its own undoing, my lord. Such is the nature of kings, and of kingdoms."

Kurash slowly clenched and unclenched his fist, studying it as if seeing it for the first time. After many heartbeats he looked up at his bodyguard, his counselor. "Then shall I not make the attempt? Shall I go back to my valley and be a quiet, contented horse-king?" There was no bitterness in the king's voice, no rancor. Only a certain quiet guardedness, such as a pupil might display at an unwelcome assignment.

"I have already said it," replied Gobhruz. "You can do nothing else than go forward. It is your fate—or your duty. But you must know, too, that it cannot be forever, this empire you are building. With men only the semblance of permanence, the appearance of eternity is possible. The wish is there, but not the capability to fulfill it. With the gods, matters may be different, but such lies beyond my seeing."

Once more a rapt, plaintive silence filled the chamber. Looking away, into a distant corner of the room or of his future, Kurash intoned softly, "Well said, Gobhruz—well said."

19

ADAD-IBNI SHIFTED UNEASILY on his cushion, eyeing the fig he held in his hand. The chief seer had taken two or three nibbles from the ripe fruit, and the sour look on his face had nothing to do with its taste.

Furtively he glanced up at the stern, pacing figure of Nabu-Naid, carefully composing his response to what the emperor had just proposed. "Everyone knows of my king's deep devotion to Lord Sin," he began, before wincing inwardly. Already he sounded too accusative. He started again. "No one has a greater appreciation than myself of the importance of reverence to the Moon Lord. But...my king well knows that the priests of Esagila would evince a certain..."—he groped delicately for a word—"*reserve*...toward such an ambitious project as my lord proposes, unless it were directed toward the benefit of Marduk. Especially now—" Realizing he had said two words too many, the mage hushed.

Nabu-Naid stared hard at the bald-pated old man. "Perhaps you wished to say, 'Especially now that the unpopular work in Haran is just completed'?"

The silence crackled with hostility in the morning-lit chamber, until Adad-ibni could tolerate it no longer. "Surely my king realizes," he said, squirming, "that by correcting the unfortunate state of affairs in Haran, he unavoidably attracted the attentions of certain malcontents seeking an excuse for the poor harvests."

The emperor sneered at his chief mage, shaking his head in wry amusement. "How hard it is for you to say what you mean, Adad-ibni," he smirked. "You of all people I would expect to appreciate my attentions to the temple, guarded so long and faithfully by my recently deceased mother." Adad-ibni bowed low in respectful genuflection at the mention of the emperor's ancient matron. She had lived so long that some half-thought her bewitched, and she finally died at the unimagined, toothless age of one hundred and four years. Her son had seen to it that her funeral was well-attended and lavishly carried out.

"My king knows I hold the utmost respect for his revered mother," said the mage. Hidden in his robes, his fingers made the sign against the evil eye.

"What you say in the silences between your many words," huffed Nabu-Naid, turning his back upon the seer, "is that you doubt the priests of Marduk will permit, without severe compulsion, the construction of a proper temple to Lord Sin within the walls of Babylon." Over his shoulder, the emperor turned a beetle-black eye upon the huddled, cringing form of the chief mage. "And we must not greatly discomfit the priests of the cherished Marduk, must we?"

The sarcastic tone of the emperor's words frightened the mage almost as much as his anger. One should not trifle with the gods, he thought. Of course, he could not verbalize such a direct reprimand to his royal sponsor. With his habitual obliqueness, he observed quietly, "My king should also consider the sizeable resources controlled by the priests of Esagila. Without their agreement to contribute to the project—"

"The scoundrels!" Nabu-Naid snorted. "They take a man's goats in security for a pledge, and when he can't pay them twice the worth of the flock they keep the whole mangy lot! There are scores of temples in this city, *my* city," raged the petulant king, "not to mention the hundreds of shrines and altars—but does Lord Sin, the Ancient One, have a house in which his name can be venerated?"

Angrily he paced to the other end of the chamber, then whirled about to add, "Don't think I've forgotten, seer: The house of Marduk gave money and materials for the building of that ridiculous edifice to Nabu in Borsip, but do you think they'd donate as much as a strip of copper if they thought Lord Sin might be so honored? Ha!" Again the emperor turned his back on the mage.

Under his breath, the mage quoted, "Nabu is the Son of Marduk, and the reflection of his glory." *This fixation of the emperor's is ill-omened*, he pondered miserably. *But how can I tell him so?* Aloud he said, "Perhaps my king should sojourn outside the walls of this city to refresh his mind—to pray to the gods and permit himself time to make a judicious disposition of this delicate matter."

Nabu-Naid, toying distractedly with the amulet about his neck, suddenly halted, staring thoughtfully at his chief diviner. The wisp of an idea had wafted its way to him. With his eyes squinted in speculation, he began smiling. "Perhaps you are correct, Lord Adad-ibni." A look of wicked relish crawled across the ruler's face.

The mage could not fathom what was taking form in the corridors of his sovereign's skull, but he suspected it could not be anything overly pleasant.

"Perhaps a tour abroad is precisely what I need," grinned the king, rubbing his hands together. "Since you mention it, good mage, there are some ruins in Teima, in the far reaches of the Arabah, which I have wished to examine for some time. I understand they have many ancient inscriptions there, preserved in the dry sands of the region. I believe this is an excellent opportunity to pursue my passion for antiquities."

The mage, apprehension clogging his chest, calculated furiously in his mind. Teima! The city lay leagues to the west, across huge stretches of desert not quickly traversed. It was already the middle of the month of Adar—the New Year Festival was only weeks away. Without the king's presence in the capital, the festival could not take place. Gasping with dismay, the mage pleaded, "My lord! You cannot possibly travel to Teima and return in time for—"

"The festival, my lord mage?" An evil chuckle hissed from

between the aging monarch's dry lips. "You may well be right!"

◆ ◆ ◆

"AND SO, MY BELOVED SUBJECTS," announced the emperor to the silent, stunned courtiers, "I shall depart on the morrow for Teima. While I sojourn away from my beloved city, I leave my son, Belshazzar"—the emperor clapped a hand on the shoulder of the loutish, smirking crown prince—"to act as steward for the kingdom.

"I charge you all," he concluded, "to obey him as you would me..."

◆ ◆ ◆

STANDING ON THE WALL of Sardis, the Lydian guard leaned back while drawing a draught of water. Suddenly the helmet slipped from his head, clattering over the edge of the battlements and finally coming to rest among the rocks below the citadel. Cursing under his breath, the sentry peered carefully about in the dusky light. *No one watching—good.* Gingerly he mounted to the top of the wall, then edged along the narrow shelf outside the battlements, more than a little mindful of the sheer drop yawning at his feet.

Reaching the corner where two walls joined, he climbed cautiously down to the rocks below the wall. This corner, known to few even among the city's guards, was the only place one could descend to the ground in a relatively easy manner. Again looking about to see that he was alone, he made his way over to where his dented bronze helmet lay among the boulders near the base of the wall. Shaking his head in disgust, he strapped the headpiece to his belt and turned about to retrace his climb up the seemingly sheer wall.

Unseen by the Lydian sentry, two Persian spies slinked away from their observation post. When they were out of sight of the walls of Sardis, they trotted quickly toward the camp of Kurash. Their lord would be pleased with the news they brought this day.

◆ ◆ ◆

KURASH CHUCKLED MERRILY, shaking his head in amazement. Rising from his couch, he said, "Scribe! Fetch me two bags containing a tenth-shekel of gold apiece." Grinning at the wide-eyed spies, he continued, "I would reward the keen vision and quick minds of these two."

For months the army of Medes and Persians had been encamped against Sardis, the glittering, seemingly impregnable capital of Croesus and his Lydians. Having won acclamation as king in Ecbatana, Kurash had quickly moved to quash Croesus' incipient attempt at a land-grab in Cappadocia and Armenia to the north. The fantastically rich Croesus had thought to take advantage of the tumult in Medea to carve out a larger territory beyond his former eastern border.

But the Lydian gambit was doomed to failure. Kurash, at the head of a reborn Medo-Persian host, had swiftly routed the effete, well-groomed forces of the gold-king. Now Croesus and his minions were holed up in the citadel of Sardis, set on a rocky ridge behind walls which had, until this moment, been invulnerable.

"Boy, fetch me Commander Gobhruz," Kurash ordered. The page scampered away. "Tonight, my fine fellows," the king of Medea and Persia said, still smiling at the two newly rich reconnaissance men, "you shall escort the general to the place you found. We shall determine how many men, and in how quick a fashion, we can place inside the walls of Sardis.

"And tomorrow," he continued, more to himself than to the men, "we shall see who is the richest king in Lydia."

◆ ◆ ◆

BABYLON WAS NOT A HAPPY PLACE. The seasons ground inexorably along, the month of Nisan approached—and still no word came from Teima, the remote desert town to which the king had hastened. For yet another year it appeared the New Year Festival would not be celebrated.

Aside from the ominous prophecies of pestilence and disaster from the soothsayers and diviners, the city's merchants and tradesmen grumbled about more prosaic matters: of lost trade and unsold goods, of profits vanished without the joyous excesses engendered by the rebirth and homecoming of Marduk. The temple prostitutes—and, for that matter, the freelance whores—were as unhappy as the others about the loss of commerce resulting from the emperor's frustrating absence.

In Esagila, far darker mutterings could be heard. Throughout the temple complex, the emperor's thinly disguised attempt at coercion caused the priests of Marduk to gnash their teeth in anger and pray unceasingly to the King of Heaven to bring down this rebellious and obstinate fool who had abandoned his people, leaving his surly and caustic son behind to pollute the palace with his ungracious presence.

But if Belshazzar was a boor, he was no simpleton. The prince-regent brutally intimidated his father's opponents. He was unblinking in his use of the military, which he wielded with the iron grip of an absolute commander. Only a month ago, as the population watched aghast, he marched a squadron of infantry into the very sanctuary of Ishtar, the heavy-breasted Lady of Uruk, and dragged out a priest known to be an open critic of Nabu-Naid. The man was hauled into the midst of crowded Aibur Shabu where he was disemboweled, and his corpse dumped unceremoniously into the Zababa Canal. Tactics such as this had had their effect; though extremely unpopular, the reign *in absentia* of Nabu-Naid was secure.

The Jews of Babylon proceeded on their way, outside the mainstream of Babylonian custom and practice, yet unmolested. Their teachers and scholars read to them from the writings of their prophets and exhorted them from the pages of their ancient Law. They continued a process of coalescence around the adamant, unremitting core of their Unnamed One and His stone-hard, profound injunctions: *Thou shalt have no other gods before Me; thou shalt not take My Name in vain; thou shalt keep My shabbat…*

♦ ♦ ♦

DANIEL GLANCED UP from his reading of the scroll, squinting his eyes and rubbing them with his fingertips. The oil lamp burned low, and the inked letters on the parchment had begun to flicker and waver before his vision with every dip and tremor of the unsteady flame. It was time to rest.

He rose, rewrapped the scroll, and placed it carefully beside the others on his reading table. Remembering the hard, worn face of Ezekiel, its author, he stroked the vellum sheath of the yellowing document, copied in the long-dead prophet's own hand. He turned toward his couch.

Beyond mere fatigue and the lateness of the hour, he felt the weariness of his years pressing upon him. For almost fifty years he had been in or near the royal court of Babylon. The drain of the constant vigilance needed to navigate safely through the subtle feuds of opposing factions and personalities, the relentless responsibility of administering the endlessly mutable policies of the emperor and the prince-regent, the shifting, slippery surfaces of uncontrollable events, and the solicitous concern for protection and maintenance of the Chosen, his brethren—all these clamored incessantly for his attention. Added to them was his overarching, lifelong sense of being a foreigner in this city which, though almost the only dwelling place he had ever known, could never be home. Such cares and burdens caused each of his years to weigh heavily upon him just now, each of the sixty years of his life tugging at him with a nagging insistence.

"Sovereign Lord," he prayed, his face buried in the scented linens of his bed, "I am so tired. Grant me the rest which is beyond sleep, beyond waking. Grant me the ease of soul which I crave; grant release, and quiet..." Unable to frame within himself the words to express his longing, he found himself remembering Mishael's lament by the tomb of old Caleb. In some ways he could almost crave the quiet, the stillness of that final couch. An end to striving. A state when worry, care—the arduous necessity of *being*—was ended.

"O my God," he continued, "Your ways are too high for me. Your will is above the highest heavens, and I am but a weak and weary old man. Once I tasted the dizzying wine of Your choosing, but now I have only the tastelessness of old age. Twice I felt my tongue ablaze with the imperatives of Your message, but now my throat is parched by the aridity of the years. And thrice I was blinded by the brilliance of Your visions, but now I witness only the gathering of darkness. O Lord of Abraham," he moaned fervently, "give me peace at last. Let me finally rest and be quiet."

Falling on his couch still fully clothed, he tumbled into the deathlike darkness of an exhaustion far beyond the physical; it was weariness of the soul which claimed Daniel, and his breath came so slowly that each might be his last.

He stood on the shore of a vast and mighty sea. Feeling a cold, foreboding tendril of air moving against his cheek, he looked far out over the restless waters of the deep. A dark bank of clouds roiled along the flat plane of the horizon, pulling within itself, mounting higher and higher, as if gathering like a black panther for a vicious spring.

Then a breeze from behind caused him to spin about in alarm. At his back, a huge cloud-beast coiled for the attack. Then he looked around, and on every horizon, all about the huge circle of the earth, the winds of creation were gathering for the onslaught.

Four huge maelstroms of the heavens rushed forward at once, smiting the sea and casting up waves as high as mountains. As he watched, terrified for his life, four hideous beasts rose from the waters of the sea where the winds had struck.

The first was like the lion of Ishtar, but with the wings of an eagle. The second was a bear, gnashing its teeth on the gory ribs of its latest kill. The third was a leopard with the wings of a bird; and the fourth —Daniel's tongue cleaved to the roof of his mouth in terror at the sight of it. This creature from a twisted nightmare was utterly indescribable; its horrific appearance sent the mind reeling in revulsion. The only features which his recoiling senses recorded were its brutal teeth of iron, with which it mauled and crushed its victims—and the ten horns on its head...

Long minutes or hours later he awoke, the echo of his awesome Guide's voice still reverberating in his mind. His heart jolted against his windpipe as the dream crossed and recrossed the window of his mind. Four beasts. Ten horns. There had been an eleventh one too, a blasphemous horn, swelling and boasting. And a glorious Son of Man, whose authority would be absolute, whose kingdom would never end...

Searching within himself for a response to the fantastic mind-journey of the night, Daniel discovered two emotions intimately entwined in his soul.

On one hand he felt exhilaration. He had tasted the power of the Eternal thrumming in his vitals—for there was no doubting the Source of the vision he had seen.

On the other hand he felt a haggard sense of foreboding. It seemed the Eternal still had a calling for His world-weary servant—and Daniel knew there was no way of predicting the paths on which such a summons might place his fatigued old feet. Some tale was yet to be told, he sensed, some vision yet to be imparted.

With deliberate slowness, Daniel rose from his couch and began gathering his writing materials.

20

PRINCE BELSHAZZAR GRASPED the glazed-clay drinking bowl, still half-full of frothy ale, and hurled it against the far wall of the chamber. Striking the baked-brick wall with a loud pop, it shattered into shards, splashing the wall with the remnants of the brew. Shocked, the others watched in dumb, feigned fascination as the white beads of foam ran in tiny rivulets down the seams between the bricks. All faces were averted, for the only alternative was meeting the furious eyes of the prince-regent.

"I ask for reports, and you bring me dung!" Belshazzar was shouting, his full lower lip quivering in rage. "Rumors, and the whisperings of foolish old women." He spat, glaring at each of them in turn. None of the counselors dared show his eyes to the son of Nabu-Naid.

Still furious, the broad-shouldered prince clutched both fists into the front of the nearest vizier's robes, half-lifting the astonished and frightened older man out of his seat. "How can I keep my father—and your king—apprised of the movements of Cyrus if the messengers you send are too fearful to make contact with him?" He shook the nobleman like a truant schoolboy. Dropping the courtier with a disgusted grunt, he turned toward the rest of them. "Must I wait until his army is encamped outside the Ishtar Gate before I can know with certainty what his intentions are?"

"My lord prince," ventured some foolhardy soul into the black curtain of silence, "Sardis is a far journey. We only dispatched the couriers two months ago, so surely they will soon—"

"I must know now!" Belshazzar bellowed, crashing his fist

to the table in front of the white-faced vizier. "The illiterate fool has already toppled Ecbatana without so much as drawing a sword! He has rolled up the territories east of the Tigris like a worn-out carpet, and now he challenges the might of Croesus!" Clawing at his face in furious frustration, the prince-regent strode to and fro like a caged tiger. "Croesus has appealed to Babylon for aid," growled the prince-regent, "and I sit here like a fat ox, with crows cawing in my ear."

"Egypt has also received an embassy from the Lydian capital," meekly ventured one of the nobles.

"Egypt!" sneered Belshazzar. "Egypt had her teeth pulled at Carchemish, in the days of Nebuchadrezzar. She won't answer the call of Croesus."

"What has the king said of these matters?" asked another counselor.

Belshazzar halted his furious pacing, glaring at the speaker. "The king…attends to other matters," he grated hesitantly, deciding that the words he really wished to say were best left unuttered. He resumed his striding, muttering to himself—or perhaps to his infuriatingly absent father. "If Sardis falls to Cyrus, he will have completely outflanked us to the north and south. How long can it be before he turns his attention to the cities of the Two Rivers?"

He halted his feverish pacing, aiming another thunderous scowl at the huddled, silent group around the table. "Well?" Belshazzar demanded. "Do you have tongues in your heads, or not? Speak, fools! Your sovereign's regent commands it!"

Chests heaving with tongue-tied anxiety, the counselors looked at each other, then at the top of the table. What could be said when all answers were wrong?

◆ ◆ ◆

PUTTING THE STYLUS ASIDE, Daniel took many deep breaths, trying to calm the trembling in his hands spawned by the still too vivid memory of the terrifying visions that had burst across his sleeping mind. Even now, with the sunlight of the spring morning drenching his chamber, the blasphemous words of the dream-beast's eleventh horn chilled his heart with a midnight darkness. Despite the gay, reassuring chirps of the sparrows in the garden outside his window, he bent only unwillingly to the task of recording the images of the frightful demons in his dream.

It was a vision of kings, this dream of his. He began writing what a Guide had explained to him of the vision:

The four great beasts are four kingdoms that will rise from the earth. But the holy ones of the Most High will receive the kingdom and will possess it forever—

His breast swelling with grateful emotion, he wrote for emphasis:

Yes! Forever and ever!

Despite the appalling fear he had felt for the winds and for the huge and dreadful beasts, the end of the dream had shouted peals of hope, of certain victory! The people of the Lord would triumph.

Daniel's hand paused in its writing. He remembered the sense he had had in his vision—the aura of vast, uncounted multitudes of victorious saints, rejoicing in the sovereignty of the just rule of the Eternal, and the vague, irrepressible intuition that the salvation promised by this triumph of righteousness would roll like a flood far beyond the borders of Judah—indeed, of Chaldea! Somehow this victory was a vindication for all creation; every piece of Adonai's handiwork would rise up together in a great shout of joy for the defeat of wickedness.

While he pondered these unnameable thoughts, a pounding came on his door. Glancing quickly about, he covered his tablet with a damp cloth to preserve its moisture, then hid the tablet behind his couch.

Opening the door, he found, to his astonishment, one of the sons of Azariah. With tears streaming down his face, the young man said, "Uncle Daniel—come quickly! Father is dying. He asks for you."

♦   ♦   ♦

IN A DAZE, Daniel entered the house on Adad street. The son had told him, on the swift journey through the streets from the palace, about Azariah's sudden, piercing cry of agony that morning at table. He had clutched at his chest, collapsing in a helpless heap upon the floor. Each breath he now drew was a battle dearly won, and the sudden, awful knowledge came unbidden to them all that he would leave them very, very soon.

At last they reached the portal. Mishael and Hananiah, already there, met his disbelieving, helpless stare with sad shakes of the head and tear-stained glances. Through the main room he walked, all sound roaring together in his ears, all sight blurring into a shapeless glare, except for the face of Ephratah and the miserable, lost faces of Azariah's children.

He entered the bedchamber. Azariah lay panting on his couch, clutching at his chest. Through pain-wracked eyes, he spied his old friend. Weakly he patted a place beside him, indicating that Daniel should sit. The vizier leaned close to his friend's lips.

"A pain...here," whispered Azariah, tapping his breast. "Like a camel—sat on me...fully loaded."

Daniel, the tears draining unheeded from his eyes, nodded at Azariah. "You should not speak, my friend," he whispered hoarsely. "You should save your breath for your family."

Azariah, impatient even on his deathbed, shook his head. "Already told them...all," he muttered. "Wanted...you."

Daniel forced a wavering smile to his lips. "Well, then... here I am."

Azariah's eyelids fluttered. Daniel, fearing the end, could not draw breath until again he saw the focused gaze of his dying friend on his face. "You need..." Several labored, wracking breaths interrupted his words. "...need to forget...before."

Daniel stared at Azariah as a decrepit host of painful memories chased each other across his face. The dying man's eyes held a knowing, reproving look. Daniel, choking on his emotion, could only nod. Again he saw Azariah gathering himself, at almost unbearable cost, to speak.

"But never forget...Jerusalem," he breathed.

Again Daniel could make no reply, other than a vigorous shake of his head. Gripping the hand of his lifelong comrade, he rained tears upon the front of Azariah's robe. Feeling a hand on his shoulder, he turned to see the entire room filled with the family and friends of Azariah/Abed-Nabu, son of Judah, counselor of Babylon.

The man on the bed moved his head slightly, taking them all in with his gaze. Then, with a tiny smile of farewell on his lips, the pain-creases on his face softened, his eyes closed. The ragged, tortured breaths halted. It was over.

Accompanied by Ephratah's soft sobbing, Mishael intoned, in a grief-clogged voice, the psalm he had uttered by the tomb of Caleb.

> *Do You show Your wonders to the dead?*
> *Do those who are dead rise up and praise You?*

"No, my friend," interrupted Daniel, suddenly remembering the victory hymn of the rejoicing multitudes in his dream. "Have you forgotten what else David says?" Daniel rose, gripping the arms of the eunuch.

> *Where can I go from Your Spirit?*
> *Where can I flee from Your presence?*
> *If I go up to the heavens, You are there;*
> *if I make my bed in Sheol, behold, You are there.*
> *If I take the wings of the dawn,*
> *and fly to the uttermost parts of the sea —*
> *even there, Your hand will guide me,*
> *Your right hand will hold me fast...*

Hananiah raised his face to Daniel's, an other-worldly gleam in his dark eyes. His chin quivering with the effort of speaking aloud rather than with his beloved harp, he chanted.

> *I will exalt You, O Lord,*

for You lifted me out of the depths…
O Lord my God, I called to You for help
and You healed me.
O Lord, You brought me up from the grave…

◆　◆　◆

STANDING ON THE HIGHEST BATTLEMENT of the citadel of Sardis, Cyrus turned to the Lydian prime minister standing at his elbow. "Well, then, Lysidias; do the terms sound agreeable to you?"

The nobleman nodded limply, unable to believe the evidence of his ears. The conqueror of Sardis proposed to leave Lydian society almost exactly as he had found it. No pillaging. No enslavement or forced relocation of masses of people. Lysidias would remain in his post, but now would report to Cyrus as his *kshatra*—satrap, as the Lydian tongue styled the odd Aryan syllables. And Cyrus said he would have allowed Croesus the same opportunity—had the Lydian king not taken the unfortunate and untimely expedient of immolating himself in the private courtyard of his suite.

The only traces of conquest Sardis would be forced to accept were the inevitable tax and the continued presence of a Persian as chancellor of the treasury and commander of the armed garrison in Sardis—a light enough load for a people who, scant hours before, had feared for their necks.

Feeling himself almost reborn with relief, the Lydian knelt before the breeches-clad king with the amber eyes. As a scribe made notation of the event, Cyrus peered toward the western horizon and remarked, "This tower commands quite a view. I suspect Croesus spent much time enjoying it, eh, Lysidias?"

The newly created satrap of Lydia replied, "No, my…my king. The king—er, that is to say, Croesus—passed most of his time in the gardens, or in the treasury. He did not concern himself overmuch with the view from the towers."

Kurash chuckled at the pungency, intended or otherwise, of the Lydian's remark. Shading his eyes, he could spy the faraway sparkle of the sea, and beyond that, a dark smudge on the most distant line between earth and sky. "What is that land yonder, Lysidias?" he asked. "There beyond the sea."

The satrap glanced in the direction of Cyrus's gaze. "That would be the isles of the Greeks, my king. Not far from the mainland of Hellas itself."

"Hellas..." The name had an odd tingle on Kurash's tongue. He felt a curious struggle within his breast. He wanted to press on from Sardis, to encounter these Greeks and see what sort of men they might be. And yet...some small corner of his soul recoiled at the thought. Some barely audible voice—his *fravashi*, perhaps—whispered that elsewhere lay destiny—for himself and his empire. Destiny...and eventual danger.

◆　◆　◆

DANIEL WAS IN A LARGE, empty courtyard. A broad, limpid canal flowed through the courtyard, its waters weirdly silent.

The vacancy, the utter absence of the noise of feet or even the most distant voices cast a pall of eeriness over the place. And yet there was something familiar about the citadel enclosing the huge plaza— as if he should recognize his whereabouts, but couldn't, quite; as if he were remembering something he had not yet seen.

He heard a footfall behind him—but not the sound of a human foot. Turning about, he saw a magnificent ram; its pelt was of glistening white wool, its hoofs and horns of gold. The nostrils of the lordly beast flared red, and dark fire flashed from its eyes. One of the beast's horns, he noticed, was larger than the other, as though it had grown in earlier than its mate.

As he watched, the ram snorted, lowering its head and charging to the east, the sinews bunching mightily along its back and hindquarters. Wheeling about in a cloud of dust, the animal bolted back in the direction it had come, raking the deadly horns along the ground as it fiercely asserted mastery over its domain.

To the four directions of the wind the ram charged, halting at last, hot breath blowing out its nostrils. With head held at a high and imperious angle, the beast surveyed its surroundings, staring through Daniel as if he had no more material presence than the air.

As he stood admiring the ram, he heard the bone-chilling sound of a bellowed challenge, the adversarial battle trumpet of the rutting season. Glancing to his right, he saw a he-goat prancing impossibly through the air as it passed over the high western wall of the court-yard, coming to rest a stone's toss from the ram.

The two beasts blared their battle cries at each other, pawing in the dust and shaking their heads in a naked display of brute hostility. He noticed that the he-goat had but one horn, albeit a large one, and it was queerly placed—in the center of the goat's forehead. The nerves in his spine unraveled as he watched and listened to the challenge and counter-challenge. Clearly there would be but one survivor of the im-pending clash.

Presently, the he-goat rushed violently at the ram, which lowered its head and bounded forward to meet the attack. When the charging beasts collided, a peal of thunder rang out; he fancied the daylight dimmed several degrees. When he could uncover his ears and open his eyes, the mighty, milk-white ram lay dead. The he-goat straddled its carcass in triumph.

No sooner had this happened than the large, single horn of the goat shattered, and in its place grew out four grotesque horns, point-ing north and south, east and west. And in their midst, another horn grew forth. As the small horn bulged outward in awful urgency, he felt the blood freezing in his veins.

For he knew its kind. He had seen this before, in the eleventh horn of the Fourth Beast. Even as the horn grew and grew, becoming a liv-ing thing, he knew what would happen. With the dreadful surety of a remembered nightmare, he listened to the blasphemies and watched the horrendous, uncontested progress of its loathsome evil.

And then a Voice was speaking, with a sound more dire and com-manding than the clash of the king-beasts. He knew the resonant tone of his Guide and listened with all his soul, for the victory of the arro-gant Fifth Horn had profoundly disquieted his spirit.

"These animals represent the kings of Medea and Persia, and the king of the Greeks to come," his Guide was saying, "and the vision you have seen concerns things which lie far in the future—in the time of the end..."

Daniel wondered to whom he should tell these things. Should he speak to the king, to warn, to chasten?

"No!" said the Guide to his unspoken question. "These things are true and trustworthy, but you must seal up this vision, for many seasons and kings will pass before its fulfillment..."

As morning light seeped beneath his eyelids, he clutched his hands to his breast. His heart pounded as if seeking explosive release from his body. His eyes were open, but the room swirled about him as for one who had drunk too much rich ale.

Again, he reflected, a vision of four! This time four horns, and the four kings they represented. Like the ten horns of the Fourth Beast in his earlier vision, the four horns of the goat were followed by a horrible fifth. Kings of Persia, and a king of the Hellenes! The frightful imagery, the tolling, diamond-hard words of his Guide swam before his fevered memory. He felt himself trapped in a sickening, helpless vertigo, drowning in the overpowering elixir of the Eternal's soul-flooding revelation.

Daniel moaned, covering his face with his hands. His clothing and divan were drenched in the cold sweat of his fear. Panting with exertion, he raised himself trembling on one elbow, then fell limply back. Gathering the tiny vestiges of his strength, he moaned aloud the name of his body-servant.

The page padded quietly into the chamber, approaching his master's bed with a worried, quizzical look.

"I...I am ill," Daniel wheezed. "I cannot appear in the court today..."

◆　◆　◆

KURASH STEPPED OUT of the low-gunwaled boat, his leg sinking calf-deep into the miry swamp. In the distance he could see rocky hills rising. "What is the name of this country?" he asked, turning to the Greek who had piloted the small craft to the mainland.

"Macedon, my lord," the wiry, dark man replied in the harsh, clattering accent of Hellas.

"Macedon," mused the Persian. He grunted with the exertion of pulling his feet out of the muck in which they disembarked. Each step made a loud sucking noise as they slogged their way toward higher ground. "Is all of Macedon's shoreline such a quagmire?" laughed Kurash. "I shouldn't think the people of this place would have energy enough to do anything save walk from one house to another, if the whole country is such a sea of clinging mud!"

"It would not do for you to speak so to the Macedonians, my lord," cautioned the Greek. "They are a quarrelsome lot—and they don't take reminders of their backward ways lightly."

"Have they frequent occasion to be reminded of their… lack of advancement?" queried the horse-king.

"Oh, the dramatists and philosophers of Athens and the other cities of the Attic peninsula delight in satirizing the Macedonian hill folk," said the guide. "It's all a sport to them. But we who live closer—in Thermopylae and in the north and east of Epirus—don't treat the Macedonians so lightly."

When they had lurched a few steps farther through the mud, he continued. "The folk of Athens can comfort themselves with their walls and their citizen armies. But we must live cheek-by-jowl with the Macedonians. One day they will tire of being seen as clowns and buffoons. And then…"

Kurash carefully noted the muted respect the Greek paid these supposedly crude Macedonians. How well he remembered the disdain with which the "civilized" Medes had jibed their mountain cousins, the Parsi! So the Athenians derided the Macedonians, did they? He fell silent, partly in thought and partly to conserve his breath for the next step through the pitchlike mud of the bog.

◆ ◆ ◆

THAT EVENING, as the reconnaissance party bivouacked in a ravine between two flinty hillsides, Kurash called Gobhruz to him.

"Old friend," said the king when the gray-bearded Mede bowed before him, "what say you? Is it time to turn back— toward Babylon?"

The older man mumbled something in his beard.

"What was that?" pressed the king. "I couldn't hear you."

The Mede stared into the flickering light of a nearby camp-fire for several moments, then glanced at the king. Unable to hold the eyes of his sovereign, he looked at the toe of his left boot, mumbling, "I said, 'Babylon has had many others; why should you be any different?'"

"What is this, Gobhruz?" asked Kurash, chuckling. "Have we come to the very western end of the world, and now you think the walls of Babylon shall best me at last? Where is the man who spoke of the fear of a star-gazing king?"

The old, sturdy Mede shook his head. "No, my king. It's not that. You will take Babylon—her time is finished. This much I know."

Kurash carefully watched his mentor's profile, as the face of Gobhruz flickered orange and black in the firelight. "What, then?" he asked at last.

"You are being taken by all this," the Mede said, gesturing widely about them. "And once you have taken Babylon, the taking will be complete."

Kurash's silence urged him to continue.

"Each victory, each new tributary takes you farther away from what you were. Makes you both more the king, and less the Parsi." The old man chewed on his thoughts for many heartbeats. Raising his eyes to Kurash's, he said, "When you were a boy, it was enough for you to have a spirited charger beneath you, and the free air of Anshan to breathe. Then you got a bit older and discovered you were the son and grandson of kings. You began to outgrow Anshan."

"If I am to be the king of Lydians and Medes—and Chaldeans," Kurash observed in a muted tone, "must I not take what is best from each part, the better to understand the whole?"

Gobhruz' hands plucked at a straggling tuft of wiry grass, twisting it to and fro as he searched his soul for the words he wanted. "I left Elam because I wished a simpler, less affected existence. I have served you with all my heart, as I swore I would to your father. And now…"

A night bird's song wafted down the hillside. A piece of green wood hissed on the crackling coals of the fire. Quietly Kurash said, "My friend, I would not bind you to an enterprise you find distasteful. You have my leave to return to Anshan, there to live out your days—"

"I cannot leave," interrupted the Mede. "I made an oath to your father, and I cannot leave."

"Very well then," said Kurash. "You will stay—and be the conscience of the king. A wise shepherd has need of much advisement. And a voice of caution is a prudent addition to any counsel. Will you do this for me, my friend—and teacher?"

Gobhruz peered long and hard into the fire, then looked down at his feet and nodded his head slowly. "Aye."

"Then…what say you?" queried Kurash, a tiny smile flickering on his lips. "Shall we turn our steps eastward—to Babylon?"

Without looking up, Gobhruz gave a weary, affirmative nod. "Aye," he grunted.

PART III

Deliverance

21

THE SMALL KNOT of priests and astrologers stood just within the Marduk Gate of Esagila, arguing heatedly among themselves while worshipers and temple functionaries scurried busily in and out of the temple complex.

"Well, at least the Festival can be kept this year," insisted a shaven-headed star-watcher, "and that, I say, is all to the good."

"Oh, certainly," scoffed another. "But only when the prince-regent bawls loudly enough to his addle-brained father about the coming of the Persians does Nabu-Naid finally see fit to return to the throne he usurped. He scurries back inside the walls of Babylon, loudly proclaiming his loyalty to Marduk, as if this miraculous change of heart might spark the forgiveness of the Great Lord—or his priests." The priest spat loudly onto the pavement, barely missing a beggar who sat in the gate. "That is for the emperor—"

The discussion broke off suddenly when a squadron of soldiers paced by. After an uncomfortable pause, the murmuring counsel resumed. "Marduk is not swayed by such double-tongued devotion as the usurper gives. Festival or no, I say the winds of change are blowing in the land—and the sooner the better."

The gaggle of robed priests and scholars moved deeper into the temple courtyard, the debate continuing with cautious vehemence and frequent guarded glances over shoulders. As they moved out of earshot, the beggar rose, dusted himself off, and limped away toward a narrow alley between two mud-brick buildings.

Making certain he was unobserved, the beggar dodged quickly into the dark, vacant recess. Swiftly he pulled a scrap of parchment out of his clothing, making a series of deft marks with the burnt end of a twig. Tucking the missive securely beneath his tattered robe, he sauntered back into the thoroughfare, glancing at the angle of the sun. Mid-morning, he observed. Not long until he met his Persian contact by the Gate of Sin. He would have much to tell.

◆　◆　◆

EGIBI STARED round the chamber at his sons. "So then: How many loans have we out to members of the royal court or to the royal family itself?"

The four sons looked at each other, their brows wrinkled in puzzlement. Clearly they had no inkling of what their father intended by such a question. Gradually their eyes returned to the face of their sire; they were plainly at a loss to answer the unexpected query.

"You don't know." Egibi shifted impatiently on his tapestried cushion, shaking his head in vexation. So old and crippled was he that he rarely left this apartment now—yet he still knew more of the outside world than did his four able-bodied sons. He sometimes despaired of teaching them anything. "Well, then, tell me this: What is our rate of collateral coverage on silver loaned to the nobility—especially the military commanders? Have you any idea?"

The sons, confused and slightly piqued by the patriarch's accusative tone, kept their eyes stonily fixed downward. *Does he think we're children?* they wondered. *Does he suppose his is the only mind capable of running the business of Egibi and Sons?*

"My sons," the old man wheezed finally, when the hostile hush had lasted long enough, "I do not seek to anger you. But have any of you thought what might happen when the Persians come to Babylon?"

The oldest yanked his eyes upward, a startled expression on his face. Smiling with his eyes, Egibi nodded. "Yes, Bel-Adan, at last you begin to see."

Bel-Adan's three brothers slowly began rubbing their beards, a look of comprehension gradually dawning on their sullen faces. "When kingdoms change," Egibi was saying, "it is well to look carefully to your affairs. Laws which may protect you today could cease to exist tomorrow. A prudent lender never willingly accepts risks which cannot be assessed."

"Perhaps we should order a current reckoning of the accounts," drawled the oldest son, ruminatively.

"Yes…and if I'm not mistaken, Lord Nabu-iddina is a trifle tardy with the payment of his debt," mused another. "I should look into the matter…"

Their father nodded appreciatively. "*Caution,* my sons," he agreed. "In times of change, caution should be an amulet about your necks."

A discreet knock sounded at the door, and a young man of perhaps twenty summers entered the room. Face lowered in submission, he said, "My father wishes to know if he should allow the doors to be opened. The sun is above the walls of the city."

Glancing from Egibi back to the youth, Bel-Adan replied, "Yes, boy. Tell him to permit them to enter." Glancing a final time at his father, Bel-Adan concluded, "We are almost finished here."

The son of Jozadak bowed, and closed the door as quietly as he had opened it.

"Very well, my sons," said Egibi, eyeing them all around. "It is time to earn our bread for another day."

◆ ◆ ◆

NABU-NAID FIDGETED NERVOUSLY with the fringe of the silk tapestry. He stared out the window, in the direction of the Sky-Garden of Nebuchadrezzar, then glanced back toward the still, black-robed figure seated on the low stool in the corner of the room. "Is this the best succor you can bring?" the old king asked, his mouth set in a petulant scowl.

Adad-ibni shrugged, his face a wrinkled, inscrutable mask. "My king, I do not create the omens," he said. "I only read them." The mage smirked inwardly. In the years he had spent in Teima, Nabu-Naid had become less a presence than the absence of one; now back in Babylon, he was almost an irrelevancy. Belshazzar, the prince-regent, was the reality, the iron-handed, mean-spirited commander of the people's obedience, if not of their wills.

The pathetic old man in front of him might be king, and his return to the capital might allow the observance of the long-slighted New Year Festival—but Adad-ibni knew the mood of Esagila, and the murmurings of the merchants along the quays of the Karum. In his long absence from Babylon, Nabu-Naid may have achieved his aim of tweaking the beards of the powerful priests of Esagila, but he had not weakened Marduk's hold on the soul of the empire.

Furthermore, reflected the seer, though Belshazzar clutched the military—and thus, the city—in talons of steel, the hearts and minds of the populace were rapidly slipping through the fingers of the cruel, brutish prince, just as they had for his doddering old father. The process having clearly begun, Adad-ibni did not need his star-charts to tell him the days of Nabu-Naid's house were numbered.

Nabu-Naid tasted, smelled the half-shrouded contempt of the wizard. "Fetch a tablet, you," he snapped, balling his fists uselessly at his sides. "I wish to make a proclamation in connection with the New Year Festival."

Impassively, Adad-ibni slouched over to a low table on which rested a moist clay tablet and a stylus. Retrieving the supplies, he waited, his hand poised, to record the words of the fading king.

"This command will be carved on slabs of basalt and taken by royal courier to the major cities of our domain," began Nabu-Naid. "It will be announced within the walls of Nippur, Borsip, Sippar, Uruk..." He listed the major municipalities of the river-lands, as the mage dutifully copied them all down.

"The proclamation herein stated shall be announced before the waning of the moon," continued the king. "Immediate compliance with our imperial and holy orders shall be expected."

Nabu-Naid paused, taking several deep breaths. Since his return, and his reluctant realization of the state of affairs within the walls of his city, he had contemplated this drastic step. Such a thing had never been done, nor even attempted. But he saw no other way to stem the growing tide of the people's ingratitude and disaffection. Now was the time for his final gambit. He resumed speaking with a firmness he did not feel.

"The gods, the holy ones themselves, shall be brought out of their houses in the temples. Ishtar, Adad, Belit-nina, Nabu—all of them shall come to Babylon, to the shelter of the strong arm of Marduk, Lord and King of All. There, with their lord and under his protection, they shall celebrate the Festival of the New Year…"

Adad-ibni dropped the stylus from his nerveless fingers. His face was a stiff, stark mask of unbelief. Could this muddled old man actually mean what he was saying? Did he truly intend to take the gods hostage?

"You have stopped writing, lord mage," noted the king, a sly, mad leer stealing slowly across his wizened face. "Are you unable to hear my words adequately?" Knowing he had gained the upper hand in the struggle of wills, for the moment at least, Nabu-Naid intended to press his advantage to the breaking point.

"My king, I… Surely you do not intend—"

"If this proclamation is not read aloud in these cities within the time of the moon's waning," growled the king, "the imperial guards shall have orders for your head." A canine grimace parted the lips of the desperate king as he glared at the anxious astrologer. Adad-ibni lowered his head and began to write in jittery, swift strokes.

"I trust, of course," said the king, his voice smeared with self-satisfaction, "that you shall in your final draft add some suitable language about omens, portents, and so forth?"

"Yes, my king," mumbled Adad-ibni, miserably.

ONCE MORE Daniel prostrated himself toward the open window—the westward-facing window. "Blessed art Thou, O Lord, our God, King of the Universe," he prayed, "who hast preserved Thy people..." Thinking again of the final words of Azariah, he concluded, "And return us, O sovereign Lord, to Jerusalem, in accordance with Thy steadfast love." Rising, he watched as the molten rim of the sun dipped below the western horizon, the sky ablaze with the gold-blue-purple heraldry of evening. A knock came on his door. Without turning his head, he called, "Come in, friends. I am here."

Mishael, old and fat and puffing with the exertion of hauling his bulk about, plodded heavily into the room, followed closely by lean, ascetic Hananiah. The two old men greeted their friend, who now motioned toward the low table surrounded by linen cushions. "Will you eat? I have plenty."

Hananiah silently shook his head, while Mishael said in his wheezy, high voice, "Well, since it's such a long walk over to this side of the city..." Selecting a handful of dates from the wooden bowl on the table, the wattle-necked eunuch settled himself across several cushions.

Daniel plucked pensively at the leathery hide of a pomegranate. "What do the Levites make of the coming of the Persians?" he asked, carefully watching the faces of his comrades.

Mishael shrugged, reaching for another handful of dates. "Opinion seems to be mixed. Some see Cyrus as the righteous judgment of Adonai upon the wickedness of this place—they seem to think it will be torn to the ground, as Jeremiah predicted. I don't know if they have asked themselves what their lot would be in such a circumstance."

Hananiah shot a dour glance at the eunuch, then looked away, shaking his head at such flippancy.

"Others," continued Mishael, "seem to care little one way or another. They keep their noses in the scrolls and rarely come out, except on the day of *shabbat* to lecture the congregations. That, and they wait to be told to return to Judah. If they have an opinion on anything else, it is difficult to tell." Mishael wiped his fingers on his robe.

Daniel looked outside, where purpling shadows fell across the streets and houses of the Old City. In his study that day, he had read from the scrolls of Ezekiel. All evening the taut, severe visage of the prophet had hovered before him. Just before his guests arrived, he had read these words:

This is what the sovereign Lord says: "I will take the Israelites out of the nations where they have gone. I will gather them from all around and bring them back into their own land...

But when? For so many years he and the other faithful Hebrews of Babylon had been posing this same question—to themselves and to the Eternal—and always the answer seemed to be, "Not yet." Now the world was in flux. And would it matter? Would the Persian conqueror, at last, be the catalyst, the fulfilling agent for the word God had announced through His tortured, persecuted servants, the prophets? Daniel wanted to believe this, and yet... So many alterations had taken place already; so many kings, so many visions in the night—and still the people of God were here, trapped in Chaldea like oxen mired in a swamp. Could the rumblings from the north be the harbingers of impending change? He hardly dared allow himself to hope.

◆　◆　◆

THE MOON was a quarter-sized crescent in the spangled sky above Babylon. It was the second watch of the night, a time when most, if not all, of the city's denizens should have been in bed.

But in the central dwelling-house of Esagila, a lamp burned in the center of a large table. Gathered about the smooth-polished surface of the oak table was a hushed, grim council of the topmost echelons of Marduk's priesthood. The flickering lamplight made bobbing shadows on the ceiling of the chamber, casting into eerie, shifting relief the creases on foreheads and faces. The men listened to the reading of a parchment held by their master, the High Priest.

"And because of my great reverence for the Lord Marduk," the message continued, "I am deeply distressed by the sacrilegious acts of your so-called king. I know that the Sun Lord has summoned me from my mountain home to right the injustices done to His people by the cruel oppressor Nabu-Naid. As my pledge toward this end, please accept this small offering as a token of my devotion."

The senior priest paused significantly, hefting from the floor beside him a camel-hide bag. As he placed it firmly on the table, the bright rattling of much silver could be plainly heard. The shaven-headed priest peered at each of his colleagues in turn. "Can we doubt, in the face of such generosity, that Marduk has touched the soul of this one who comes at such a troubled time?"

He let the parchment slip from his fingers, to fall upon the table. It was sealed, the priests could clearly see, with the winged-circle symbol of Cyrus the Persian.

22

THOUGH IT WAS ONLY a morning in the month of *Nisan*, the day was already hot enough to be midsummer. Even such unseasonable heat, however, could not keep the people of Babylon from massing along Aibur Shabu to celebrate the first New Year Festival in so many seasons. With an almost hysterical jubilance, the capital city awaited the appearance of the reborn Marduk.

Sunlight flashed from the polished brass bells of trumpets as the heralds raised the instruments to their lips. But instead of the expected royal fanfare which traditionally announced the entry of Marduk, the musicians played a slightly different flourish. The celebrants closest to the Ishtar Gate, within easy earshot, turned to one another, puzzling among themselves as to the meaning of this unfamiliar prelude.

And then the reason became clear. From the shadows of the huge gate's narrow passageway, the image of Ishtar, the fertile Lady of Uruk, rolled into view, seated atop her gold-maned lions.

An amazed, awed murmuring swept the crowds on either side of the Processional Way. This was no proxy image, no mere emblem of Ishtar. This was the great goddess herself, brought inexplicably from the grand temple in Uruk, the city of her patronage. How could it be? How could the priestesses in Uruk allow it? What would become of the city without the presence of its Lady? As the masses tried to digest this portentous anomaly, another strange shout rang from the brazen throats of the trumpets at the Ishtar Gate.

Now Nergal, dread lord of the nether regions, came into view. If the people's consternation was great before, it was positively overwhelming now. No precedent existed for such a fearsome spectacle as this procession of the gods themselves through the streets of Babylon.

One after another they came, a formidable parade of the most potent, ancient icons of Chaldean culture. The festive atmosphere was forgotten in the dreadful solemnity of the display. The throngs along Aibur Shabu were cowed into silence by the incomprehensible, foreboding presence of the deities. When at last the familiar fanfare came, heralding the entry of Marduk, the celebratory air with which the day had begun was in tatters. The image of Marduk moved along the awed hush of the broad avenue like a funeral barge along a spectral river. Here and there a few less-reflective souls made a futile effort to applaud, but to no avail. The procession of the gods had done its work. This long-overdue renewal of the New Year Festival bore the pall of something momentous and severe—something final.

◆　◆　◆

KURASH SAT ON HIS CHARGER, gazing serenely across the flat, turgid expanse of the Euphrates. The beast tossed its head, jingling the bits and linkages of its bridle. The king, with the automatic attention to the disposition of his mount which is the horseman's habit, grinned at the impatient, flickering ears of his horse.

"Are you so eager to cross?" he said to the charger. "Do you sense that across this river lies the heartland of our adversary's domain? Are you anxious for the battle call, the swift charge into the enemy's ranks?" In reply, the animal stamped a forefoot and blew a loud, fluttering snort. Kurash laughed aloud.

At his back lay Carchemish, the far northern outpost of the Chaldean Empire. His host, with its newly conscripted Lydian and Greek contingents, was drawn up in marching array, waiting only for his command to begin the fording of the Euphrates.

His plan was to drive across the land from north to south. Starting in Haran, he intended to engage any resistance he found and continue to the very gates of Babylon. From the reports he was receiving from his agents, he expected to meet scant opposition in the outlying regions, whose garrisons would have little will to fight for their absentee sovereign or his brutal son. Things might get a bit more difficult, he reasoned, as he approached the capital city. Belshazzar had stationed commanders in the nearby cities who were more loyal to himself, and they might be counted on to contend more sternly with the Persian advance.

Even so, Kurash was optimistic that his overtures to the nobility, the priesthood, and the merchant classes would not be without effect. With some satisfaction, he had heard that the cities of Borsip, Cutha, and Sippar—none more than a two-day's march from the walls of Babylon—had not complied with Nabu-Naid's edict concerning the relocation of the empire's city-gods. He hoped that gold, silver, and well-chosen words might blunt the edges of the Chaldean swords.

The taut sense of anticipation in the pit of his stomach told him he stood on the knife-edge of destiny. The urgent momentum of his life had brought him to this hour; he felt the vibrant calm in his soul known only by those who stand at the pulsing nexus of fate. The mighty towers of Babylon were the last obstacle in his path. Like a tree with dry rot at its core, the empire of the Chaldeans would topple, despite its formidable walls and the deep, ancient learning of its sages. Kurash, the Shepherd from the mountains of Persis, would reign from the mountains of the Hindush to the blue-green sea of the Greek islands.

With the breath of empire flaring hot in his nostrils, Kurash squeezed the withers of his charger with his knees. The beast, tossing its head and nickering eagerly, pranced into the brown waters of the Euphrates. The final campaign was begun.

◆ ◆ ◆

AT LAST the welcome shadow of evening crept across the scorching sands beside the Tigris, falling like a sigh over besieged Opis and the hosts of Kurash which encircled her. For a week now the invading army had encamped against this city, which was the first line of defense for Babylon.

Kurash, sweating in his campaign tent, cursed the Chaldean summer for the thousandth time. The unrelenting heat bore down upon them, complicating the already difficult task of maintaining vigilance over the beleaguered city. The midday heat threatened to broil the brains of his Greeks inside their bronze battle helmets; he had been forced to allow them to remove their armor unless a sortie from the fortified walls manifested itself.

Opis sat on a narrow spit of land at the confluence of the Tigris and her tributary, the Diala. From the west bank of the Tigris, the line of fortifications known as the Medean Wall stretched toward Sippar, scarcely hid beyond the southwestern horizon. The presence of this wall was what made the siege of Opis so devilishly complex. As long as the wall remained intact, Belshazzar was free to shuttle men and materiel back and forth from Sippar to Opis. Yet Kurash was not entirely at liberty to attack the supply route, for to do so would risk inviting a counter-assault launched from within the walls of Opis. He might well find himself pinched between the the defenders of the city and the defenders of the wall. And so he sat outside, beneath the searing rays of the Chaldean sun, fuming as the summer wore away at the morale of his troops.

Though night had fallen, still the heat shimmered in the pavilion, an invisible, inescapable oppressor. Impatiently Kurash sponged his face with a linen cloth soaked in the tepid waters of the Tigris. Squeezing the moisture down the back of his neck, he glanced up as he heard the bodyguard outside his tent challenge an approaching footstep.

Through the open flap at the front of the pavilion stooped a shaven-headed, black-robed Chaldean. Sighting Kurash, the heavy-set man made obeisance. "Lord Cyrus, he whose coming is foretold in the stars," the fellow mumbled, his face in the carpet at Kurash's feet.

"Who are you?" the Persian asked testily, "and how did you manage to leave a city under siege?"

The obsequious Chaldean rose to his knees, touching his breast with both open palms. "I am Sheshach-latti, priest of Marduk in Opis. I come with a message from the High Priest of Esagila, in Babylon."

Kurash scrutinized the man's seamless face, then strode to the open doorway of the pavilion. "Fetch Commander Gobhruz," he ordered. One of the guards scurried away into the darkness.

◆　◆　◆

"THEREFORE," the black-robed priest was saying, "you will find the Diala Gate unguarded. No one in the city will hinder you. The garrison will be at your mercy."

Above the head of the kneeling priest, the eyes of the king and his commander locked in a voiceless moment of question and answer. *So*, Kurash thought, *the silver sent to Esagila found its mark.*

◆　◆　◆

AFTER THE SLAUGHTER of the garrison at Opis, the military command in Sippar found itself in a most untenable position. Convinced by the priests that the coming of Cyrus was foreordained, the common folk of Sippar began to resent the impious insistence of the prince-regent's cronies upon the need for opposition to the onrushing Persian flood.

Officers suffered bouts of insubordination from the men under their commands. Military rations were pilfered or spoiled. More than one commander found scorpions in his bed. When one of Belshazzar's trusted henchmen was discovered lying in a pool of his own blood, his throat slit, the remaining generals needed but little encouragement from the priests and astrologers to strike terms with the advancing Persian army. The city capitulated to Kurash without a struggle.

The late summer days of *Elul* now shortened into the waning-time of *Tisre*. In the sunset of that autumn, the shadows of the Persian host stretched inexorably across the flat lands of Chaldea, relentlessly reaching toward the mighty walls of Babylon.

◆　◆　◆

"MORE BEER!" bellowed Belshazzar, slamming his drinking bowl onto the table. A slave boy grabbed at the bowl and scampered away toward the cask of ale.

The prince-regent had been in an unquenchably surly mood since receiving news of the craven surrender of Sippar.

Let a few priests interfere, he thought, let them whisper in the ears of the superstitious peasants, and the manly blood of trained soldiers turned to water. He had depended on these cowards! He had trusted them to deny passage of the Northern Wall to the unlettered Persian. And they had meekly offered Cyrus the keys to the gate!

A black gush of fury swelled within his foggy mind. He lurched upward from the table, upsetting the foaming bowl of beer the slave had just placed in front of him. "Guards!" he shouted, staggering toward the doorway of the room. "Guards! Bring my sword! I'll find those traitors who fled like rats from the face of the enemy! I'll spill their guts in the street—"

Belshazzar was brought up short by the shrivelled, stooped figure of his father, the king. As the slaves behind him fell to the floor, the prince stood swaying, blearily eyeing the figure of his sire.

"Can you find no better use for your time," spat the venomous old man, "than drinking yourself into a stupor?"

Belshazzar belched sourly, then looked away from Nabu-Naid. His voice dripping with sarcasm, he said, "What would you have me do, Father? Lead the mighty host of Babylon out onto the plain to face the Persians?" The prince gave a drunken giggle. "At the sight of a *real* foe, they might soil themselves." Belshazzar threw back his head and laughed.

The old king, unable to contain his futile anger, reached out with a withered, blue-veined hand and slapped his son across the cheek. Belshazzar's bloated laughter halted as abruptly as a knife thrust. The prince's eyes widened in shock, then anger.

"You are not fit to be called the son of Nabu-Naid," the brittle old king hissed, shaking his finger in Belshazzar's face. "You are worthless to me! I curse the day of your birth, you useless drunkard!"

Belshazzar, his lip curled in a wild snarl, grabbed the wrist which wagged the finger. With the strength of mindless fury, he squeezed his father's arm until he heard the dry old tendons begin to crackle. Nabu-Naid's face was a frozen mask of pain and helpless anger. The drunken prince-regent spoke in a voice like the growl of a rabid dog.

"So you disapprove of my drinking, do you? You, the king who rules Babylon from the midst of the Arabah! You, who have spent more time sifting through the potsherds of dead kings than concerning yourself with the matters of living ones! You, the fool who invites the wrath of the gods by bringing them into this city from their own temples! You find me unworthy, do you, Father?"

Giving the king's arm a final, excruciating twist, Belshazzar sneered. "I shall continue to drink, Father. In fact, I shall see that everyone in Babylon has opportunity to drink. Perhaps I should proclaim a banquet. Would you like that, Father?" A conniving smile twisted his lips. "Yes—a feast!" he leered. I will invite the nobility—nay, the gods themselves!—to a feast in honor of Nabu-Naid, the Great Emperor. I will call upon one and all to witness the glory of the one who has brought about the downfall of Babylon. We shall feast while the carrion birds gather upon the walls of the city."

Nabu-Naid stared in fearful agony at the purpling, madly grinning face of his son. The king appeared to shrivel, to diminish. He lost all pretense of royalty in that moment, fully transformed into a despairing, dying old wretch. Belshazzar saw the change in his father's countenance, and again laughed his drunkard's laugh.

"Chamberlain!" shouted the prince, striding from the room. "Summon the scribes and heralds! I wish to proclaim a day of celebration..."

Nabu-Naid grimaced, gripped in a torment of body and soul, as he tenderly massaged his wounded wrist. Then he turned and limped dejectedly from the room of his violent, crazed son.

◆　◆　◆

SEATED IN THE COUNCIL CHAMBER of the citadel of Sippar, Kurash thoughtfully studied the lowered face of the Chaldean who stood before him. The fellow had the full lips and kinky beard of the Semitic denizens of these lands of the Two Rivers. He was an engineer, an overseer of the official buildings and canals of the city of Sippar.

"What can you tell me," the Persian now asked, "about the disposition of the canals of Babylon?"

The engineer's brow furrowed for a moment as he considered the request. "If memory serves," he mused, "they are much the same as the canals in Sippar: about ten cubits in width, lined along the bottom with bitumen-coated brick." He scratched his beard, squinting upward in an effort at recollection. "With the exception of the Zababa Canal, most of them are rather straight, running either roughly parallel or perpendicular to the Euphrates, whose waters feed them and the moat surrounding the walls."

Kurash nodded appreciatively. "Very good, Master Sharuk. The depth of your knowledge is astounding, indeed!"

The Chaldean grinned shyly. "My Lord Cyrus is too kind..."

"Tell me this, then, my good man," urged Kurash, testing the engineer as he recalled his own observations of Babylon during his secret visit with Gobhruz years before. "What of the walls? Is it true what they say? Can two chariots be driven abreast along the top of them?"

Sharuk nodded solemnly. "Aye, Lord Cyrus. And along the walls, at hundred-cubit intervals, are fortified turrets. A company of men can march from turret to turret with great ease, shielded by the battlements along the top of the walls."

Kurash cupped his chin in his hand, his elbow resting on the arm of the ebony-wood chair. The fingers of his other hand drummed ruminatively on his knee. "And what of the walls' foundations, Sharuk? Can they be undermined?"

The engineer grimaced. "Not without great difficulty, my lord. Like the canals, the footings are sheathed in bitumen, and their depth is very great. Further, you will be exposed to fire from the turrets." The Chaldean shrugged expressively. "This is an old land, my lord. Men have been settled here for countless generations. We have had much time to practice and refine the art of fortification."

Kurash remembered the rocky heights of Sardis, and the clattering fall of the guard's helmet which had betrayed its secret. He had not come so far to be thwarted now. There must be a way into Babylon, and it would be found!

His voice acquired a sudden edge of impatience. "I suppose the city will now be shut up as tightly as a fist. Are you certain there is not some flaw or weak point you have forgotten?"

Flustered by the change in the conqueror's tone, the engineer's face fell, his fingers twined nervously about one another. "I...I cannot recall anything," he stammered. "Perhaps if my Lord Cyrus could speak to an engineer of Babylon—but of course that is impossible now. Nothing and no one enters or leaves Babylon, save the river itself."

"Yes, impossible," drawled Kurash, looking away. After a moment of silent consideration, he looked sharply back at the Chaldean. "The soil hereabout—what is its nature?"

Sharuk, confused by the apparently unrelated question, peered questioningly at the Persian. Shaking his head in slow bewilderment, he said, "Quite sandy, my lord—typical river silt, deposited by the flooding of the Euphrates—"

"Then the soil is easily dug?" interrupted Kurash sharply.

"I...I suppose so—"

"Aha!" Kurash leaped from his chair, striding back and forth, shaking his fist triumphantly. "That's it, then!" Whirling about, he gestured at an attendant. "Get Commander Gobhruz!" The page hurried to obey, even as Kurash halted him with another blurted command. "And bring a shekel of gold for Master Sharuk"—he grinned at the dazed Chaldean—"who has given me the key to the great city of Babylon." The boy scurried away.

"Sit down, Sharuk, sit down!" Kurash ordered. "I will have meat and wine brought! You must eat with me today, most excellent fellow!"

239

Numb with relief, befuddlement, and elation, the engineer slowly sank down on the nearest cushion, smiling hesitantly at his bewildering benefactor.

Kurash halted pacing. He looked into the dazzled eyes of Sharuk, threw back his head, and laughed.

23

"THEY'RE DOING WHAT?" Belshazzar cried, incredulous. A wild burst of hope careened about within his breast, his face flushed—for once—with other than beer or wine.

The courtier bowed even lower. "They have halted their march toward the city, and are engaged in the construction of some sort of earthworks near the Depression of Eshunna."

Belshazzar, struggling to contain the bubbling enthusiasm that was threatening to breach his control, pondered frantically the unimaginable reasons for the stalling of Cyrus's advance. Did the fool think that Belshazzar would sally out of Babylon to engage him on the plains by Eshunna? What possible reason could he have for building fortifications in such wide open, indefensible terrain?

For so long Belshazzar had felt the impending arrival of the Persian host as a constant, overhanging shadow upon his every thought. The coming of Cyrus was certain, imminent. And until this moment he had seen no alternative course—given the manifestly uncertain disposition of the general populace—other than to prepare for a long siege. Within Babylon he could maintain a strict, enforceable control. He had hoped the virtual impossibility of overrunning Babylon, coupled with the need to maintain a large army to enforce the siege, would debilitate the Persian, allowing opportunities for cracks to develop in the control of his far-flung satrapies. This would buy Belshazzar the commodity he most craved—time.

And now, this! Was it possible that the invincible Cyrus was capable of miscalculation? That he would waste his resources and dissipate the energies of his men in constructing unneeded fortifications?

"See that the developments in the Persian camp are observed closely," ordered the prince. "In a few days I will hold my banquet. Then we shall see what may be done about Cyrus and his earthworks."

♦ ♦ ♦

THOUSANDS OF TORCHES illumined the great central plaza of Esagila, making the courtyard almost as bright as day.

Though row upon row of banquet tables groaned under the weight of the richest meats and cheeses, and though the wine of Syria flowed like water in the courtyard of Marduk's house, the god's priests were nowhere in sight. Instead, Belshazzar and scores of representatives of the noble houses of Babylon laughed and cavorted, guarded on all sides by dour-faced bodyguards.

The prince had gone far beyond the bounds of decency in the misbegotten ordinance of his festival. It was less a banquet than a debauchery, a carousal. Temple prostitutes, their perfumed limbs tantalizingly visible beneath the gauzy fabric of their gowns, sauntered among the rows of revelers. Belshazzar had even brought his wives to Esagila, to sit in plain view of other men, eating and drinking like common harlots! Despite the tight-lipped disapproval of the priests, the event had been carried forward; no matter how huge their disdain of Belshazzar and his crude tastes, the priests were little able to avoid the spectacle in the plaza, as long as the palace guard's armed and menacing presence prevented interference.

As if the impious frolicking were not disgraceful enough, the prince had ordered the gods to be brought out of their guarded chambers within the citadel, and had them set up all about the courtyard of Esagila—divine witnesses to his folly! All about the perimeter of the plaza the regal images looked on. Full-hipped Ishtar watched as her laughing female servitors pandered to the drunken, lustful nobles. Ninurtu gazed on in grim disapproval at the uncustomary merriment. Shamash, Adad, Belit-Nina, even Lord Marduk himself—all were silent observers of the crown prince's vulgarity.

The high priest heard the echoes of the orgy, his lip curling in disgust. Though he had walked to the side of the temple complex farthest away from the revolting scene in the courtyard, still the noise of the hated feast carried to his ears. He walked along the river wall in the darkness; below him was the Euphrates.

A foul odor wafted to his nostrils from the darkness at the base of the wall. Puzzled, he paused and peered downward. The moon was full, giving sufficient light for him to see—and to gasp.

The river was vanishing! The smell which had attracted his notice was spawned by hundreds of dead and dying fish, stranded in the strangling air by the retreating waters of their home. The slow, broad stream of the Euphrates was now no more than a stone's toss wide!

His face froze in apprehension: Surely this was the anger of the gods, the manifest consequence of Belshazzar's folly! Chest pounding in urgency, he began to run back toward the temple. If the wrath of Marduk rained down on Belshazzar, they might all perish in its fury. He must gather the priests and singers. It was time to pray.

♦ ♦ ♦

KURASH NODDED in satisfaction. The operation had worked exactly as he had envisioned. Three days ago, the canal con-

242

necting the Euphrates with the Depression of Eshunna had been completed. He had signalled the workers to strike down the bulkhead restraining the river waters from the newly built ditch. The brown Euphrates shunted eagerly into its new pathway, coiling quickly toward the bottom of the ancient, dry lakebed.

With the lowering of the river's level, a whole host of gates into Babylon would be created. Outside the city walls his men, stationed in the darkness beside the canals and along the banks of the Euphrates, would be able to walk easily into Babylon. The river which had nourished her for so many generations would be the means of her undoing, the pathway of her conqueror.

"Gobhruz," he murmured to the armed and mounted Mede whose charger stood quietly beside his own, "I shall allow you to be the first to enter the city. Since you despise the effects of too much civilization, you shall have opportunity to decide which of its edifices will stand and which will fall."

The old man grunted and looked away. "Foolishness," he muttered. "I will do nothing which my king does not command. This is your city, not mine."

Kurash grinned in the darkness.

◆　◆　◆

"MORE WINE!" bellowed Belshazzar, his arm twined about the waist of a dark-eyed temple courtesan. He was thoroughly enjoying himself. This banquet, which he had originally imagined as a massive insult to his feeble father, had taken on for him the air of a pre-victory celebration. After all, was not Cyrus at this very moment squatting at Eshunna, unaware of the absurdity of his position? *Anything is possible*, thought Belshazzar, guzzling another cup of the rare Syrian wine he had ordered for the evening. In his gorged, wine-fogged imagination, he had persuaded himself there might yet be hope. And none of the revelers who reeled from table to table in the courtyard of Esagila did anything to dispel his notion.

Lurching unsteadily to his feet, Belshazzar called for a fanfare from the nearby trumpeters. The brassy flourish produced a pause in the noisy gamboling among the tables. Bleary, sated faces turned expectantly toward the dais. Framed by the two huge glazed-brick dragons on the wall behind him, Belshazzar held up his arms for silence.

"My lords, who have gathered here for this, my feast day," he shouted; "look about you! Salute the gods, who bless you this night with their mighty benediction!"

A drunken cheer rippled across the courtyard, as Belshazzar seated himself unsteadily. Quickly the rowdy revelry began anew.

Looking about in confusion, the prince queried a nearby page, "Where is the god of that western province—Judah, is it? What image signifies his presence?"

The page shook his head in consternation.

"Have you failed to carry out my orders, you wretch?" bellowed the prince. The courtesan in Belshazzar's embrace tittered with amusement. "Find me the god of Judah," the prince went on, "or I will gut you on this very table!" Nearby, one of his wives blanched at hearing such a threat. The slave took to his heels, the raucous laughter of the prince chasing him past the gate of the courtyard.

Soon the boy came racing back, his arms laden with cups and goblets of gold, inlaid with precious gems. Spilling them upon the table before prostrating himself at the feet of the prince, the runner panted, "My lord, these are all I could find which belonged to Judah. A scribe in the citadel vault told me these utensils were sacred to the god of that place—I know no more!"

"Sacred, eh?" mused Belshazzar groggily, hefting one of the gold flagons. "Well then, I suppose these will have to do..."

♦ ♦ ♦

CAUTIOUSLY THE MAN looked about him to make certain he was not followed. Satisfied, he sidled along the wall of the house on Adad Street, slipping like a shadow into the entryway. The gatekeeper studied him carefully, then nodded and allowed him to pass into the central courtyard.

From the doorway to the main room, the flickering light of a single tallow lamp shone. The man followed the light across the packed earth of the courtyard, peering around the corner of the portal.

Around the low table in the center of the room sat Ezra, Sheshbazzar, Zerubbabel, Jozadak, and several other leaders of the Hebrew community. Each brow furled in concern, they huddled in a low-voiced conference while Ephratah, the widow of Azariah, looked on from a corner. Their faces lifted to acknowledge the latecomer. Ezra rose from his place at the head of the table, opening his arms to greet the one who had just arrived.

"Daniel! Thank you for coming! You know of the reason for this gathering?"

The old man nodded, his eyes silently greeting each of them, lingering a moment longer on the face of his friend's widow. Then he hurried to the table as the others shuffled about to make room.

"My brothers," Daniel said in a low voice, "matters at the palace have become fearfully grave. The emperor does not leave his chamber—no one, not even his body-servants, have seen him for the past two days. The crown prince is beyond the reach of sensible men. He follows some course of his own choosing, hearing only what he wishes to hear, seeing only such things as his drink-befogged vision allows. No one in the palace or citadel seeks anything but his own way—there is no authority. Belshazzar yet controls the palace guard, but many of the generals—though they would deny it with their mouths —have made secret peace with the Persians." Aiming a significant look at each of them in turn, Daniel concluded, "The days of the royal house of Chaldea are drawing to a close, my brothers. We have arrived at a time of great change."

"Did you notice the river when you came here?" asked Sheshbazzar.

Daniel nodded. "The Persian is cunning. Let us pray he is also benevolent."

"One king or another, it makes little difference," observed Jozadak darkly. "No matter how clever Cyrus may be, still he is an infidel, an unbeliever. How can his coming improve our lot?"

"The Lord says, 'I will bring Judah and Israel back from captivity,'" quoted Zerubbabel softly, peering intently at Jozadak's scowling face, "'and will rebuild them as they were before...'" Cutting his eyes toward Sheshbazzar, he continued, "'David will never fail to have a man to stand before Me...'"

Sheshbazzar—who traced his lineage to the royal house of Judah—ducked his head, an upsurge of emotion forcing tears from his eyes.

"The prophet Jeremiah also said this," mused Daniel after a moment's pause:

> *"Babylon will be captured;*
> *Bel will be put to shame,*
> *Marduk filled with terror...*
> *A nation from the north will attack her*
> *and lay waste her land.*
> *No one will live in it;*
> *both men and animals will flee away..."*

The men fell silent, each contemplating the momentous events swirling about them and wondering whether the morrow would bring deliverance—or disaster.

◆ ◆ ◆

A BAND OF JUGGLERS dazzled the crowd in Esagila's plaza. The bright-colored tunics of the performers shimmered in the torchlight as they tossed painted sticks, torches, sharply glittering knives, and even—to the uproarious delight of all but the unfortunate victims—drinking cups filched from the lips of the celebrants. With consummate skill they caused the objects to hurtle through the air from hand to hand.

As the jugglers exited to the enthusiastic salutation of the feasters, a conjurer leapt upon the dais and began drawing feathers from the sleeves of his robe, and brilliantly dyed silken scarves from behind the ears of Belshazzar's surprised and delighted wives. A skillful illusionist, the fellow awed the throng with his dexterity. Tossing fistfuls of powder on a nearby brazier, he produced bursts of colored smoke and flame, to the appreciative applause of the prince and his courtiers. To the clamorous accompaniment of the musicians at the foot of the dais, the performer deftly entranced the gathering, proceeding apace to more and more dazzling feats, to greater and more enthralling pyrotechnic stunts.

As the magician's display drew to its frenzied climax, a finger of flame lanced from nowhere toward the wall above Belshazzar's head, leaving a burning, smoking tracery of letter-like markings in the glazed bricks. The awed throng broke into loud, riotous applause, plainly astonished, even in the dregs of their wine-steeped merrymaking, at the astounding skill with which this last breathtaking illusion had been accomplished.

Belshazzar, cheering with the rest, looked at the face of the conjurer—and froze. The magician, staring white-faced at the fire-chiseled characters in the wall above him, was quaking with fright. Even to the drunken prince, the fellow did not display the attitude of one who had successfully executed a stunning sleight-of-hand. Rather, he appeared as one who stared into the shimmering, fearful terrain of the Unknown. When the magician turned tail and fled the dais like a whipped dog, Belshazzar felt the chilled breath of fright stinging his nostrils.

Slowly a sobering realization began to dawn among the banquet tables: The glowing letters on the wall of Esagila's courtyard had not been produced by the conjurer. As they saw Belshazzar stagger upward from his place, yelping in helpless panic, they began to murmur among themselves. A party of armed guards raced pellmell from the dais toward the dwelling halls of the priests. Staring about in superstitious dread at the encircling figures of the gods, the now subdued mob pondered the enigma etched in flame upon the huge wall.

And the cold, clammy fist of fear slowly tightened its grip about the throats of the revelers of Babylon.

◆　◆　◆

"LET US BIDE, THEN, my brothers," Ezra was saying. "Perhaps the wind at the backs of the Persians comes from the Eternal. It may be that Cyrus comes at this precise time to accomplish the purpose of Adonai…"

Daniel, listening carefully to the words of the priest, suddenly remembered a *shabbat* meeting in a palm grove, and how the gold of the sunset splashed upon the robes of this man as he read from the scroll of Isaiah. With a breathtaking rush of clarity, he relived the scene, hearing once more Ezra's reading:

> *I am the Lord, who has made all things…*
> *who says of Jerusalem, "It shall be inhabited,"*
> *who says of Kurus, "He is My shepherd…"*

Cyrus!

Daniel felt his heart slamming against his ribs. He knew the clarion-call, no less awesome for its familiarity, of *El Shaddai*. Again the summons had come. As he stiffened, listening with the ears of his soul to the cascading, torrential muster of the Almighty, a small moan of awe escaped his lips. The others stared at him, their eyes widening in alarm.

At that moment, a runner dashed breathlessly into the room, followed by the protesting gatekeeper. Ephratah lurched to her feet, staring an unspoken question at the intruder.

"I tried to stop him, mistress," apologized the hapless doorman, "but he threw me aside. He says he has come—"

"Lord Belteshazzar!" the herald panted, falling beside the still-seated Daniel and clutching at his robes. "You must come at once to Esagila! The crown prince has summoned you—his wife has said you are the only one who can help!"

The others stared in gaping wonder from the messenger to Daniel. After a frozen moment, Daniel rose, an expression of dire purpose on his craggy, wrinkled face.

His eyes shining with a calm, brilliant urgency, he nodded

at the runner. "Take me to the prince, boy. There are things which must be said."

24

BY THE TIME Daniel and the page arrived at Esagila, most of the places at the banquet tables were vacant. An apprehensive pall hung over the place like the echo of a mourner's wail. With deliberate steps, Daniel approached the dais where Belshazzar huddled in dejected confusion. A small knot of priests and astrologers were gathered about him.

As Daniel paced toward the platform, his eyes swept across the legend charred indelibly into the wall. Four words. A heaven-sent motto whose meaning, even now, budded within his mind like a harbinger of fate.

Stepping onto the dais, his eyes took in the scene: the careless clutter left in the wake of the carousers; the sullen, motionless images of the city-gods; the nervous, untoward expressions on the faces of the mages and seers. Even Adad-ibni was here; like Daniel, he had been summoned hastily by the panic-stricken Belshazzar. As his eyes glided over the visage of the chief mage, Daniel noted the sullen resentment which festered in the eyes of Adad-ibni like an old wound.

Then his glance fell upon the upturned cup lying in a puddle of spilled wine atop the table where Belshazzar and his wives had sat. A surge of anger rippled outward from his stunned heart, bringing a flush of heat to his cheeks. Though he had never seen it during his childhood in Jerusalem, he knew the style and design of the jewelled gold chalice. Like the other Hebrews of Babylon, he had grieved over the reports of Nebuchadrezzar's sacking of the Temple, his pillaging of the sacred utensils from the Holy Place. And now Belshazzar had brought the cup and its mates to this place of abomination, using that which was dedicated to the Holiness of Israel to drink a polluted toast to the images of Marduk, Ishtar, and Nergal!

As if hearing from a distance, Daniel realized that the crown prince had spoken to him. Reluctantly, striving to veil the righteous indignation in his eyes, Daniel pulled his vision away from the spoiled Temple utensils, and made a grudging salute to Belshazzar.

"I have heard," the prince was saying in a nervous voice, "that the spirit of the holy gods is in you, Belteshazzar; that you have insight and wisdom. These"—he gestured vaguely toward the mages and astrologers huddled nearby—"could not read the writing which appeared on the wall. Can you?"

Adad-ibni ground his teeth in impotent rage. Again! Once more he must stand idly by while this foreigner garnered the glory! The dull fires of lifelong resentment burned acridly in his stooped old frame as he listened on.

Daniel had made no reply to the prince's anxious request. Still he stood, staring from the words on the wall to the chalice on the table, his jaw tensing and relaxing as if he would not willingly answer Belshazzar.

The prince, discomfited even more by Belteshazzar's reticence, moved a half-step closer to the old Hebrew, his voice rising to a strident pitch of desperation. "If you can read this writing, Hebrew, I shall reward you richly! I shall give you..."—he cast about within himself for an adequate enticement—"a gold chain! And...and a purple robe!"

Still Daniel made no answer.

"I will make you the third ruler in the kingdom!" Belshazzar crowed in despair. "I must know what this message means!"

Adad-ibni could not believe his ears. Third ruler in the kingdom! Was the prince mad?

Daniel's fingers reached out as if to caress the toppled gold cup, then pulled back. As his stature lengthened and stiffened, his eyes shifted to Belshazzar's face. A force burned outward from Daniel, a radiant aura of holy power which at this moment gave him absolute command of every ear and eye in the room.

"You may keep your gifts," he said with quiet vehemence, "and reward someone else. But I shall read the writing for you, Prince Belshazzar, and give you the meaning.

"*El Elyon*, the Most High, gave Nebuchadrezzar, your master, sovereignty and greatness and splendor. Because of the regency given to him, peoples from every land and tongue learned to fear him. He held the power of life and death over them, the power to make great and the power to abase."

Daniel leaned toward Belshazzar then, so close to the prince's breast that none could have prevented him from plunging a dagger into the heart of the heir to Nabu-Naid. But such was the power of his presence that even the prince's bodyguards could do no more than listen, mouths agape, to the steely words of the aged counselor.

"But when Nebuchadrezzar grew haughty," Daniel was saying, the last word spoken like a lash, "he was deposed from his throne. The great and powerful Nebuchadrezzar"—Daniel's tone signified that the one he now addressed could never dream of being the equal of the long-dead emperor—"then squatted among the weeds like a brute beast. He ate fodder like an ass and the dew of heaven soaked his beard, until he learned to fear the Most High who is sovereign over the kingdoms of men, and who makes and breaks kings as He pleases."

The next words came in a near whisper that seemed to crackle throughout the whole courtyard of Esagila. "And you,

Belshazzar, have learned nothing from the example of your betters! You have set your face against the Lord of heaven!"

Daniel seized one of the defiled goblets from the table, shaking it in his fist as he continued. "You have taken these cups that were consecrated to the service of the Most High, and have drunk wine from them to the honor of these deaf, dumb, and insensible images of silver and gold and bronze!"

The priests standing nearby looked stricken, but were as powerless as the others to interrupt the adamant old man.

"You have allowed your wives and concubines to defile that which was holy to the Lord," Daniel continued, "and you have not known Him who holds the very threads of your life in His hands. This is why He has made this inscription—for *you*."

At the awful intimacy implied by Daniel's words, the crown prince staggered backward a half-pace. Daniel glared at him for two breaths, then turned his face upward, toward the giant letters above their heads.

"The first two words are these," he pronounced, in a voice that rang out like a warrior's cry. "*Mene, mene.*" Turning a dour eye upon the quaking prince, he said, "This means that God has counted out the days of your reign like the *minas* of silver in the hands of the bankers, and He has declared your debt due and payable.

"*Tekel*," Daniel went on, "means that you have been weighed on the balances of God's justice—and your measure is faulty."

"*Parsin*," Daniel finished, as Belshazzar gasped like a wounded man, reaching limply for the shoulders of his bodyguards, "means that your kingdom is no longer yours, but is parceled out to the Persians. Your time is finished—theirs has begun."

◆　◆　◆

GOBHRUZ RODE NORTH at a swift walk along the Street of Nabu. With each step his mount took, clumps of moist river mud fell from its fetlocks to be trod upon by the company of foot-soldiers who paced quickly behind their commander.

They had forded the muddy canal and passed along the river-bed, entering the city beside the Borsip Gate. Thus far, they were unchallenged.

The commander glanced up to his right: Above his head he could see the silhouettes of his men against the stars, marching rapidly along the tops of the walls. Their mission was to secure, as efficiently and quietly as possible, the command posts and fortifications situated at intervals along the broad surrounding ramparts.

He turned west onto a broad thoroughfare, then north again between the corridor walls of Aibur Shabu. Unlike in the days of Nebuchadrezzar, the Processional Way was dark now, its torches extinguished at the beginning of the second watch of the night. Only the razor-thin crescent of the moon and a shining riot of stars lit the broad avenue along which he and his hand-picked troops patrolled, their every sense wound to a taut-string pitch of readiness.

His task was to secure the citadel. They had awaited the dead of the second night-watch before entering the city by the newly opened paths created by the draining of the river. Babylon would awaken with the dawn to find her new masters in control of every fortification, every street, every rooftop—or so ran the plan. As many Babylonian commanders as possible had been bought or otherwise neutralized, but conquest was inherently an inexact science. Thus far no opposition had been encountered, but Gobhruz did not imagine this state of affairs could last.

They came abreast of the walls of the huge Esagila complex. As they neared the silent gateway of the temple, Gobhruz's vanguard sighted an armed band hurrying toward them along the intersecting Avenue of Marduk. Gobhruz's fist went to his sword, then relaxed as his men signaled; the approaching patrol was their own, having entered the city by the Marduk Gate.

The combined forces swept along the broad street. Crossing the Zababa Bridge before the gates of the palace, Gobhruz counted a mere handful of guards standing sentry. These few, seeing all too clearly the futility of their position, threw down their arms and prostrated themselves before the eerily silent armed horde which poured into the courtyard fronting the gate.

His archers standing guard with arrows notched against an ambush from behind or above, Gobhruz watched impatiently as his troops went to work on the sealed gates of the palace. Sinews straining, the men pried and grunted, driving wedges into the crack between the two halves of the massive iron-bound doors. They made noisy, splintering progress—and still no sentry challenged, no defender impeded their efforts. For all the outward evidence, they might have been forcing their way into a house of tombs safeguarded only by the restless spirits of the dead. When at last the soldiers won through the final barricade, the huge portals swung open upon a courtyard huge, imposing—and empty.

Gobhruz pointed to three lieutenants. "Each of you take a hundred men apiece. Search the palace and citadel for—" Hearing the noise of a shod foot against pavement, the commander glanced above him. He could see the shadowy figures of men moving along the tops of the barricades. Softly one of them called out—in Parsi. He gaped in wonderment. Could his men have already encircled the entire length of the city's walls? Had there been no Chaldeans on guard? He sent a runner to summon one of the men to him.

"No, my lord," panted the infantryman softly, when he had clambered down into the courtyard where the amazed Gobhruz waited. "We saw no one, heard nothing. It was..." The fellow's brow wrinkled in thought as he searched for the words. "It was as if the hand of a god went before us. Time and again we came upon the guard-stations along the walls, only to find them abandoned, with weapons and armor lying on the floor. Something has happened to them—all of them." The eyes of the men standing nearby rolled white, staring about in superstitious dread at the vast, empty courtyard.

"Steady, lads," growled a grizzled old sergeant in their midst. "If the gods want to wipe out Chaldeans for us, why not let them?"

Nervous laughter stuttered from the throats of the men as Gobhruz smiled grudgingly at the well-timed joke. He turned to the lieutenants he had chosen earlier. "Off with you, then. Look sharp!"

The three companies of men moved off in different directions, each disappearing into a separate corridor of the palace. Gobhruz watched them go, rubbing his beard in wary bemusement. Could it really be this easy?

◆ ◆ ◆

DANIEL PACED BACK AND FORTH in his chamber, as sleepless as if it were midday. As he turned beside his couch, he again spied the robe of purple linen, the heavy gold chain lying atop it.

He snorted with disgust. After he had arrived back at his suite from Esagila, a timid knock had come at his door. A messenger from Belshazzar entered, meekly bearing the bribe of the crown prince. As if the word of the Almighty might be averted by paltry gifts! Shaking his head, the aged vizier resumed his pensive pacing.

He heard the scuffling of booted feet outside his door. Going silently to the portal, he laid his ear upon its planking, listening carefully as a seemingly interminable succession of footsteps scooted past in the corridor without. He heard whispered voices speaking in the exotic tongue of the western mountains. So! The Persians were in the very palace! His heart pounded with the enormity of the realization. Again the ominous tolling of the words on Esagila's wall resounded within his mind. Only four words—and the world was changed.

◆ ◆ ◆

FROM THE RICH FURNISHINGS, the lavish murals, and the decorative cast of the wall-lamps, the lieutenant knew his patrol was in the wing of the palace where the imperial family resided. Nervously he loosened his sword in its sheath, for he fully expected to be met around the next corner by a company of bodyguards. The torches borne aloft by the men behind him cast black, wavering shadows at his feet as they moved along the darkened corridors.

Ahead was a large portal, the door sheathed in tooled bronze and the surrounding wall inset with gaudily colored glazed bricks. Gods and cherubim festooned the archway in which the door was set, presumably affording divine protection to whomever sheltered within. The lieutenant reasoned that this was the emperor's private suite. His mouth dry with apprehension, he scanned the corridors on either side, stretching mazelike into the darkness beyond the torches' flickering light. Nothing. Only the same eerie emptiness and silence through which they had moved since entering this huge, puzzling city.

Drawing a deep breath, he stepped aside, nodding to the four burly men bearing the battering ram.

The four men lunged forward, the ram striking the door with a fearfully loud crash. Again and again they dashed the thick pile against the door, until at last the hinges gave way, groaning as the battering ram's blows drove them from their sockets in the walls. The door caved inward, falling forward into the room with a resounding crash.

The soldiers spilled into the chamber, swords drawn. The lieutenant bolted forward behind his men, as they searched the folds of the silken hangings and plunged behind the tapestries, searching out a foe which did not appear.

"Sir!" one of the men shouted. "Come here!"

The lieutenant followed the sound of the voice, finding the infantryman standing beside a gold-sheathed mahogany couch.

On it lay an old man—or the dried-out husk of what had once been an old man. His eyes gaped glassily in death, while his tomb-pale hands gripped a golden scepter; it was as if, even in dying, Nabu-Naid could not willingly surrender what he once had seized.

BELSHAZZAR HEARD THE TREAD of many feet outside his door. *Where are my sentries? The villains have deserted—everyone has deserted!*

Panting with fear, he picked up a sword in clammy, nerveless fingers. He heard the strange voices, the fearful gabble of Persian words which announced his impending doom. He did not want to die! Why had the gods turned against him?

"Father!" he shrilled as the ram clanged against his door. "This is your doing! Your stupidity has brought this upon me!"

The ram smashed through into the room, and the door fell inward with a crash that raised a cloud of masonry dust. With a shriek of madness, the prince rushed forward toward the black hole that had opened into the corridor. He saw the dark, shadowed faces of the invaders, and the points of their arrows aimed at him. There was a screaming, crimson flash of pain. Then nothing.

25

THE MARTIAL ANNOUNCEMENT of the trumpets was lost in the huge roar of acclamation which rose, as if of a single immense throat, from the vast crowds thronging the walls of Aibur Shabu.

From between the massive, dragon-emblazoned columns

of the Ishtar Gate—as if the strength of Babylon herself had somehow given him new birth—rode Cyrus the conqueror astride a jet-black Nisayan charger. He was surrounded on all sides by the bristling hedge of his bodyguards' lances.

As he rode through the deafening wall of adoration, Cyrus fancied the mob's exuberance was not entirely feigned. He had correctly interpreted the currents of mistrust and hostility engendered by Nabu-Naid's misguided policies and the coarse harshness of his son. As in Ecbatana, he was looked upon as a deliverer, a people's king, a remedy to the oppressive hand of a tyrant. And he knew, with the instinct of a performer, how to draw their even greater admiration for this, his latest conquest. Before this day was over, he would be enthroned not only in the Great Hall of Babylon, but in the hearts and minds of her citizens.

The cortege moved slowly along the Processional Way, showered with the praises of Babylon. As he drew near the huge archway of Esagila, Cyrus reigned his steed to a halt and dismounted. The throngs quieted, watching attentively as their new monarch, now leaving behind the diligent phalanx of his bodyguards, walked into the huge plaza of the House of Marduk.

In the center of the courtyard a company of priests awaited the coming of Cyrus. At the forefront stood the chief priest of Marduk, who watched anxiously as the solitary, commanding figure strode purposefully toward him.

Cyrus reached the priests and received their obeisance. In a loud voice, he said, "I greet Marduk, the great lord, who has brought me safely and peacefully within the walls of this city. It is my wish that all men know of my reverence for the gods—and I hereby order the immediate return of the holy ones to the cities and temples which are their proper residing places. Let it be done!"

He turned on his heel, striding back the way he had come. He heard the gratified sighs of the priests at his back. Permitting himself a tiny smile, he continued toward his waiting bodyguard.

◆　◆　◆

LATER THAT DAY Cyrus entered the throne room, as the waiting courtiers fell to their faces. With measured tread he paced toward the Dragon Throne, carefully eyeing the facade behind the dais. His Aryan sense of proportion was gratified by the four stylized palm trees, and by the striking contrast between the deep blue of the glazed-brick background and the bright reds and yellows of the trees themselves. He seated himself upon the throne, resting his palms upon the cool gold of its carved dragons' heads. His amber gaze imperiously roved the vast chamber, as his subjects quietly rose from their obeisance.

By ones and twos they came, the nobility and other leaders of Babylonian society. Merchants, generals, landowners, shaven-headed representatives of the god-houses—all making the quiet pilgrimage of devotion to their new lord. Quietly they whispered the formulas of homage as they knelt before the Dragon Throne. Gravely Cyrus received them, nodding his mute benediction upon each of them in turn.

Adad-ibni, as chief seer, was responsible for producing the chronicle of Cyrus's conquest in accordance with the approved signs and portents. He was acutely conscious of the importance of this first interview with the new emperor, and he felt his palms sweating as he approached the dais, his head lowered in respect. When he reached the edge of the platform he knelt, holding before him a clay tablet covered with script in the Old Babylonian language used in court since the days of Nebuchadrezzar.

"My lord Cyrus, please accept the humble labor of your servant Adad-ibni, chief of his majesty's seers, soothsayers and mages," came the wrinkled voice of the black-robed old man. "As my lord Cyrus knows, his coming was foretold by the mighty gods themselves, was writ large in the skies for all to see. Your humble servant has made a history of these omens and foreshadowings, and he now offers these to the mighty Cyrus, for his reading, approval, or amendment."

Cyrus stared down at the shaven, parchment-like scalp of the venerable mage. *Is this a veiled insult?* he wondered. Did the Chaldeans, so prideful of their ancient learning, attempt to tweak him subtly for the illiteracy of his Parsi heritage? He looked up at Gobhruz, standing near his right shoulder. The commander returned his gaze stoically, as if to say, "You have sought the kingship of this place. How will you respond?" The gray beard of his mentor twitched, but he offered not a word, not a gesture.

"Bring me the tablet," he commanded, and an aide jerked forward to place the proffered document in the king's outstretched hand.

Cyrus made a show of scanning the tablet, his mind furiously churning to find a way past this dilemma. The request had been couched most eloquently by the old man—he had not seen any previous hint that the Chaldean nobility or priesthood wished him anything other than the utmost respect. Yet his pride bridled at openly displaying the disadvantages of his semi-nomadic legacy. He was ruler of the greatest empire the world had ever known! How could he admit, in this renowned seat of age-old knowledge, that he could not read even the Aramaic spoken by all his vassal lands, much less this archaic language of dead Chaldean kings?

The notion of such an indignity was so repugnant to him that in desperation he decided upon a brazen bluff. Handing the tablet to the aide, he indicated that it should be passed back to Adad-ibni. Without looking up, the chief seer accepted the tablet and bowed himself backward from the dais, returning to the silent, deferential ranks of the courtiers.

In a ringing voice, Babylon's new ruler said, "This writing pleases us. Be it known to all that I, Cyrus, the Great King, the king of lands, monarch of Sumer and Akkad, and the One ascribed as Darius the King of Medea and Persia, say this: The word of the Medes and Persians, which shall henceforth govern this place and all places which lie under our beneficent rule, shall not be broken, nor may they be changed. Once written, the word of the Medes and Persians shall stand forever. So let it be done."

Carefully Cyrus studied the manner and bearing of the Chaldean courtiers. They had received the bold proclamation in awed silence; no glimmer of anything other than submissive acceptance showed in their faces or attitudes. *Good*, he thought. *They shall see that I respect the written word as much as any trained scholar.* A look of calm satisfaction spread across his features—until his eyes found the face of Gobhruz.

The old Mede would not look at him. Eyes averted, his air was one of mute reproach to the presumption and dissimulation of his king. Invisible to all but himself and Gobhruz, a trace of the satisfaction left Cyrus's features. Chastened, he turned his attention toward another nobleman who now approached the dais mumbling, as had the many preceding him, the contrite litany of subservience to the great King Cyrus.

◆ ◆ ◆

"BUT WHEN THE SEVENTY YEARS are fulfilled, I will punish the king of Babylon and his nation, the land of the Chaldeans, for their guilt," declares the Lord, "and will make it desolate forever. I will bring upon that land all the things I have spoken against it, all that are written in this book and prophesied by Jeremiah against all the nations. They themselves will be enslaved by many nations and great kings; I will repay them according to their deeds and the work of their hands..."

Daniel laid aside the scroll, a deep sigh surging upward from his roiled soul. For the first time in many years the sad, noble face of Jeremiah rose up before him. How amazing it was to contemplate: Though his body had lain in an anonymous crypt in Egypt for scores of years, that great, troubled man of God still spoke to Daniel's spirit, just as surely as he had spoken on that Syrian night so many lifetimes ago! Daniel gently stroked the scroll of the prophet's words, as if by doing so he stroked the beard of the long-departed man who had striven to bring comfort to a frightened boy.

And how surely the sweeping scythe of God reaped the very harvest foretold by Jeremiah during the days of Daniel's youth! The downfall of the nations opposing Nebuchadrezzar, the ruin of Zion…And then, the fall of the lineage of Nebuchadrezzar—indeed, of the entire Semitic hierarchy! The rise of the Persian nation, and its great king, Cyrus. All shown to Jeremiah so long ago.

But the words which haunted Daniel, which summoned the heartsick, nameless storms in his soul, were the last ones he had read:

I will repay them according to their deeds and the work of their hands…

Who could stand before the righteousness of the Almighty? With a melancholy certainty, Daniel knew the uncleanness of his own heart, the craven desire for self-preservation, the words withheld which should have been spoken, the passivity when action should have been taken, the secret enjoyment of the power and prestige of his rank.

And he knew his experience was not unique. Ezra, Shemaiah, and others of the elders and teachers of the Hebrews had discussed this painful subject with him at length. All felt the disquiet—sometimes vague, sometimes as pointed as a red-hot dagger—of the immeasurable chasm between the fitful glimmerings in the soul of a man—even a good man—and the white-hot, unapproachable purity of *Adonai Elohim.*

How then was it possible that this God, this utterly blameless Presence, could tolerate the proven faithlessness, the wearily redundant disobedience of this people Israel? Why should He rebuild Jerusalem and bring them back from the myriad places to which He had scattered them, if they were so powerless to maintain His standards? Why should it be any different this time?

A deep, soul-wrenching moan tore at the moorings of his spirit. Daniel fell face-down on the floor of his room. His arm reached beseechingly toward his window, through which the burnished light of the setting sun cast its fading glory—reaching west, toward Jerusalem. Crying aloud, the words crowded past his lips in a surge of shame.

"O Lord, the great and awesome God who keeps His covenant of love with all who love Him and obey His commands: We have sinned and done wrong; we have been wicked and have rebelled; we have turned away from Your commands and laws. We have not listened to Your servants the prophets, who spoke in Your name to our kings, our princes, and our fathers, and to all the people of the land.

"Lord, You are righteous, but this day we are covered with shame—the men of Judah and people of Jerusalem and all Israel, both near and far, in all the countries where You have scattered us because of our unfaithfulness to You..."

The sun sank on a purple and gold cushion into the west, and still Daniel poured out the groanings of his soul before the Lord. Against all hope, against all the contrary tide of his own unworthiness, Daniel pleaded mightily with the God of his people, begging earnestly for a fate he knew with all surety was better than they—or he—deserved.

"Now, our God, hear the prayers and petitions of Your servant. For Your sake, O Lord, look with favor on Your desolate sanctuary..."

He thought of the emptying of the temples of Uruk, of Nippur and Opis, and of the deep resentment the foolish proclamation of Nabu-Naid had engendered. How much more terrible, how much greater the anguish spawned by the desolation of Zion! And that was done not by the edict of an addled old king, but by the severe, burning hand of the True God Himself —as if the stench of His people was so great that He must unremittingly cancel all evidence of His habitation with them, even to the extent of ravaging the house of His own Name!

A black wail of misery gushed from between Daniel's lips, as his prayer continued. "Give ear, O God, and hear; open Your eyes and see the desolation of the city that bears Your Name.

We do not make requests of You because we are righteous, but because of Your great mercy."

Drained of words, emptied almost of thought itself, he concluded with a plea the more impassioned for its directness.

"O Lord, listen! O Lord, forgive! O Lord, hear and act! For Your sake, O my God, do not delay, because Your city and Your people bear Your Name."

Almost insensible with grief and exhaustion, he buried his face in his arms, still prostrate on the floor of his suite. As he drifted toward a black chasm of unconsciousness, a diamond-hard spear-point of light stabbed into his aching brain. And for a third time he felt the terrifying, onrushing precursor of the Eternal's presence within his mind.

Again the ringing, thundering voice of the Guide called his name, in tones as huge and frightening as eternity. He spoke to Daniel of the rebuilding of a city, of the passage of ages and seasons, of the wickedness of kings and the coming of an Anointed One. The brilliant hues of the Almighty's grand tapestry absorbed him, drew him helpless into its dazzling vortex. It swirled about him with wonders beyond understanding, visions beyond retelling. Finally it ebbed away from him, casting him ashore on the familiar shoals of his own overburdened senses.

And then Daniel slept.

◆   ◆   ◆

HE AWOKE with the early light of dawn tracing its pink hues along the walls of the palace. Looking down, he realized he had fallen asleep fully clothed. He lay half on his couch, half on the carpeted floor beside. Rising, he winced at the stiffness of his old joints, made the more severe by the awkward position in which he had lain. As he sleepily rubbed the back of his neck, a knock came upon his door.

A page entered, holding out a message cylinder sealed with the winged-circle impression of Cyrus's royal signet. Taking the cylinder, he scanned the Aramaic script, and heard the ominous muttering of fate at the back of his skull. The emperor wished to see him. Today. Alone.

◆　◆　◆

CYRUS PEERED into the highly polished brass mirror on the wall of the chamber. Though his thick, straight locks still retained much of the robust, sandy-brown shade of his youth, the white filaments of age proliferated more and more. Only to be expected, he realized, in a man who had passed three-score years.

And yet his vigor was unabated. He still felt able to ride and to wield the lance and scimitar as well as ever. Why might he not continue to rule for many years over this vast kingdom he had forged?

Behind him came the sound of shuffling feet and the tap of a cane. He wheeled about to see a stooped, white-bearded old man enter and make obeisance—as best his feeble knees would allow.

"My king, I am Daniel, who is called Belteshazzar," the old fellow was saying. "I have answered the summons of the king."

"Ah, yes," replied Cyrus, taking his seat on a nearby cushion. "Please rise, Vizier Belteshazzar—or do you prefer your native name?"

Visibly pleased at being asked, the old man answered, "Daniel, my king. It is the name my father gave me, and it gives me much pleasure to hear it spoken aloud."

Cyrus smiled in an open, boyish way. "Very well then, Daniel. You must be curious as to why I have called you here alone."

The dark, watery eyes of the old man blinked, but he made no other reply.

"A king is but a man, Daniel," began Cyrus. "He sees only what is visible to a man. Yet his eyes and ears must be all about. He must be able to hear the words of his people, even those that remain unspoken. And he must see what will happen in the future, as well as what is happening in the present."

265

Remembering the words spoken so long ago by another counselor, Cyrus mused, "A king, if he is to remain a king, must be ever attentive to those he governs. When he ceases to be so, he ceases to be a king. He may remain in power, may continue to exercise authority by force of arms—but he is no longer a king."

Daniel, gazing down the long corridor of his memory, nodded to himself. Then Cyrus was again speaking.

"A king must be a student of men, Daniel. I have examined many men under many different circumstances. Even in this court of Babylon I have closely observed the nuances of expression, the subtle outward suggestions of what some might wish to conceal. I know there are many within these ancient walls, Daniel, whose words and professions of loyalty mask motives which have little to do with allegiance to me."

Now Daniel stared directly into the probing eyes of this perceptive, engaging conqueror.

"I have heard men speak of you, Daniel," the king was saying. "It is said you have a wisdom beyond that of ordinary men. If this is true, I will have need of your counsel."

Daniel bowed his head in respect. "My king has but to command, and his humble servant obeys."

Cyrus studied the downcast face of Daniel for ten long breaths. In some ways this old fellow reminded him of Gobhruz, his lifelong servant, friend and mentor. He found himself wishing to strike a deeper chord of familiarity with this venerable veteran of the Babylonian court. "My father gave me a name, too, Daniel," said the king with a smile, changing his tone to a lighter, more intimate timbre in an effort to establish some bond with Daniel beyond that of king and courtier. "Do you want to know what it is?"

A premonition of inevitability turned a page within Daniel's mind. His nostrils flared with the fragrance of the Eternal. Silently he nodded.

"In these parts they say 'Cyrus,' but in Aryan my name is 'Kurash,'" the king said. "In the language of the Persians, it means 'Shepherd.' That is what a king ought to be, Daniel. Not a butcher who terrorizes the herd, but a shepherd who guides his—" He stopped, frozen in mid-thought by the entranced expression on the face of Daniel, whose mouth opened to speak.

...who says of Jerusalem, "It shall be inhabited..."

The old man was half-whispering words in some strange tongue, intoning in awe an incantation summoned from some memory too powerful to be suppressed. As Cyrus listened in curious confusion, Daniel went on:

...who says of Kurus, "He is My shepherd,
and will accomplish all that I please..."

Now Daniel was staring at him with eyes glittering with import, with the suggestion—or perhaps the realization—of some momentous purpose. For some reason beyond conscious decision, Cyrus asked, "Those words you said just now—neither Aramaic nor Chaldean. What language were they?"

"I spoke Hebrew, my king—the tongue of my people."

"You are not Chaldean? Your appearance is similar to that of the rest—"

Daniel shook his head. His white, bushy eyebrows protruded toward the king, his intense gaze honing his words like carefully chosen weapons. "No, my king. I am a Hebrew. Like the men of Chaldea, we are children of Shem, but scores of ages ago our clans diverged. Our most ancient father Abraham was called out of this country to go to the land promised him by the Most High."

Suddenly, unaccountably, Cyrus felt less like a king examining a vizier and more like an infantryman who sought to pass some hitherto-unknown muster. With the disconcerting sense that his next words were expected, perhaps ordained, he asked another question.

"Why, then, are your people here, Daniel? And how did you, a foreigner, come to be in the high councils of the kings of Babylon?"

Daniel smiled. His head cocked as if he were listening to another voice, he waited long before replying. Finally he said, "The Almighty One, the God of heaven, caused us to be brought here from our own land because of our disobedience. It is He who has placed me within the halls of the kings of this place." His eyes drilled into the very core of Cyrus's being as he concluded, "And it is He who has brought *you* here, O my king, to accomplish the further unfolding of His will."

For ten heartbeats, then twenty, the eyes of the king and those of the old man were frozen in a stare as inexorable as the tides of time. Cyrus found himself remembering the face of the holy man at the mountain shrine—remembering his words about a calling and a purpose, and his restless, beyond-seeking vision. The gaze that now gripped him was like that of the priest of Ahura Mazda, only more potent—as if what Diravarnya sought so relentlessly had been found at last by this man who now spoke to him...

With a start Cyrus pulled his eyes away, striving to regain control of his emotions and the conversation. "Many gods have brought me to this day, Daniel," he said, his words ringing false, even to his own ears. "Already the priests of Marduk have commissioned a stone tablet celebrating the Sun Lord's sponsorship of my victory." He pressed on: "And in every temple in Chaldea my name will be associated with the triumphs of the local deity." Willing his face to remain impassive, he stared coolly at the old man. "Now you are telling me that your god is the next in this long line."

Daniel shook his head, still smiling his enigmatic smile. Patiently, as if teaching a child, the vizier said, "My king does not understand. The astrologers and seers come to him with portents and omens reinterpreted in the light of what is already known." Leaning forward on his cane, Daniel's next words came in a whisper as focused and brilliant as the light in the eye of a god. "The words I quoted were written by a prophet of my people—almost eight-score years ago."

The king's mind reeled. Eight-score years! Was it possible?

How could a man so long dead, living in a land neither Cyrus nor his fathers had ever seen, ascribe him service to a god whose name, even now, he knew not? The expression on Daniel's face, the incontrovertible aura of holiness emanating from his every feature, told Cyrus more surely than the endorsement of a hundred witnesses that the words spoken by the aged vizier were dependable.

Cyrus's next words were spoken quietly, without inflection, as if in that intimate striving of visions he and his servant had changed places, reversed roles—as if he, and not Daniel, must now attend to the wishes of the King.

"What, then, does your God require of me?"

26

THE SHRILL BLAST of the trumpets brought a sudden halt to the raucous babble in the bustling courtyard. Egibi's oldest son, leaning against the doorway of the counting-house, broke off the conversation he had been having with Jozadak, his father's chief overseer. Along with everyone else in the crowded street, the banker and his gray-bearded employee craned their necks to see the imperial herald as he cried aloud whatever pronouncement Cyrus had composed for him.

"Cyrus, the Great King, the King of Lands, has made a proclamation and has put it in writing, so that it cannot be changed!" The fellow shouted his message, holding above his head a clay cylinder imprinted with the winged-circle of the Persian monarch. "This word shall be announced throughout all the realm of Cyrus, to all the lands and nations which know his just and gracious rule!

"This is what Cyrus, king of Persia, Medea, Lydia and Babylon, says:

"The Lord, the God of heaven, has given me all the kingdoms of the earth, and He has appointed me to build a temple for Him at Jerusalem in Judah. For any of His people among you—may their God be with them. And let them go up to Jerusalem in Judah and build the temple of the Lord, the God of Israel, the God who is in Jerusalem.

"And the people of any place where Hebrew survivors may now be living are to provide them with silver and gold, with goods and livestock, and with freewill offerings for the temple of God in Jerusalem."

Slowly the din of the marketplace returned, most of the buyers and sellers exchanging quizzical remarks and queries about the place referred to in the emperor's edict. Few had ever heard of Jerusalem or Judah. Within a few moments, amid shrugs and shakings of the head, the odd announcement was forgotten. Urgent matters of commerce superseded useless speculation about the king's intent concerning this unknown place.

Bel-Adan, the son of Egibi, turned to ask Jozadak what he knew of these strange goings-on, but halted before he could speak, his eyes widening in surprise. Tears were streaming down the face of the older man, as over and over again Jozadak whispered, in a voice choked with joy, a single Hebrew phrase.

"Hallelu-Yah!"

◆　◆　◆

BEFORE THE SUN SET that day, breathless word came to the leaders of the Hebrew community in Babylon of the miraculous proclamation of Cyrus. Before the next *shabbat*, the message had reached the Jews of Opis, Sippar, and Nippur. Not since the legendary days of the Departure from Egypt had such a scurrying, joyful bustle been seen. In every Hebrew household the discussion was of which families would make the return journey to Judah and which would not, what to take and how much, how to dispose of things that could not be taken—and all the myriad intricacies accompanying the mass relocation of an extensive population.

In the house on Adad Street it was a bittersweet time. Joel, oldest son of Azariah and Ephratah, had decided to remain behind in Babylon to care for the ailing Ephratah. His sister Milcah and her husband—a fine, vigorous Hebrew of Benjamite stock—would join those repatriating Judah, as would their younger brother, yet unmarried. Many were the quiet conversations, many the memories of things past and the conjectures on things to come. The air was full of plans, hopes, and dreams—and of the wistful sorrow of parting. Their days were a transient mix of joy, sadness, and apprehension.

◆　◆　◆

THE DAY CAME when Ezra, Jozadak and his son Yeshua, and a large band of Levites and priests gathered in the courtyard of the imperial palace, their faces those of men about to see a cherished dream become reality. Presently a line of porters headed by Mithredath, chief steward of the imperial treasury at Babylon, came into view, each porter bearing one or more sturdy wooden casks. Under the watchful eye of Mithredath, the servants carefully placed the casks on the ground at the feet of the eagerly waiting Hebrews.

Slowly, reverently, Jozadak lifted the lid on the nearest cask. Glowing softly within were ten of the solid gold dishes forged in the days of Solomon—consecrated for use in the Lord's Temple. A gasp of awe escaped his lips as he beheld these, some of the most ancient and holy artifacts of his people.

The other containers held the silver and gold dishes, tongs, and other utensils of the Temple pillaged during the fall of Jerusalem. After a generation they were at last returned to the hands of those who knew their proper employment. The

Levites looked at one another, unable to put their emotions into words.

Jozadak and his son returned to the house of Egibi with hearts full almost to bursting. As they entered the main room, Jozadak was startled to see old Egibi himself, frail and near death, lying on his couch just outside the door to his private rooms. Everyone in the counting-house—indeed, every merchant in the banking district—knew this illness would be his last. Since its onset Egibi had scarcely been glimpsed outside the sanctuary of his rooms. And it was better so, for on the recent rare occasions when he had come to the areas where business was conducted, the entire establishment became subdued, cast under the pall of its owner's looming death. Even now the normally bustling main room of Egibi and Sons was as quiet and somber as a gathering beside a crypt. Each scribe and errand boy paused in his routes, arrested by the cold ambience of finality wafting outward from the bed of the master of the house.

Weakly, Egibi gestured toward Jozadak, beckoning him. Jozadak whispered to his son, "Go along, Yeshua. I will attend our patron." Needing no other urging, Yeshua hurried away, anxious to leave the vicinity so overshadowed by impending death. Not quite knowing what to expect, Jozadak approached the berth where Egibi lay.

When Jozadak had reached the side of his employer, Egibi signaled limply to the four servants attending his bier. Carefully they raised the couch and carried the sick man toward his rooms. Not knowing what else to do, Jozadak followed.

When the servants had gently placed Egibi's couch on the floor in his chamber, the ill banker dismissed them with a waggle of his fingers. They left, and Egibi whispered throatily to Jozadak, "Close the door." Jozadak closed and secured the door, stepping quietly back to his employer's side.

For long moments Egibi said nothing, peering up into the face of his oldest and most trusted employee. Jozadak could hear the tattered sound of the air rattling in and out of Egibi's lungs. The skin of the dying old man's face, once so taut with the pudgy evidence of his prosperity, now lay in pallid folds along his jowls and beneath the darkening caves in which his eyes crouched. Those eyes, still keen despite the fading of the light behind them, gripped Jozadak's face with an almost palpable pressure. At last, with an effort painful to watch, Egibi gathered breath to speak.

"You are going back with the others," he rasped.

Jozadak confirmed the statement with a silent nod.

"Why?" It was a single word, but the expression on Egibi's face was eloquent with layers of meaning. *Have I not been good to you?* the face asked. *What can there be in Judah for one who has lived all his life in Babylon? Who will help my sons maintain this trade I have spent my life nurturing?* And just perhaps, Jozadak thought, there was a trace of wonderment in the sallow visage of Egibi—a haunted musing: *Is there a god truly worth all this bother, all this upheaval?* As the shadows of death lengthened on his horizons, could Egibi be listening to some faint echo from the forgotten past of his Israelite ancestry?

As gently as he could, Jozadak tried to clarify. "Honored patron, though my body was given birth in this land between the Two Rivers, my soul was born in Judah, atop the hill of Zion. I can no more forget Jerusalem, though I have never seen her, than I could forget the name of my father. I am of the line of Aaron, my master Egibi. Do you know what that means?"

The confused squint of Egibi showed he did not. Inwardly Jozadak sighed for the impoverishment of this man's heritage. When Sargon of Nineveh had carried his forebears to this place he had robbed Egibi of something—robbed him so completely he had never noticed its lack.

Quietly Jozadak explained. "I am of the priestly caste of Israel. It is my role, and that of my son Yeshua after me, to minister in the House of Adonai—in Jerusalem." Merely saying the words, Jozadak felt a thrill ripple along his spine. For a moment, his eyes glazed over in wonderment. *Soon!* he thought.

Then Egibi was tugging at his sleeve. "Once, in this very

room," the dying man wheezed, "you spoke to me of the god of Israel."

Jozadak winced, remembering the awkwardness of that evening so many years ago.

"I have remembered that conversation," gasped Egibi, "and the heat of your words."

For many heartbeats, the only sound in the room was the labored breathing of Egibi. Finally, he gathered himself for another attempt at speech. Feebly aiming a trembling finger at a brass-bound wooden box in the corner of the room, he breathed, "Open it."

Puzzled, Jozadak went to the box and raised its cover. Inside were stacks of silver strips. To Jozadak's practiced eye, the sum appeared to be on the order of forty *mana*, if not a full talent. Replacing the cover he returned to his master's bedside, his brow furled in bafflement.

"Beneath the talent of silver," said Egibi, his voice thin and dry as old parchment, "there is another—of gold."

Jozadak nodded, but he still failed to comprehend.

"Take it," sighed Egibi in a breath-starved whisper, "and use it…as you see fit." Exhausted, the banker fell back on his couch, fighting for air.

Jozadak felt his face stiffening in shock. A talent of gold and one of silver! More wealth than he could imagine—being placed in his hands!

"My patron!" he whispered in a voice swollen with astonishment. "Are…are you certain? What will your sons—"

With a curt movement of his hand, Egibi cut short his overseer's question. Gathering his breath, he said, "My sons need not be concerned in this. I have but few sunrises left, but such as remain to me, I will use as I see fit." Glaring imperiously at Jozadak, he sucked feebly at the air before finishing: "This is yet the house of Egibi!"

Abashed and overwhelmed, Jozadak lowered his head, his chest heaving with a storm of emotions whirling too fast to be named. When he managed to regain his voice, he said, "Very well, my master. I will do as you say. And…" For several moments, he tried to find a way to squeeze the words in his mind past the constriction in his throat. "And, honored patron, I pledge to you…"—again he struggled with the surge of feelings which now forced burning tears from the corners of his eyes—"I pledge to you that I will say a *qaddish* for you, atop the holy hill of Zion." Completely overcome at last, Jozadak grasped the cold, limp hand of his patron, bringing it to his lips in a kiss of gratitude.

Something like a smile bloomed faintly across the parched cheeks of Jacob-Egibi, dying merchant of Babylon.

◆ ◆ ◆

DANIEL HEARD THE SHUFFLING STEPS behind him, and turned around. It was Hananiah. As soon as he saw his old friend, he knew what he would say.

"Will you not come?" the aged musician asked, his eyes dark pools of concern.

Daniel sighed, looking away. Slowly he shook his head. "I cannot, my old friend."

The silence was as long and compelling as a shared lifetime.

"Why?" queried Hananiah finally.

Daniel glanced at the other man, then limped over to a chair, groaning as he lowered himself carefully into it. "Come, sit," he beckoned, gesturing toward a seat adjacent to his. "My old knees are too stiff for getting up and down from cushions, Hananiah. As you can see, I now prefer higher seating. Less stylish perhaps, but easier on old men like us, eh?"

Hananiah slowly seated himself, his eyes never leaving the face of his friend. Daniel swallowed, then peered into the familiar, time-worn face of Hananiah. "I am too old and tired—"

"We are the same age," interrupted Hananiah curtly. "Since we buried Mishael two years ago, you and I are the only ones left who made the long journey of exile. Will you not complete the circle with me, back to Jerusalem?"

It was the longest speech Daniel had heard Hananiah make

in many years. It was a measure of the tremendous sentiment between the two men that he was so voluble. Daniel felt the tendrils of confusion and apprehension reaching from Hananiah's soul toward his own, groping for understanding, for reassurance. He felt them twine securely about his heart, evoking and intensifying the poignant pangs of leave-taking which were his constant companions in these days of parting.

His throat aching with emotion, he said, "I cannot, Hananiah. I am too deeply embedded in this place." A pain-filled chuckle escaped him. "It seems that I have, at last, become a creature of Babylon."

The wounded, puzzled expression on Hananiah's face twisted the knife of sadness piercing his friend's heart. "Oh, my brother," Daniel cried, his voice breaking on the edge of his grief. "How many the times I have stared out that western window yonder and longed for Judah as a lost child longs for its mother! Each day Jerusalem has been a prayer on my lips, an ache in my breast! And now—now that the Eternal has taken up Jacob in the palm of His hand to bring him back to the land of promise—He has shown me that I must remain behind."

A gulf, a vacuum as hushed as darkness, yawned within the quiet places of their souls as the two old friends helplessly pondered this enigmatic tragedy that was all but lost in the festive preparations for Israel's homecoming. That one who desired so much to depart must remain behind...

From the quiet musician came a single word: "Why?"

Daniel massaged his eyes with the tips of his fingers, then shook his head, looking away. "I cannot say, old friend. Something He desires of me, some task yet remaining..." He groped for more words, a more fitting explanation, but his hands gestured mutely in the air.

The two old men sat staring at the void that soon would gape between their spirits: the impending parting—their final parting. So many leagues, so many years they had shared...

"Daniel, I must go. I have waited for this day—"

"Of course you must!" Daniel asserted. "Of all people I need the least explanation of your motives. You must go back.

"And I will ask this of you, Hananiah," said Daniel, after another pause. "When you arrive at Zion…when you see the sun rise over the hills of Benjamin…will you think of me? Will you say my name there, atop the mountain of the Lord? Will you again bring the name of Daniel before the Lord there, in the place where His name dwells? Will you do this for me?"

The two aged men exchanged a long, liquid look brimming with all the pain, joy, grief, fear, and quiet understanding of two long lifetimes of brotherly love. A lambent tear trembled in the eye of Hananiah, then broke, spilling raggedly down his cheek, becoming lost in the labyrinth of wrinkles on his face. His fingers quivered, striking the invisible strings of a nonexistent harp—as he plucked from the chords of their hearts a haunting melody, pregnant with fathomless sorrow. He nodded at Daniel. There was no more to be said.

27

FROM ALL THE FAR-FLUNG territories, from the four corners of the world, they came—armed caravans and ranks of liveried footmen, troops mounted upon richly caparisoned horses and bravely bedecked chariots. In silken palanquins and beneath gold-tasseled canopies they came: all the high and mighty lords, officials and advisers of Cyrus answering the call of ingathering. With every scrap of splendor they could muster, they descended to the plain beside the Ulai River, to the terraced battlements and high-walled citadels of Shushan, capital of the Persian Empire.

Making the journey were erudite Chaldeans, aristocratic Medes, gold-adorned Lydians, swarthy Scythians, skin-clad Bactrians, fair-skinned Ionians, and the dark, quiet dwellers by the Indus. All the myriad tongues and tribes in the empire were represented. All answered the summons of the Aryan conqueror, the people's king from the mountains of Persis who had bound them together into the greatest single realm the world had yet known. They gathered here in Shushan of Elam to hear the word of Cyrus the Persian, heir of Achaemenes, the Great King, King of Lands, Ruler of the World from the snowbound passes of the Hindu Kush to the warm, sparkling tides of the Great Sea in the west.

Daniel, swaying back and forth in his sedan chair, studied with interest the paving stones of the roadway leading toward the gates of Shushan. *So,* he thought—*this is the royal highway Cyrus has begun.* At its completion the road was to connect the central regions of the empire with its western terminus at Sardis. The highway would cover some twenty-score leagues, traversing the hot plains of Medea and the craggy mountains of Cappadocia and Anatolia. An ambitious project, Daniel mused. And yet he had learned, in the year of his association with this king, not to scoff at his designs, however unlikely they seemed at the time. The envoys from every nation under the sun, now winding their way to Shushan in obedience to this road-building king, were eloquent testimony to the danger of underestimating Cyrus's vigor and determination.

◆ ◆ ◆

ONE HUNDRED TWENTY satraps and viziers, along with all their chief advisers, counselors, and functionaries, were now gathered in the huge central courtyard of the imperial palace in Shushan, awaiting the arrival of their monarch. Pacing back and forth in a chamber just off the courtyard, Cyrus nervously rehearsed his intentions for this crucial audience, the men who would be the mainstay of his dominion over the huge, daunting diversity under his rule.

In all the satrapies, his method of organization was the same: The satrap was the administrator, the governor; he was directly answerable to the emperor. Further, the treasurer and commander of the garrison in each capital were carefully selected by Cyrus himself for their unquestioned loyalty. They, too, answered directly to him, not to the satrap. In this way the governance, the purse strings, and the military force of each satrapy rested directly in his hands. Thus he would discourage an ambitious satrap from becoming too independent in his stewardship of the land.

Beyond this, Cyrus planned yet another level of organization. He would this day, in the presence of all the primary officials of the realm, appoint three men who would stand between the emperor and the provinces—the "eyes of the king," he called them. These super-administrators would be given extraordinary powers, and would have their own agents, informers, and messenger networks. They would oversee the satraps, the garrison commanders, and the treasurers to ensure Cyrus that his wishes and best interests were being served throughout his empire. Their word and judgments would be in every respect more weighty and far-reaching than those of the governors and satraps, and of only slightly less import than those of the king himself.

For this reason he had summoned the assembly in the courtyard. He would announce, before them all, the three men who would be his eyes and ears throughout his vast dominion. No one could doubt that the three he called would have the absolute backing of the King of Lands, and have at their disposal, with regard to the oversight of the satrapies, all the authority he himself might bring to bear. Confirming to himself once more the wisdom of his plan, he turned to the chamberlain. "Have the heralds announce my entry."

Throughout the spacious plaza, the nobles of Cyrus's empire fell to their faces as the trumpets hailed his entrance. Pacing slowly beneath the canopy carried by four brilliantly liveried slaves, he approached the ceremonial seat, its high back emblazoned with the royal seal of Achaemenes: a man—symbolizing the king—seated on the circle of the world, guarded on either side by two winged, lion-bodied cherubim. Above the trio hovered the representation of Ahura Mazda, seated on a winged throne.

With regal deliberation Cyrus seated himself on the throne, as the chamberlain cried, "Behold your king: Cyrus, heir of Achaemenes, King of Lands. May he live forever!"

At this signal the nobles rose slowly, dusting their robes and rearranging their clothing. When all was again still in the courtyard, Cyrus spoke in a voice that carried clearly to each listening ear: "I, Cyrus the King, have called and appointed each of you here. I have summoned you to my service that the peoples and lands under my protection might be well served…"

Adad-ibni, in his place with the Chaldean delegation, listened only sketchily to the words of his lord. Most of his attention was focused ahead to where the hated Belteshazzar sat in his sedan chair at the forefront of the nobles of Babylon. How it rankled him to see this Jew, the bane of his existence, in the preeminent position! *How did he do it?* the mage wondered. This wretch wormed his way into the closest confidences of every king, every ruler in power. It was the more infuriating for its inexplicability. If it were not worth his life to do so, he might have refused to attend this convocation, thus avoiding the despised sight of the maddeningly indestructible Hebrew—a constant, chafing reminder that he was Adad-ibni's superior.

"Therefore it has pleased me," Cyrus was announcing, "to appoint and affix three men, superior in wisdom and of proven loyalty, as my ambassadors extraordinary to all the realm—to see and act in all manner with my express authority, for the greater benefit of the kingdom. They shall be answerable only to the king, and shall have power to act on my behalf in any satrapy, any territory, any precinct of our vast empire."

A greater stillness had enveloped the throng in the courtyard. The three persons named by the king would indeed be forces to be reckoned with. Surreptitiously, all the nobles began cutting their eyes about at each other. Who showed some hint, some gleam of self-satisfaction? Who gave any evidence that he knew his name was about to fall from the lips of his sire? Who in the next moments would be exalted above all in the empire, save the king himself? What shifts in allegiance would take place? Who would find himself in closer proximity to the emperor, perhaps by virtue of enjoying the good graces of one whose name was yet to be announced? Rapid, silent calculation buzzed about beneath the skulls of the emperor's listeners as each judged his chances, or those of a friend—or an enemy.

"In the western reaches of the kingdom," rang the voice of the king, "I appoint Lysidias, of Sardis in Lydia…"

The purple-robed Lydian, in a display of extreme self-control, kept his face impassive. But inside, the release of pent-up tension caused his heart to clamor within his ribs like a mad beast.

"In the east, I now call Hushtaspa, of Kermani…"

The Persian, of a kindred clan to that of Cyrus, did not appear surprised by the announcement, nor did he seem overly gratified. The vast, empty lands of the east—comprising the arid plateaus of the Aryan homeland, the desolate country of the Bactrians, and the Hindi frontier—were not generally considered a particularly rewarding post. There were constant incursions by the steppe-peoples from the north, and scant rich country to support an opulent lifestyle. It was a necessary post, little more.

"And in the center, the heartland of the empire, I name Daniel-Belteshazzar, of Babylon…"

Daniel, seated in his chair, allowed his cane to fall from suddenly numb fingers. He bowed his head. "Lord God," he prayed silently, "please…I don't want this—I'm too old." Even as the words formed in his mind, he had another impression: To this he was called. He might not refuse the summons, for One greater than Cyrus had so ordained. With a sigh he leaned over and retrieved his crutch.

Adad-ibni's face went slack with horror. Surely his ears had deceived him! Surely the name the king pronounced was not that of the cursed Jew! But no—those around the sedan chair now evidenced attitudes of greater respect, a more profound deference to the gnarled old fool! The seer wanted to tear his robe, to gash his cheeks and wail aloud—but instead he stood quietly in impotent rage, his vitals burning with the fervor of his hatred that had grown all the stronger and more cankerous in his old age, after the long years in which he had honed the futile blade of his envy.

♦　♦　♦

THE CONGREGATION GATHERED atop the crest of the hill, surrounded by the debris of a ruined city. Although tears flowed freely on many faces, they were not all tears of sadness nor despair. Rivulets of joy coursed down many cheeks—mingled with grief-spawned tears for some, perhaps most. They rejoiced at a homecoming to a place most had never seen, and wept at the absence of many who should have come. They sang songs of celebration at the return to their ancient and holy homeland, and moaned dirges of heartache for the derelict condition of the sacred city. Such was the tangle of emotions known by those who had made the long journey: these exiles of Babylon, now come back to the despoiled, burned, weed-grown object of their longing—Mount Zion in Judah.

Earlier in the day a group of elders and heads of clans had gathered atop Mount Moriah. At the feet of Jozadak and the other priests they had heaped silver, gold, and bolts of purest-white linen. Jozadak, as he stacked a portion of the gold and silver given to him by the dying Egibi, felt grateful tears overwhelming his eyes. As he watched the bringing of the gifts devoted to the Temple's rebuilding, he remembered his oath to his employer, and quoted softly to himself:

O Lord, the God who saves me,
day and night I cry out before You;
turn Your ear to my cry.
For my soul is full of trouble
and my life draws near the grave...

Evening fell. As the returnees drifted toward their tents and makeshift shelters built against the night's chill, one old man remained in the ruined city. Like a lost soul, he drifted among the broken walls, the weed-choked places which had once been bustling courtyards and marketplaces. As if searching for something lost among the fragments of the city's destruction, Hananiah wandered along the broken, dust-drifted streets which had once been so full of life. For a full generation now, the only sounds these alleys and avenues had heard was the occasional bleating of strayed goats or the yip of hunting jackals.

The shuffling elder hummed softly as he ambled aimlessly along the pathways of his dim youth. Now and again a word or half a phrase would pass his lips, the only outward evidence of the music which flowed, full and lush and enthralling, within his mind:

By the waters of Babylon we sat and wept
when we remembered Zion...

"Mishael, do you remember when we used to play here, when we were children?" he spoke aloud, though no other person was present. He had momentarily halted his wandering, and was gazing out across a courtyard paved with cracked, upthrust stones, and rimmed by a smashed wall. In his mind, two laughing boys raced across the expanse. He blinked, and the image was gone. He turned to go.

He has set His foundation on the holy mountain;
the Lord loves the gates of Zion
more than all the dwellings of Jacob.
Glorious things are said of you, O city of God...

Leaning against the place where the Ephraim Gate had been, he recalled a day when he and Azariah had stood atop the wall which once rose here, their eyes huge and glistening with distress as they watched the entourage of Nebuchadrezzar's envoy riding into the city. Scant days later, they would find themselves marching away to a future that loomed before them as threatening and implacable as the shrouded gates of Sheol. Terrified boys would look in misery over their shoulders, striving through tear-shimmering eyes to catch a last glimpse of their mothers and fathers, to fix in their fright-shackled minds a last memory of the blessed gates of the doomed, glorious City of the Name.

With new tears rolling down his leathery cheeks, he staggered away from the jagged, broken, impotent columns of the gate.

> *You have rejected us, O God, and burst forth upon us;*
> *You have been angry—now restore us!*
> *You have shaken the land and torn it open;*
> *mend its fractures, for it is quaking...*

The streets leading to the Temple mount were choked with crumbling debris. By the time Hananiah reached the scattered bones of what was once the New Gate, the moon was halfway up the star-scattered velvet night sky. He thought of the festival days, the high days of the Lord, the days when celebrants came with songs of joy to the crest of Moriah:

> *I lift up my eyes to the hills—*
> *Where does my help come from?*
> *My help comes from the Lord,*
> *the Maker of heaven and earth...*

> *The Lord will watch over your coming and going,*
> *both now and forevermore...*

How long? he wondered. How long before the throngs of worshipers could again make that mirthful ascent to the beautiful gates of the Lord's house? Would he live long enough to see again the clouds of smoke, to smell the rich, soul-fattening scent of the freewill offerings roasting on the altar?

Once he and Daniel had stood here, their tiny hands enfolded in those of their fathers; with the nobility of Judah they had watched the priests, clad in their dazzling white garments —the very image of the purity and majesty of *El Elyon*—performing their duties with a solemn delight which throbbed like a heartbeat throughout the great courtyard of the Temple.

"Daniel, my friend, my brother...I am here again, at last," he mumbled aloud. "I have come to the ruined center of all that we were, and I have brought my memory of you here with me..." He clenched his fist to his chest, as if reassuring himself of the location of a secreted treasure.

He thought of the piercing bliss of the homecoming, of the ecstasy of again standing on the soil of Zion—an ecstasy mixed with jagged shards of anguish: anguish for those left behind, for the many who had died before seeing this day; anguish for the awful reality, its horror dimmed scarcely a whit by the passage of three-score and ten years of the dreadful, holy wrath which had burned against this city.

The duality, the essential melding of profound pain and profound joy, moved mightily within Hananiah at this moment —as if the sleeping spirit of Mishael stirred within him, strove through his living hands and lips to utter that which was denied those in Sheol. As if Daniel, still far away in the land beyond the Two Rivers, now reached out to link souls with him. As if Azariah roused from his slumber amid the tombs of Babylon to join in a final hymn of homecoming.

A song formed within his mind, a song woven of all that he was and all that he knew, all that he had kept and all that he had lost—the sum of the losses and keepings which had brought him surely to this very instant in time. The indissoluble union of loss and gain—of losing *in order* to gain—crystallized within his wondering spirit, clothed itself with bone and sinew. As if summoned by his need, by the gaping vacancies and choking passions in his heart, melody and words looped together within his mind.

> *When the Lord brought back the captives to Zion,*
> *we were like men who dreamed.*
> *Our mouths were filled with laughter,*
> *our tongues with songs of joy.*
> *Then it was said among the nations,*
> *"The Lord has done great things for them."*
>
> *The Lord has done great things for us,*
> *and we are filled with joy.*
>
> *Restore our fortunes, O Lord,*
> *like streams in the Negev.*
> *Those who sow in tears*
> *will reap with songs of joy.*
> *He who goes out weeping,*
> *carrying seeds to sow,*
> *Will return with songs of joy,*
> *carrying sheaves with him…*

A shaft of rapture held him in breathless wonder. He sat down on a broken wall stone. Tomorrow, he knew, would be soon enough to seek pen and parchment—he would not likely forget the words, etched as they were in the fabric of his soul. Again he breathed, in a voice hollow with awe, "The Lord has done great things for us…"

◆　◆　◆

"I TELL YOU, he has bewitched the king!" Adad-ibni's eyes were yellow with fury, and flecks of spittle spattered from his trembling lips, thinned with age and anger. "If we don't act, Belteshazzar will hold absolute power over our fates! Do you relish such a prospect?"

His mad stare dared them to disagree. Slowly the other mages and counselors seated in the darkened chamber shook their heads. One of them hesitantly opened his mouth to speak.

"Lord Adad-ibni…I have lived all my life in Babylon, in

the imperial court. And I have never known Lord Belteshazzar to seek vengeance on anyone. Indeed I have scarcely known anyone who had ill to speak of him. How then can you say—"

"But don't you see?" interjected the wrinkled mage, the words hissing insistently between his missing teeth. "The very absence you mentioned—that is the mark of his cunning!" Several brows at the table curdled in confusion. Slapping the table in impatience, the gnarled mage pointed a crooked finger at the one who had just spoken. "You—Lord Shatak! You are under-satrap in Babylon, are you not?"

The noble, blinking in surprise at the mage's vehemence, nodded.

"And how long have you been in the court of Babylon?"

Shatak calculated silently. "Almost two-score years and ten. But what—"

"And in all that time," Adad-ibni pressed, "how many kings has Belteshazzar served?"

"Cyrus," mused the satrap, "and before him, Nabu-Naid; there was Nergal-Sharezer, and before him, Awil-Marduk, and the first, Nebuchadrezzar."

"Don't forget Labashi-Marduk," put in one of the others.

"Oh, yes," amended Shatak, "I always forget him—such a short time…"

"Six!" shouted Adad-ibni, a mad grin of triumph stretching across his gap-toothed face. "Six kings—all but one now dead! Don't you see the implication?"

The others stared dumbly at the animated face of the aged seer.

"Fools!" spat the old man. "Are you all meek, trusting children? Belteshazzar has outlived six kings and the coming of Cyrus unscathed because he is so crafty, so subtle in his maneuvering, that no one can detect him!"

"Old man, you are crazy!" laughed Shatak. "Just because Belteshazzar has survived your spite these many years does not indicate that he is anything other than what he seems to be: an honest, intelligent, diligent man. You have spent too many years mumbling over star charts. Your eyes see signs that don't exist." Chuckling in derision, Shatak got up from the table and walked toward the door. Turning about at the entryway, he said, "The hour is late, and I have better things to do this night than listen to the hateful prattlings of a skin-headed old stargazer." Casting a final glance about the room, he left.

Adad-ibni was apoplectic. Trembling with rage, he stared death at the one who had just departed. He shook a knobby fist at the closing door. "I am still chief mage of Babylon," he hissed. "I know the ways of the mighty ones, and of the demons in their lairs. He who does not heed my words is an ass." His livid gaze swung toward those who remained in the chamber with him. "I tell you: Belteshazzar will soon be the mightiest man in the empire. Do any others of you here question the vision of the First Seer of Babylon?"

The nobles looked from one to another. No one was willing to contradict the furious mage—who, after all, seemed deadly sure of the truth of his allegations. And indeed, he *was* a very learned man, whose business it was to read portents and omens invisible to common men. One after another, they slowly shook their heads. They would not impede Adad-ibni in his dark design.

"Very well, then," the mage crackled. "This is what must be done..."

Secretly, one of the mage's listeners made the sign against the evil eye.

28

CYRUS FINGERED HIS BEARD, staring thoughtfully at Daniel. "So…you are saying I should bring the satraps of Armenia and Cappadocia here, to Shushan, and force them to speak to one another in my presence until they have settled their differences over their common border?"

The aged Hebrew nodded. "Many generations ago, a king of my people said this: 'Starting a quarrel is like breaching a dam; so drop the matter before a dispute breaks out.' It would seem to be rather too late for preventing a dispute—better to have the disagreement occur here, under your eyes and control, than out in the provinces where matters might progress in a less constructive fashion."

Cyrus nodded pensively, looking away, then glanced back at Daniel, smiling. "This wise king of yours—has he many such pithy sayings as the one you have just quoted?"

Daniel smiled. "Yes, my king. His name was Solomon, and it is said the Queen of the South once came and sat at his feet to hear the words he spoke." Daniel's wrinkled face darkened as he muttered, looking away, "A pity he did not learn to heed his own advice…"

"What do you mean?" asked Cyrus.

Daniel sighed. "The beginning of Solomon's days were better than the ending. In his latter life he forgot the fear of the Lord, and forgot to teach his sons after him. Those days began the ending of our nation…" Daniel's voice wandered off into the past like a candle flame down a dark street.

Cyrus remembered the words of Gobhruz—now dead these three moons past—about the beginnings of kingdoms, the transitory nature of dynasties. He sorely missed the counsel of the taciturn Mede. His passing was something the old horseman seemed to decide for himself—as if, now that the cultured and ancient cities of the plains were conquered, Gobhruz felt he was no longer needed. Cyrus had wept openly at the funeral of his oldest and most trusted friend.

Perhaps that was why the emperor had taken such an immediate liking to the wizened Hebrew who sat before him. He sensed in Daniel the same durable wisdom, the same unclouded, dispassionate view of the well-mannered facades of court life, as those he had come to value so highly in Gobhruz.

"How I wish my son Kanbujiya could sit at your feet, Daniel," Cyrus said finally. "I have sent the wisest teachers of the realm to his court in Parsagard, but I believe they fall short of the wisdom in that gray old head of yours."

Daniel shrugged, a bit embarrassed at such lavish praise. "Solomon has also said, 'Even a fool is thought wise if he keeps silent, and discerning if he holds his tongue.'"

Cyrus threw back his head and laughed. He was still chuckling when a slave entered, carrying a bowl of sweetmeats and dried fruits.

Daniel rose to leave. "No! Stay!" said Cyrus, waving the satrap back to his seat. "Take meat with me—I want to question you further about this Solomon of yours."

Daniel bowed in acquiescence, lowering himself stiffly to his chair. The slave proffered the painted ceramic bowl, and Daniel took a handful of raisins and a few dried figs. These days, he reflected ruefully, his ancient bowels craved fruit above all else.

"Tell me then, my good friend," began Cyrus, leaning on one elbow as he dropped almonds into his mouth. "What was the transgression of this wise king Solomon, that your God should be at such pains to punish his progeny?"

Daniel paused long before answering. "He forgot the ways of the Lord, my king," he replied finally. "His heart was turned to other gods and away from the worship of the Most High God."

"I see," mused the king, toying with the stone of a date. "This Most High you refer to—He sounds much like Ahura Mazda, the chief god of Persia. Are they the same?"

Again Daniel thought long and carefully before responding. "He is the One Lord, the Most High, the King of Heaven."

Cyrus saw the discomfort, heard the hesitancy in Daniel's voice as he worded his enigmatic, oblique response. The king shifted on his cushion, considering a way to alter the tone of the conversation. "Zarathushtra, a long-dead prophet of Ahura Mazda, has spoken of a Day of Reckoning," he remarked lightly, "when all men living and in the grave shall stand before the Wise Lord to receive reward or punishment. Does your Hebrew God say anything of this?"

Again he saw he had unwittingly broached a subject to which Daniel could not make easy rejoinder. The older man seemed to huddle within himself, as if at odds with his own opinions. After interminable rumination, he said quietly, "Another king of our people—the father of Solomon, in fact—once sang, 'My heart is glad and my tongue rejoices; my body also will rest secure, because You will not abandon me to Sheol, nor will You let Your holy one see decay...'" After another pause, Daniel continued: "This king also said, 'Vindicate me, O Lord, for I have led a blameless life; I have trusted in the Lord without wavering...'" Daniel's voice halted, and his eyes found those of Cyrus. "And yet, the king who uttered these words died and was buried. His tomb lies among the ruins of Jerusalem." The satrap's words framed a plea, a plaintive riddle which admitted of no solution, as if even Daniel were at a loss to resolve the paradox presented by this unjustified confidence of a dead king.

Then he looked up, above Cyrus's head and away into a place hidden from other eyes. "Once I thought there might be ...something else," he breathed, his vision clouded with longing. "But," he finished, lowering his face and rubbing his eyes with his fingertips, "it was not shown to me. I know not..."

Cyrus was oddly moved by the groping ache in Daniel's

gaze, by the catches in his voice as he spoke of what he had half-seen. "May your God reveal to you the things you desire to see, Daniel," he whispered.

Daniel smiled ruefully. "Perhaps my desire is not what it pleases the Lord to reveal," he said. "Another proverb of Solomon is this: 'All a man's ways seem right to him, but the Lord weighs the heart...'"

◆　◆　◆

GRINNING TO HIMSELF, Adad-ibni waited in the anteroom outside the king's council chamber. The plan would work — he felt it in his bones. And this time there would be no second chances, no opportunity for Belteshazzar to evade the snare laid for him.

The door to the chamber swung open, and the mage and those accompanying him entered and bowed before Cyrus.

The emperor dismissed the counselors with whom he had been conferring, looking up in curiosity at the delegation which now knelt before him. At their forefront was an ancient, shriveled man dressed in the robes and with the shaven head of the Babylonian astrologers. Out of habit, Cyrus glanced at his bodyguards to make certain they carefully observed the movements of this unexpected group of petitioners. One couldn't be too careful.

"O King, may you live forever," the seer was hissing in a dry, time-worn voice. "I am Adad-ibni, faithful chief mage of the emperor's city of Babylon. I have given my life to the study of the signs of sky, earth, fire, and water. These servants of my king's"—the old man indicated the uncomfortable-looking knot of men that had entered with him—"and I have come to the king to tell him of a dire portent which your humble servant has divined in the movements of the stars of heaven." The mage crossed his hands on his breast and bowed his head toward Cyrus.

"Well—what is it?" asked the emperor impatiently. Something about this wizard's manner and intonation grated upon him; he could not specify the source of his irritation, but a voice at the back of his mind whispered caution.

Adad-ibni smiled beatifically. "My king must know that the conjunction of Marduk and Ishtar, while normally most propitious, has this time occurred within the sphere governed by Nergal." He paused significantly, to allow this vital fact to impress his audience. Unfortunately, its importance was completely obscure to his listeners.

"What of it?" snapped Cyrus, quickly growing weary of this sniveling, wrinkle-pated lizard.

"The meaning is this, my king," hurried Adad-ibni, swallowing his annoyance at the king's obtuse manner. "The next cycle of the moon is one of some danger to your imperial person. Precautions should be taken."

Cyrus's nostrils flared in irritation. "The loyalty of my people and my bodyguards' vigilance are my precautions, lord mage," he sniffed. "I do not think it necessary to employ the incantations of wizards to protect myself."

"Doubtless the loyalty of most of my king's people is beyond question," glided Adad-ibni, "but I have made a life of study upon these matters, and the portents do not equivocate. There is danger during this moon. Those of us here are unanimous in our conclusions, as well as in our concern for the welfare of the empire. Surely my king will not be angry at his servants for being solicitous of his benefit?" Again the crossed hands, the infuriatingly subservient bow.

Cyrus stood up from his place at the council table and paced to a nearby window. Sighing, he recollected words of Gobhruz: of the Mede's refusal to become embroiled in the matters of the gods. *By far the best policy,* reflected Cyrus. Sometimes he became so confused by the myriad customs and practices of the multitude of deities reverenced by his diverse people that he hardly knew in which direction to bow in which city, or what things were repugnant to whom on what days. It was a wearisome nuisance, all this to-do with gods and demons—good for little, he had decided, except providing employment for tiresome pedants such as this Adad-ibni. Of all the religious practitioners he had encountered in his travels, only two had made much sense to Cyrus: the guardian of the flame at the mountain shrine of Ahura Mazda…and Daniel. Again he saw in Daniel's haunted eyes the soul-bleeding longing for his mysterious, nameless God…

Ah, well, he thought. *I have always insisted that the religious proclivities of my people be protected. Perhaps it is best to let these benighted conjurers of Babylon do as they think they must. What harm can come of it?* He wheeled about. "Very well, Adad-ibni. What do your signs tell you ought to be done?"

Breathing a quiet sigh of relief, the mage said through his missing teeth, "My king is truly wise in his judgments! Now then—let the king decree as follows: For the next cycle of the moon, no man shall pray or bow down to any god or man except my lord Cyrus. As the regent of the gods on earth, this will ensure the absolute safety of my lord Cyrus and the order of his realm. Any man who refuses the terms of this decree should be punished for his disloyalty by being thrown to the lions."

Cyrus stiffened. Was this truly necessary?

"Furthermore, my lord Cyrus," oozed Adad-ibni, "the decree should be put in writing, and announced throughout the satrapies of Medea and Persia…"—a crafty gleam came into the seer's eye—"and most definitely here, in Shushan." *After all,* thought the mage with evil glee, *is not this where the hated Belteshazzar resides—here in the very house of the king?* "Yes, in writing, O king, according to the ordinances of the empire, so that it cannot be altered by any man." Crossed hands and the pious bowing of his head indicated that Adad-ibni had concluded his bizarre prescription for the safety of the empire.

Cyrus shook his head, staring in disbelief at the captain of his bodyguard. The soldier made a slight shrug. Cyrus, wishing to be instantly rid of the aggravating presence of this reptilian stargazer, said in a tone dripping with exasperation, "Very well. Send in a scribe." A bodyguard hastened from the room to obey.

Adad-ibni, his old heart rattling in triumph, allowed himself a secret sneer.

◆　◆　◆

"O LORD GOD, place Your blessing on those who are in Judah," Daniel prayed, kneeling beside his western window, his face resting on his clenched hands. "And speed the building of Your Temple, that Your Name may again be adored in Jerusalem. Protect Your people, and preserve them alive, according to Your steadfast love and Your abundant promises..."

Grunting at the stiffness in his knees, he rose from the straw mat by the window and rearranged his robes. For a moment he gazed out his window toward the west, then turned to go back to his duties.

Shuffling down the corridor to his audience room, he heard the cry of the herald. "Give ear! Give ear! A proclamation from our Lord the King, Cyrus the Achaemenean, Ruler of Lands! Give ear! Give ear!" Hurrying to the Great Hall, from whence the call issued, Daniel arrived with others like himself who hastened to hear the latest edict of the emperor.

Standing in the midst of the vast hall, the herald, flanked by two officers of the imperial guard, held a parchment from which he read. Daniel could see, dangling from the bottom of the script, the winged-circle seal of Cyrus's own signet.

"The King, Cyrus the Achaemenean, the Great Lord, has caused to be written this day a proclamation for all the lands of the Medes and Persians. This word is written and may not be altered, according to the ordinances of Cyrus the King—may he live forever!

"For the next cycle of the moon, no man in Medea or Persia may pray or bend the knee to any god or man except Cyrus himself, the bounteous earthly regent of the gods. No man may make petition to any except Cyrus, nor may he sacrifice or do reverence to any idol or deity except Cyrus, the Great King. Any man who fails to comply with the gracious command of

Cyrus the King shall be cast among the lions for his disloyalty. Let all his faithful and devoted subjects hear this decree, and obey!"

Daniel's heart froze. How could this be? Why should the king—who was not, as Daniel knew in his inmost heart, in need of such vain pride-stoking—make such pointless, frivolous use of the authority granted to him by the Lord of heaven? Daniel's mind fled down the corridors of memory, back to a day long ago, when he had stood alone and panicked in his chamber on Adad street, frantically pondering the dilemma imposed on him by another such decree of a now-dead monarch.

Pulling away from the anxious memory of a time before, his eyes roved across the hall, among the muttering, departing ranks of nobles and courtiers.

Adad-ibni!

The mage stood in the shadows across the way, grinning at Daniel with a wicked, knowing look. Daniel's mind flashed back once again: this time to a council chamber in Babylon, and the leering, calculating visage of a much younger but no less hateful Adad-ibni—smirking as he related his "vision" of the necessity for a loyalty-oath to Nebuchadrezzar, of a golden image on the plain of Dura, and of a furnace...

With a sinking certainty Daniel realized that the seer—his ancient, unsought enemy—had engineered this disastrous proclamation, just as he had masterminded the ceremony on the Dura plain, to avenge himself on Daniel for whatever supposed injury had originally engendered such rancid malice.

Daniel turned to go. Across the huge chamber he could hear the fiendish sound of the mage's chattering laugh.

For the remainder of Daniel's day, the figures and tallies on the documents in front of him were a blurred succession of meaningless scratches. Over and over again his mind returned with a dreadful insistence to the lethal shape of his quandary.

For a third time in his life his feet were tangled in a trap not of his own making. The first time he had surrendered abjectly to the voice of panic. He had lied to save his own life, allowing his friends to face the danger without him. The second time, in the matter of Nebuchadrezzar's madness, he had spoken the words of God, but the fist of fear had choked them from his throat in a graceless, debasing babble of unnerved hysteria.

What would be his response this time? He had lived his life by now, it was true; often the fatigue of dragging about his worn-out body was almost more than he could endure. And yet…the dark, yawning void of Sheol was terrifying to contemplate. And when he was gone, what would remain to remind the earth he had existed? He had no offspring, no sons to say *qaddish* over his remains. And there was the horrifying way he would die: the hot, fetid breath of the lions, the terrible sharpness of their teeth, the rending pain of their claws! To be torn limb from limb, screaming in agony, watching with terror-widened eyes as the growling beasts ripped at one's living flesh…

By the end of the day he knew what he must do. The appointed time came, and he rose from his place, dismissing his assistants. Panting with trepidation, now and again leaning upon the walls of the corridors, he made his way toward his suite.

Entering his rooms, he made directly for the woven mat beside his western window. He fell to his knees, clenching his hands in a white-knuckled grip. Resting his forehead on his fists, he prayed:

> *Have mercy on me, O God, have mercy on me,*
> *for in You my soul takes refuge.*
> *I will take refuge in the shadow of Your wings*
> *until the disaster has passed…*
>
> *I am in the midst of lions;*
> *I lie among ravenous beasts—*
> *men whose teeth are spears and arrows,*
> *whose tongues are sharp swords.*
> *Be exalted, O God, above the heavens—*

Daniel heard the door to his rooms creak open. He knew,

without looking, who stole inside his suite—and why they had come. He did not so much as glance upward from his mat, but continued in a louder voice the ancient *miktam* of David:

> *They spread a net for my feet—*
> > *I was bowed down in distress.*
> *They dug a pit in my path—*
> > *but they have fallen into it themselves…*
>
> *I will praise You, O Lord, among the nations;*
> > *I will sing of You among the peoples,*
> *for Great is Your love, reaching to the heavens;*
> > *Your faithfulness reaches to the skies.*
> *Be exalted, O God, above the heavens;*
> > *let Your glory be over all the earth.*

29

ADAD-IBNI COULD HARDLY WAIT for morning's first light. As soon as it was decent to do so, he rushed to the audience room of the emperor, demanding of the chamberlain to be admitted.

When Cyrus saw the sniveling face of the mage, a foul grin seeping across his features, he felt a cold shaft of apprehension lance through his chest. "What is it, lord mage, that brings you with such urgency to my chamber?" he asked, not knowing why he dreaded the answer.

A bubble of mirth rose to the top of Adad-ibni's throat, but he sternly repressed it. Feigning as stern a face as he could, he said, "O King, may all your enemies perish! Only yesterday, did you not issue a decree concerning a ban on worship of any god or man but your imperial self?"

The knot of dread twisted tighter in the king's gut. "Yes—what of it?"

"And did my lord the king not put this decree in writing, so that it cannot be amended or retracted?"

The sly old wizard was clearly enjoying this little charade, despite his feeble attempts to conceal the fact. Hating the sound of his own voice, Cyrus answered, "Yes."

"Then my lord the king must know: Belteshazzar, called Daniel by his own people—one of the king's three closest counselors!—was found in his room on the very evening of the decree of my lord the king, praying to his Hebrew god, in direct and flagrant defiance of the command of my lord the king." Adad-ibni crossed his hands on his breast and bowed his head, less in respect than to hide the smirk of triumph which he could not keep from his lips.

Cyrus was horrified. He leapt from his seat and strode to the kneeling mage, grasping the old bag of bones by the front of his robes and hauling him forcefully to his feet.

"Villain!" the king shouted. "You have twisted my words into a snare for my most trusted adviser! I should have *you* thrown to the beasts for creating such a treasonous trap!" As he spoke, Cyrus shook the seer back and forth, violently rattling the few teeth Adad-ibni had remaining in his head.

Then the king allowed the mage to fall to the floor like a sack of kindling. His head throbbing, his breathing heavy, Adad-ibni jabbered, "My lord...the king...must realize...the empire cannot...long endure...inconsistency on the part...of the king. Laws...must be upheld..."

Cyrus realized, despite the white-hot fury of his rage, the

truth behind the wretch's words. Cursing Adad-ibni, cursing himself, cursing the words he had uttered which had unknowingly damned his most valued official, the king turned his head away. "You have done what you came to do," he grated. "Now get out of my presence." He did not turn until he had heard the sounds of the seer crawling out the door, closing it behind him.

Cyrus found Daniel in his rooms, lying face-down on a mat of woven straw beneath a westward-facing window. Realizing that his beloved counselor was in prayer, he sat quietly until the old man had finished and risen from his devotions. Turning about, Daniel saw the king, and began to make obeisance.

"No!" said Cyrus, going to Daniel and lifting him by the elbow. "You must not bow to me—not after what I have done to you."

Daniel peered into the anguished face of his king for several long breaths. A wistful, faraway look came across his weathered features, and he almost smiled.

"My lord," the old man said, "you must not fear for me. My God is able to save me, if He so wishes. And if not…" Eyes downcast, he could say no more.

"He deceived me, Daniel!" cried Cyrus, in a voice thick with distress. "I thought it merely some silly ceremony, some meaningless placation of a few shaved-headed stargazers in Babylon. I had no idea…" Groping about within the desolation of his soul, the king fell silent. At last he muttered, "I will revoke this misbegotten decree."

Daniel laid a hand on Cyrus's arm and stared pointedly into his eyes as he slowly shook his head. "My lord, another proverb of Solomon: 'The lips of a king speak as an oracle, and his mouth should not betray justice.' You cannot go back on your word, my king. It is not possible for such as you."

"But where is the justice in this—this calamity?" Cyrus cried.

"An empire must be governed by law, my lord. Laws must be upheld by the king."

Shuddering at the echo of the hated Adad-ibni's words,

Cyrus stood. "I will spend the day with my advisers," he said. "If there is any path out of this morass, I will find it." A single tear escaped the eye of Cyrus, tracing a shining path across his cheek and into the steel-gray thicket of his beard. "Daniel, my ...my friend—I would never have intended—"

"I know," assured Daniel. "You should go now. The matter lies in the hands of God."

Looking long into the eyes of Daniel, Cyrus finally turned and left.

◆　◆　◆

AS THE SUN'S DISC turned from yellow to orange with the approach of evening, Cyrus remained huddled with his counselors and advisers. All day they had debated the problem, coming repeatedly against the blind wall of the written decree. Once written, the word could not be changed. How Cyrus inwardly berated himself for the crude vanity which had caused him to formulate such a simple-minded premise!

A quiet knock sounded on the door of the chamber. They all looked up, and there stood Daniel. With a faded, fear-blanched expression on his face, he said, "My king...it is time."

Looking helplessly around the group, Cyrus struggled to force words past the grief-blockage in his throat. "Very well," he managed at last. "Summon the guards. We will go."

Word had raced around the palace and citadel of Shushan: how the king's wisest, most trusted counselor had disobeyed the edict; how the king, despite his aversion to doing so, would indeed enforce the law against one said to be very dear to him. As the party of guards, the condemned man, and the emperor himself exited the arched entryway of the citadel which led to the beast pens, a large, hushed crowd awaited. They lined the causeway much like onlookers at a funeral procession.

It was an odd, pathetic entourage. The aged satrap Daniel, hobbling feebly along, leaned heavily on his smooth-worn cane while his other hand gripped the shoulder of Cyrus. His face was ashen, starched with fear. The emperor's visage was only slightly less pallid than Daniel's—like that of a man about to amputate his own hand with a dull knife. Between the guards they walked, the very representation of hopelessness.

With sympathetic sorrow for the strange twist of fate which had embroiled the unwilling king and his confidant, all who saw the sight were driven to pity. All, that is, except Adad-ibni. The wizened seer exulted at the dour, despairing cast of Belteshazzar's features, congratulating himself for the subtlety of his plan. At last the hated Jew would be utterly defeated, his flesh and bones ripped asunder, his name disgraced and completely forgotten. Standing at the back of the crowd, he could not withhold a gratified chuckle—a sound as out of place among the silent crowd as a birthing-cry in a tomb. Even the Chaldeans with the mage looked at him askance, wishing he could better contain himself.

The setting sun was disappearing behind a low bank of clouds on the horizon when the group reached the barred gateway to the wild beasts' compound. Cyrus had the stockade constructed as a holding place for his menagerie—animals he had collected on his journeys of conquest, and those brought to him as gifts by tributary delegations. The wildlife of the Aryan central plateau was represented here: the ostriches and the wild cattle and donkeys that roamed the wide, arid plains of the Kermani and Parthian satrapies; elephants brought from the low country along the Indus River; dromedaries, Bactrian camels, gazelles, and pea fowl—a vast profusion of animal life assembled here in homage to Cyrus, the Great King.

And lions. The lank, tawny beasts were locked into a secure enclosure of stone and iron, and were fed huge, dripping haunches of meat passed through the barred walls of their den on long, pointed poles. In the fading light, as the party of men approached the den, the deep rumbling of the great cats could be heard as they worried the bones and scraps left from their last feeding.

The imperial gamekeeper fumbled with the keys on his belt, seeking the one which would open the lock securing the gate to the lair. The emperor gripped the shoulder of Daniel, gazing with wounded eyes at the aghast face of the old man. "May your God save you, my friend," he whispered. Daniel, mute with dread, only nodded. Then the gate was unlocked.

When the old man had shuffled wretchedly inside the dark entryway, the gate was secured behind him. "Let a stone be brought and placed before the gate," ordered Cyrus. "And let a guard be posted outside the compound, so that no one—not even your king—may enter during the night and free Daniel." The stone was rolled into place, hot wax was dripped onto the corner where it contacted the wall, and the signets of authority affixed. As Cyrus pressed his ring into the soft tallow, he felt he was driving a dagger into the heart of the innocent man trapped inside.

All official procedures observed, Cyrus wheeled about in remorse and revulsion, half-running from the place, his guards struggling to keep pace with him.

As he strode toward his palace, Cyrus reflected on the true reason for the stone before the gate: It was not to prevent rescue, but that he might not hear Daniel's tortured shrieks. Hating himself more with each step, he fled to his private chamber. "I will see no one this night," he ordered the chamberlain. "No meat, no drink, no women—no one. I wish to be alone. See to it." The chamberlain nodded, fastening the door behind him and deploying the guards to ensure the king's wishes.

Cyrus went inside, pausing in the dark solitude of his room. After a moment's reflection he paced to a window—a westward-facing window. Kneeling, gazing toward the darkening line of the horizon, he groped within himself for a way to begin. What was the name Daniel used? "Most High God," he managed finally, "I, Cyrus the king...I—I beg You...spare Daniel's life..."

◆　◆　◆

DANIEL HEARD THE GATE-LATCH click into place behind him, heard the gravel crunching beneath the stone as it was rolled across the entry. Peering into the darkness, he saw the baleful yellow orbs of the lions' eyes reflecting the low light that entered through the open-air run at the opposite end of their enclosure. His bowels turned liquid in a rush of terror. He smelled the rank, acrid odor of the beasts, heard the huge, hoarse sound of their panting. As his eyes adjusted to the dimness, he could make out eight or ten shaggy forms ranging about the enclosure in various attitudes—some reclining, some standing, some sitting on their haunches. All were staring at him with the same brutish interest, the same dispassionate, predatory evaluation.

Their nostrils flared as they tested his scent. He knew they could smell his fear—he could smell it himself. He could hear the breath gasping in and out of his lungs, could feel his frenzied heart battering in his chest like a frightened bird in a wicker basket. As his eyes widened in horror, one of the beasts —a large male—rose lazily to its feet and padded toward him, its great pink tongue licking along its chops. Daniel staggered backward against the bars of the gate, closing his eyes. His neck tingled in terrified anticipation of the pounce, the hot breath, the swift clamp of the fanged jaws...

A burst of light inside his chest announced the arrival of a presence more terrifying, more immediate and imperative, than ten thousand lions. The brightness inside him forced his unwilling eyes open, compelled him to view the appalling glory of the one who now stood between him and the lion— which now lay meekly on its belly, its ears tucked close, its eyes averted from the shining one, just as a cub avoids the gaze of a lord of the pride.

Much like the lions, Daniel fell to the ground, overcome with awe. "My Lord!" he whispered.

"No!" said the angel in a voice like sunlight and the clash of armies. "Do not worship me! I am the servant of *El Shaddai* —as you name Him—who has sent me to watch over you this night, and deliver you from the mouths of the beasts."

The Guide! It was the same voice which had called to him in the visions! *Could this be—? But, no!* He felt the gravel of the den beneath his hands, smelled the sour, musky reek of the lions. This was no dream.

And then the Guide spoke again.

"Daniel, your prayers have been heard. Adonai..."—the shimmering one bowed his head in respect when he spoke the word—"has given heed to your many petitions and your faithfulness. Because of your fidelity, all the peoples and lands of the domain of Cyrus will hear of the name of Him Who Is." Again the lowered head, suggesting the reverence for Adonai which must be the habit and joy of heaven.

Daniel marveled within himself. Could this be the calling, the purpose for which he was detained from the repatriation of Judah? That he, such an unworthy vessel as he felt himself to be, should be the means to extend the honor of the Most High —it was too wonderful to contemplate!

Almost simultaneous with the astonishment came the old shame, the gnawing sense of unworthiness. He again relived the accusing memory of a self-serving lie, the ignominy of cowardly bleating where confident boldness would have better served. Shivering in the holy glare of the messenger's otherworldly radiance, he felt naked, contemptible, unclean.

"Daniel!" said the Guide in a voice of velvet and thunder, "do you not remember your own words?"

Daniel tried to look into the angel's face, but could not, because of the brightness. With downcast eyes, he asked, "What words are those, my Guide?"

"The words you offered to the Most High as you lay on your couch in Babylon: 'We do not make requests of You because we are righteous, but because of Your great mercy...'"

Daniel gasped, hearing the words of his petition in the mouth of this blazing messenger of heaven.

"Not because of your merit has He heard you, son of Jacob," the angel continued, "but because of the boundless reaches of His grace, and because it pleases Him to do so. In the same way, He sent me to your friends in the furnace of Nebuchadrezzar—not for their own sakes, but because He purposed it in His will to be thus. It is not your unworthiness, but His absolute worth which pertains. You are the instrument of His will, O Daniel, not its essence. He alone is to be praised in all things."

Daniel felt hot tears spilling like the oil of Aaron down his cheeks. With his breath coming in great, white draughts of relief and awe, he whispered, "Glory to Adonai!"

"Glory and honor to Him," echoed the angel, head bowed. "And now, Daniel, you must rest. You will need strength for the moment of your witness."

A great, comfortable drowsiness, like an old, familiar cloak on a cool night, settled warmly about his shoulders. Slumping down against the wall of the lions' den, he felt as peaceful as if he had been upon his own couch. As his mind drifted toward sleep, his last thought was, *I...Even one such as I...* Then the grateful darkness took him.

◆ ◆ ◆

CYRUS, LEANING WEARILY against the window sill, lifted his head from his forearm. Impending dawn was the merest gray suggestion in the starlit dome of the sky. His eyes were two burning, chafed, sleepless sores—as if he had, during the night, trudged through one of the howling sandstorms of the Aryan steppes.

He had indeed passed through a storm during the dark, silent watches—a storm within his soul. Like a blind man seeking a twisted path through a copse of briars, he had stumbled after Daniel's God. Many the promises he made, many the vows he swore to an unknown entity, seeking to vouchsafe the safety of his beloved counselor. And despite his strict attempts at piety, despite the dogged solemnity with which he had approached the unfamiliar presence, he was met again and again with the same impression: He did not suffice. For the first time in his life of ambition and conquest, Cyrus knew the midnight isolation of helplessness. The answer, the remedy, lay completely beyond his power—as distant as the dimming stars from the depths of the sea. It was a shattering ordeal for the horse-king, this brutal encounter with the limits of his capacity. How humbling it was to be so utterly ineffectual in a circumstance where he wished desperately to avail.

As the faintest blush of pink rose in the cheeks of the day, he rose from his vigil. Without washing his face, without changing the rumpled, disheveled garments of his night-watch, he strode to the door of his chamber.

"We go to the menagerie," he snapped, pacing briskly down the hall. The guards came rapidly alongside, rubbing their tired eyes in the dim half-light of broadening morning. "Page!" the king called to a boy dozing against the wall of the corridor. "Go to the gamekeeper and summon him, with all speed, to the lions' den." The boy scrambled to his feet and dashed away.

◆ ◆ ◆

A PONDEROUS SCRAPING SOUND intruded upon Daniel's slumber. He stirred and sat up, the echo of the Guide's last words still reverberating faintly in the chambers of his soul: *Glory and honor to Him…strength for the moment of your witness…*

Stretching, his gaze fell upon the still-sleeping forms of the lions, their fanged mouths agape, the deep, slow breaths hushing heavily in and out of their chests. In a strange twist of emotions, he felt himself somehow akin to the beasts which had been intended as his destroyers. Had they not bowed together, in reverence to a common superior?

Then the key rattled in the lock of the gate, and a voice was calling his name.

"Daniel! Daniel! Has your God, whom you serve faithfully, been able to save you from the mouths of the beasts?"

The king.

"O, my king, may you live forever!" Daniel called, glancing back toward the lions. Oddly, the animals had not stirred from their languorous inertia, despite the commotion at the gate. "My God sent His angel, and he shut the mouths of the lions…"

As the lock slid back, Cyrus gripped the bars of the gate

and threw them wide open, heedless of the beasts inside. Those with him gasped and shrank back from the dark opening which might at any moment pour forth angry, wild lions. But the only being to emerge from the cavern was the rickety old figure of Daniel, shuffling into the morning light, shading his eyes with a wrinkled hand.

"They have not hurt me," the satrap was saying, "because I was found innocent in His sight..."

As Daniel stepped clear of the entryway, a nervous game-keeper shut and secured the gate.

"Nor have I ever done any wrong before you, O my king," Daniel finished quietly.

Cyrus grasped Daniel in an embrace of gratitude and relief. Then he turned to a man standing behind his left shoulder, one whom Daniel recognized as the imperial physician. "Examine him," Cyrus ordered. "For every wound this faithful man bears, I will exact treble retribution from his persecutors."

Over Daniel's protests, the physician carefully inspected his person. When he had satisfied himself of Daniel's condition, he turned to the king. "He is whole," the physician stated in a calm, professional voice. "There is no mark on him."

"Very well," said Cyrus, his eyes flashing a hazardous amber. A hot torrent of rage gushed into the place where his anxiety had been. "Guards, you will find the men who have accused Daniel—especially their leader, the Chaldean mage Adad-ibni." His voice dropping into a perilous growl, he continued, "You will bind them, and bring them to me in the throne hall. I will order the chamberlain to assemble the court..."

30

*"AND IN EVERY PART of my kingdom people must fear and rever-
ence the God of Daniel.*

"For He is the living God and He endures forever;
"His kingdom will not be destroyed,
"His dominion will never end.
"He rescues and He saves;
"He performs signs and wonders in the heavens
and on the earth—
"He has rescued his servant Daniel from the power
of the lions."

The herald's voice resonated into silence among the glazed
tiles on the high ceiling of the throne room of Babylon. Daniel
watched from his seat beside the empty throne as the cautious
glances of the nobles silently queried his face, found their answer, and turned aside.

Daniel did not deceive himself: The Most High would not
suddenly replace Marduk either in the Chaldean pantheon or
in the hearts and minds of these listeners—nor was such the intent of this decree of Cyrus. The proclamation was far from
meaningless, however. At least during the lifetime and memory of the Persian kings, the worship of Adonai could not be
persecuted or hindered without risking the punishment of the
emperor. The solemnity of Cyrus's written word would not be
questioned, despite its somewhat inconvenient implications for
the Esagila establishment. If *El Shaddai* was to continue to be ig-
nored by the majority of Babylon's denizens, at least His faithful might not be harmed.

Again Daniel silently thanked the Holy One for His gracious provision. By his entry into the lions' den, he had been a channel of blessing for all of Jacob's children.

Daniel allowed a few moments for the import of the herald's message to be absorbed, then announced in a voice no less firm for his great age, "You have heard the edict of Cyrus, the Great King, the King of Lands, in whose name I administer this land of Chaldea, and all the lands between the Two Rivers." He gestured toward the ceremonially vacant throne of Cyrus, who had remained in Shushan. "Let his word be obeyed." A moment more he sat, still holding them by the authority of the proclamation, the force of his imperial and divine protection, and the weight of his venerable and storied wisdom. Then he stood, giving them leave to return to their duties.

As he limped back toward his suite, leaning heavily on his cane, he thought of the aftermath of his deliverance. If Cyrus's relief had been great, so had been his wrath, his determination to render justice on the accusers. With a shudder Daniel heard again the eager snarling of the lions, the screams of the wives and children of Adad-ibni's accomplices...and then—the horrible silence. Daniel had found little comfort in the grisly demise of his lifelong foe. Even though it fell upon such a craven scoundrel as Adad-ibni, Daniel could not find it within himself to rejoice in such a dreadful vengeance.

Reaching the door to his quarters, he paused to allow one of his bodyguards to open the way for him and to check within to ascertain the security of the suite. This done, Daniel went inside, groaning with the weight of his years as he slowly sank into the cushioned chair beside his table. He began sifting through the documents brought before him for his inspection.

He had arrived back from Shushan to find a messenger from Judah awaiting him. Hananiah was dead—his last words were that Daniel should be notified. It was a black time for the last survivor of the four young boys who had come to Babylon so very long ago. He alone was left, and the sudden onslaught of loneliness drove him to his couch for three weeks. He took only enough food to maintain life, and he would not allow his attendants to minister to him with salves or baths or anything which might bring him comfort. For he mourned more than the passing of Hananiah: A time, a life, a past had been finally taken from him by the death of this last friend of his youth and old age. Again the obscurity of Sheol whispered its message of inevitability into his grieving ears.

Only in the last two days, since the written edict of Cyrus had arrived, had he returned to his court duties. During his convalescence the matters of state had accumulated, awaiting his attentions.

Daniel's secretary, a young man of perhaps twenty summers, entered. "My master," the youth began, his head bowed in respect, "the overseers of the city of Opis have requested that you come and inspect the repairs to the fortifications there, which have recently been completed. When will it be your pleasure to grant their request?"

The old man sighed. *It never ends,* he thought—the round of tours, inspections, appearances. Necessary, though, and part of the trust placed upon him by the emperor. His elbow to the table, Daniel cradled his forehead in his outstretched hand as he pondered the most propitious time for an excursion up to the city between the Tigris and the Diala.

It was the month of Nisan. Since the year had just turned, the sun had not yet reached its full power—the spring days were not so unbearably hot as to make travel a misery for his old bones. "Why should I not leave today, when the sun has passed its zenith?" he asked. "The city is quiet, the people content; is there any reason Babylon could not spare my presence for the overland trek to Opis?" He looked up at his young assistant, awaiting his answer.

The secretary tapped his chin thoughtfully for several moments, staring into the middle distance. "I can think of no reason," he concluded, finally. "Will my master wish me to make the arrangements?"

Daniel nodded. "See to it." Quietly the boy left.

◆ ◆ ◆

THE WALLS OF OPIS loomed ahead. Daniel, swaying back and forth in his silk-hung palanquin, peered out at the approaching city. Allowing the drape to fall again into place, he leaned back into the cushions on which he rested, sighing wearily. It was a hard two-day's foot journey from Babylon to Opis, and despite the relative ease of the sedan, his age protested such dislocation.

Since nearing Opis and the Tigris, Daniel had felt a vague sense of impending astonishment, as if the shadow of some hovering wonder fell faintly upon the corner of his mind. Far from being alarmed by such a premonition, Daniel found himself queerly annoyed. He was too old and tired for such dire activity, wasn't he? This late in life, he thought, could a man not fade quietly and peacefully into the void without any more bother from the unseen realms? Sternly he quenched such feelings, and tried his best to ignore the vague muttering at the threshold of his consciousness.

As they neared the river, he identified the sound of water slapping the hull of a boat, and the clatter of oars in their locks. Then his men stepped onto the barge to cross the river into Opis.

The inspection of the fortifications proceeded smoothly, with the usual round of banquets and receptions in honor of the emperor's archsatrap. Daniel endured such fetes, eating as little of the rich food as decency would allow. He would smile at the proper times, and nod when such was called for. As usual, all was in order. Opis was being governed in an orderly and sedate manner by her overseers, and Cyrus's ordinances were well-maintained.

Daniel noted with mild displeasure that the temples still asserted their dominance over lending and much of the trade of the city—as was true in much of Chaldea and Akkad. One day, he knew, the god-houses would not be able to sate their ever-increasing appetite for lands and herds taken in pledge, nor to justify their widening rates of usury. When the people were burdened beyond their ability to continue, they would seek redress—either rising up themselves, as did the northern kingdoms in the ancient days of Solomon, or by alliance with a new king, whose conquest might be expected to bring relief. But such problems would not arise in his day, Daniel thought. It would be for those who came after him to solve such difficulties.

On the second day after his arrival, he went for a tour of the canals surrounding the walls of the city. These had recently been drained, and the bitumen-and-tile linings patched and replaced where needed. A group of the city's engineers walked about as Daniel's men carried his sedan chair, pointing out this or that feature of the elaborate system which provided drainage, defense, and water for the city.

Suddenly a hush fell over the company, like an invisible, awesome cloud. The engineers and officials with Daniel stared at one another with fear-starkened eyes. An irresistible, unreasoning trembling took them; without knowing why, they fled in heart-pounding panic from the unseen, inaudible source of their inexplicable fright.

Daniel scarcely noticed the frenzied flight of the others. His eyes were fixed with avid consternation on the piercing, exigent visage of his Guide, who stood before him in a manifestation whose power pinioned Daniel, body and soul, to the spot where he stood.

The brilliance the divine messenger had exuded in the lions' den was only a shadow compared to the appalling, beautiful, terrifying radiance in which the Guide now showed himself. It was as if he had worn a shroud in the den, but now stood unveiled before Daniel, allowing the full, potent glare of heaven's majesty to pour from him in a voiceless paean of victory. He was clad in the habit of a Levitic priest. The heartbreaking purity of his white linen robe and the breathtaking radiance of his gold belt were the soul-wrenching realities symbolized only feebly by the garments of the Judean priesthood.

His body glowed through his clothing—or perhaps, Daniel

thought as he looked, his clothing and his body were somehow one, as if what seemed to be robes and belt were in fact the visible portrayal of his vital, holy essence. The gleam was like the luminous glow of a polished gem. From his eyes, the white-hot flame of righteousness burned forth, and his legs and arms had the burnished, unyielding appearance of forged bronze. His voice was the war cry of a battle-host.

"Daniel! You who are highly esteemed—listen carefully to what I will tell you today! Stand up! I have been sent to you!"

As the Guide's words struck his consciousness like molten hammer blows, Daniel realized he had fallen face-down on the ground. He felt something like a huge hand clasping him about the waist, raising him to his knees with a touch as gentle as a mother's smile, as strong as the rays of the summer sun.

Daniel leaned upon his cane and levered himself to his feet, where he stood swaying with awe. His face was blanched, his eyes wide and unblinking as he listened to the pealing voice of the angel, speaking words of comfort, of explanation—of revelation. There was a pause, and Daniel understood that a reply was expected of him. Alas! His tongue was cleaving to the roof of his dry mouth, and his parched throat could not even begin to form words. As well might he be expected to leap over the walls of Opis as to parley with this majestic, dreadful messenger. Then a touch came—a calming, healing touch, unlocking the hasp of dread which sealed his lips.

"I…I am overcome with anguish because of this vision," Daniel stammered, "and I am helpless. How can your servant talk with you? My strength has fled, and I can scarcely draw breath!"

Again came the bracing, soothing touch. Daniel felt vitality and serenity coursing together through his being—a warm tide of comfort buoyed him, bore him up.

"Do not be afraid, O man highly esteemed! Peace!" he commanded. And it was so. "Be strong now; be strong."

No more had the words left the angel's lips than Daniel's trembling ceased, the palsied shaking of his limbs steadied. His

314

wonder unabated by his newfound composure, Daniel said in gratitude, "Speak, my lord, since you have given me strength."

And the angel spoke.

He told of the coming of three kings, and of a fourth who would surpass the rest in grandeur. He told of a king of the Greeks whose power would be irresistible, whose kingdom, while great in glory and extensive in domain, would not survive his own mortality. He told of the four kings who would divide that empire among them, of the wars and conflicts between them and their descendants—a dizzying, bloody exchange of invasions and battles, of alliances made and broken. He told of threat and danger to the Beautiful Land, and a time of desolation.

And then the messenger spoke of a final, unimaginable deliverance. Daniel's breath caught in his throat as the Guide told of the awakening of hosts who slept in the dust of the earth, of a great rising up, a vast partitioning which would take place before the Judge of all the earth.

He felt the salty tears of joy brimming in his eyes. At last! The word whose echo he had heard so faintly, so very long ago! It had not been a fantasy, nor a wishful dream. It was real! The darkness of Sheol was not the final lot of the Lord's faithful ones! *O, Mishael!* he thought. *If only you, too, could have seen this day—and Azariah, and old Caleb, and...*

He caught himself up short. What was he thinking? Of course they would see this day! Had not the angel just said that those who slept would one day be awakened? Might not they, even now, be awaiting the summons, the glad rush of quickening which would draw them forth from the embrace of the earth, gleaming in newness like the very hosts of heaven?

A spontaneous cry of joy escaped his lips; he felt his insides quivering with elation.

And then two other shining ones were there, bracketing the Tigris with the radiance of their presence. With huge voices that inspired awe they asked, "How long until these things come to pass?"

Daniel's Guide now appeared to hover in the midst of the waters of the river as he gave his answer. He swore an oath so potent that Daniel's ears shuddered to hear it, invoking the Name of the One Who Lives. "It will be a time," he said, "times, and half a time. When the power of the holy people has been finally broken, all these things will be completed."

It was far too much for Daniel. So much to see, to remember—his mind was overwhelmed with the grandeur, the sweep, the appalling totality. In the only words his mind could frame, he said, "My lord, what...what will be the...the outcome of all this?"

The angel's eyes reached toward Daniel, and the flame in them dimmed to the soft, comforting glow of hearth-embers. "Go your way, Daniel," he said in a voice redolent with comfort. "These words you have heard are closed up and sealed until the end-time. Many will become pure, but most will remain wicked. To the wicked, understanding will remain hidden, but to the wise, understanding shall come.

"As for you, Daniel: Endure until the end. You will rest; and then, at the end of the days, you will rise to receive your allotted inheritance."

♦ ♦ ♦

THEY FOUND HIM lying beside the canal in a crumpled heap. Swiftly he was carried to a chamber in the citadel. Physicians were summoned, incense and ointments were applied. Those who were with him when the terror came told of the torrent of dismay which had ambushed them from some unidentifiable source.

On the third day, to the great relief of all, the parchment-thin eyelids of the archsatrap fluttered open. Recognition was in his eyes as he peered at them from his sickbed. A tiny smile lifted his cheeks, and the old, dry lips parted to speak.

"Where is my secretary?" Daniel whispered.

"Here, master," answered the youth, coming forward to kneel beside the couch.

"Have you your writing materials?" Daniel asked, his voice a barely audible sigh.

Puzzled, the aide answered, "Yes, master, but…why do you ask?"

Shaking his head with a gentle smile, he said, "No questions. There isn't time." Again peering about at the anxious, hovering faces, he said to them hoarsely, "Leave us."

With many a worried glance, the room emptied of all except the youth and his patron. When the door closed, Daniel turned to the boy. "Write what I tell you," he murmured. The secretary turned to gather his equipment.

As the young man fetched his tablet, a sound from the outside fell upon Daniel's ears. *Tap-tap. Tap-tap.* The cane of the beggar! Was his ancient summoner come at last to take him home? He half-raised his head, the better to hear.

"What is that sound?" he asked his aide.

The lad turned, a puzzled expression on his face. "What sound, master?"

"Ah, never mind," whispered Daniel. "Let us begin." He allowed his head to fall back upon the pillow.

Four visions, Daniel reflected. It was apt. Apt, also, that this fourth one should be the last, the completion. When its message had been recorded, he knew, the task for which Adonai had placed him on this earth would be ended.

As he remembered the words of the angel, the glorious hope burst again into vivid bloom in Daniel's fading consciousness. Unlike the brief, evanescent whisper by the grave of Caleb, unlike the faint, tentative intimations of wishfulness, the Guide had shouted this final message in tones of overcoming jubilation: *El Shaddai*, the All-Sufficient One, who could save from flame and sword and beasts and the hands of kings and men, was able to deliver even from the cold clutches of the tomb. Adonai wished all men to know: Hope lay ever beyond.

The youth returned to his bedside. "Master," asked the secretary, his eyes dark and wide with concern, "why the urgency?" A look of panic flared suddenly on the boy's face. "Are

...are you dying?... We...we should send immediately for the emperor!"

Again the smile, the calm shake of the head. "Tell Cyrus this: At last I have seen. I will rest...And then I will rise."